CLINICAL
ASPECTS
OF CHILD
DEVELOPMENT

CLINICAL ASPECTS OF CHILD DEVELOPMENT

*AN INTRODUCTORY SYNTHESIS OF
PSYCHOLOGICAL CONCEPTS AND
CLINICAL PROBLEMS*

by

Melvin Lewis, M.B. B.S. (London), D.C.H., F.A.A.C.P.

*Professor of Clinical Pediatrics and Psychiatry
Child Study Center, Yale University*

Lea & Febiger  *Philadelphia*

to DOROTHY

Preface

This book is written primarily for medical students. Other students may also find it useful. Its goal is to provide the student with an introductory synthesis of certain basic psychological concepts and their use in understanding the wide range of behavior seen during the stage of human development we call childhood. To the extent that sound diagnosis and treatment are based upon the principles and findings in child development, this book will also serve as a basis from which principles of management may be inferred. However, no attempt will be made here to describe specific techniques of management.

Many medical students have an urge to learn "first things first" and, since they want to become doctors, "first" to their minds means basic functioning, normal and abnormal. It is recognized that to teach a course of normal development without any reference to deviant or pathological patterns is often thought at best to lack correlation, and at worst to be quite irrelevant. On the other hand, to teach psychopathology before the student has an idea of normal psychological development is to leave the student floundering in a sea of symptoms and signs, with no normal reference points by which he can chart his course.

The obvious resolution is to teach normality and abnormality simultaneously. An attempt, therefore, is made here to paint in broad strokes the essential framework, or skeleton, for such a resolution. At the same time, this overview should enable the student to fill in for himself the gaps in his knowledge, the gaps in the teacher's knowledge, and the gaps in any course on the subject.

In working toward this goal I have had, of course, to be selective in the material used.

Others will differ from me in the selection and emphasis made. I have changed the balance several times myself. Each year students come to medical school better informed. Curricula in many medical schools are themselves in a state of flux. Further, the introduction of new findings and new concepts and the challenge to old beliefs are changing the face of medicine more rapidly than ever before. Nevertheless, I have tried to present the broad range of material fairly and consistently within a more or less unified theoretical frame of reference.

This brings me to a special characteristic of this book. The original literature is now so large that it cannot be encompassed by one person. Moreover, the mere physical act of trying to retrieve original works, papers, etc., from a library is enormously time consuming, if not actually frustrating. Yet, if the medical student only reads someone else's synthesis, he is the poorer for the development of his own ideas.

In an effort to reduce this difficulty, a series of 18 "notes" consisting of more or less extensive, but hopefully always relevant, quotations from the literature are appended at the end of each chapter. In this way I hope the student will at least get a taste of the joy of reading an original contribution, and perhaps be encouraged to make further explorations as he proceeds in his studies.

Implicit in this book is a particular pedagogical concept. This concept views medical education as a kind of spiral process, in which the student first goes once over lightly, and relatively briefly, the broad sweep of the curriculum. At subsequent periods he can then go over similar ground, this time with more familiarity and greater depth. This concept underlies some of the thinking, for example, of the new curriculum at Yale University School of Medicine. It is hoped, therefore, that this text will form the basis for such a first go-around by the student interested in human behavior. And as such it is purposefully brief. In fact, it contains the essential information and concepts presented in a 36-hour course consisting of lectures, demonstrations, interviews, clinical exercises and seminars, given during the first 9 weeks of medical school. It may also serve as a "refresher" course when the student returns to the basic sciences in the "track system" now in use in the clinical years.

Many colleagues and friends have helped me in the preparation of this book, and of course the literature belongs to us all. If I have not assiduously connotated every thought, concept, or finding uttered or written by everyone I have listened to or read over the years, it is because I have come to regard many of them now as part of the common domain of accepted knowledge. Yet, I have tried to indicate certain landmarks in the literature that might be used as a guide for those who wish to explore the subject further.

My thanks go especially to my wife Dorothy for her ideas, her stimulation, and her encouragement. I also wish to thank Herbert D. Kleber, M.D., Ernesto E. Pollitt, Ph.D., Milton J. E. Senn, M.D., and Randall M. Zusman, medical student, for their helpful criticisms and suggestions. My particular thanks go to my secretary, Mrs. Arthur Eberlein, for her unflagging enthusiasm and helpful suggestions, as well as her astonishing capacity to keep things in order and correct my errors. Lastly, I thank Lea & Febiger for their unfailing courtesy and cooperation.

Melvin Lewis

New Haven, Connecticut

Acknowledgments

I should like to express my thanks to the following individuals and firms for permission to use the material quoted in the Notes.

Note 1

D. Hartmann; International Universities Press, Inc.

Note 2

M. J. E. Senn; Josiah Macy, Jr. Foundation.

Note 3

Paul B. Hoeber Medical Division, Harper & Row, Inc.

Note 4

E. H. Erikson; International Universities Press, Inc.

Note 5

J. Bowlby; Penguin Books Ltd.

Note 6

R. A. Spitz; International Universities Press, Inc.

Note 7

J. Piaget; International Universities Press, Inc.; Delachaux & Niestle.

Note 8

D. W. Winnicott; Tavistock Publications Ltd.

Note 9

A. Freud; D. Burlingham; International Universities Press, Inc.

Note 10

Sigmund Freud Copyrights Ltd.; The Institute of Psycho-Analysis; The Hogarth Press; Basic Books, Inc.

Note 11

B. Bornstein; International Universities Press, Inc.

Note 12

G. H. J. Pearson; Bulletin of the Philadelphia Association for Psychoanalysis.

Note 13

S. Peller; The Psychoanalytic Study of the Child; International Universities Press, Inc.

Note 14

   Sigmund Freud Copyrights Ltd.; The Institute of Psycho-Analysis; The Hogarth Press, Ltd.

Note 15

   J. Piaget; Basic Books, Inc.

Note 16

   E. H. Erikson; W. W. Norton & Company, Inc.

Note 17

   C. F. Settlage; Journal of the American Academy of Child Psychiatry; International Universities Press, Inc.

Note 18

   D. G. Prugh; E. M. Staub; H. H. Sands; R. M. Kurschbaum; E. A. Lenihan; American Journal of Orthopsychiatry.

Contents

CHAPTER 1—Prior to Birth   1

Prenatal development; prenatal environment; mother's personality; acceptance
of pregnancy; reaction to pregnancy; expectations of the child; modifying
factors; role of father; grandparents and siblings; environmental variables;
anticipatory guidance.

    NOTE 1   6
    NOTE 2   7
    REFERENCES   8

CHAPTER 2—Early Infancy—The First Year   11

Concept of development; critical period; maternal deprivation; maturation;
motor sequence; adaptive sequence; language sequence; personal-social development; role of activity; role of stimulation; stimulation and language
development; stimulation and visual activity; influence of infant upon the
mother; infant's needs; sleep; modes of need satisfaction; signs of unmet needs;
early personality development and the sense of self; origins of reality testing;
development of object relations; stranger anxiety; early object relations and
object constancy; early defense mechanisms; beginning of thought; thumb
sucking; infantile fantasy life; infantile anxiety; infantile autism; maternal
insufficiency; social deprivation.

    NOTE 3   35
    NOTE 4   43
    NOTE 5   44
    NOTE 6   45
    NOTE 7   45
    REFERENCES   47

CHAPTER 3—Infancy—1-3 Years   51

Motor sequence; adaptive sequence; language sequence; personal-social behavior; fantasy life and play; manifest object relations; peer relations; parent

development; body image; gender identification; sense of self; object constancy; sense of autonomy; cognitive development; developmental tasks; aggression; toilet training; difficulties in the parents; difficulties in the child; pleasure principle, reality principle; separation; separation and reaction to hospital; separation and maternal depression; crucial developmental tasks; symbiotic psychosis; inadequate parenting; accidental poisoning in children; encopresis; perennial developmental tasks, environmental stresses, and individual characteristics.

NOTE 8   74
NOTE 9   78
REFERENCES   79

CHAPTER 4—Early Childhood—3-6 Years   83

Maturation; childhood sexual theories; manifestation of sexual theories in food attitudes; family romance; oedipal fantasies; prototypical fantasies of boys; prototypical fantasies of girls; consolidation of the superego; factors influencing oedipal fantasies and feelings; special situations; adoption; the one-parent child; play characteristics; functions of play; cognitive development; signs of anxiety; nightmares, night terrors, and bad dreams; dreams and R.E.M. sleep; child's concept of dreams; guilt; origin of guilt; purpose of guilt; guilt and socialization; masturbation; origins of masturbation; masturbation fantasies; masturbation and fantasies of being beaten; masturbation and social rules; spankings; bed wetting; major developmental thrusts; phobic organization; defense hierarchy.

NOTE 10   108
NOTE 11   110
REFERENCES   114

CHAPTER 5—The Elementary School Age Child   119

Maturation; personality development; latency; superego development; relationship with parents and peers; imaginary companion; social preparation; play development; cognitive development; prerequisites to school learning; developmental strain and developmental imbalance; ego psychopathology; learning difficulties; learning and maturational readiness; learning and lateralization; learning and C.N.S. integration; minimal cerebral dysfunction and learning disabilities; learning and intelligence; emotional freedom to learn; language problems and learning difficulties; temperament and learning disabilities; school underachievement; anxiety and aggression; anxiety and depression; anxiety and the appearance of stupidity; anxiety and symbolic association; anxiety and truancy; anxiety and school phobia; ego and superego deviations; sexual difficulties; homosexuality; transvestite behavior; sexual promiscuity in girls; superego problems; stealing; lying.

NOTE 12   140
NOTE 13   142

Note 14   142

References   142

CHAPTER 6—Early Adolescence   147

Maturation; cognitive development; personality development: universal ego tasks; identity; reactions to identity tasks; alienation; separation and feelings toward parents; further reactions to the task of separation; love relationships; unresolved love relationship behavior; mastery of impulses and body; drive regression; intellectualization as a defense; adolescent turmoil; reactions of parents; society and adolescents; adolescent conflicts and physical illness; attempted suicide; illegitimate pregnancy; homosexuality; anorexia nervosa; conversion reaction; delinquency; drugs; glue sniffing; narcotic usage; motivation for drug use; normality.

Note 15   176

Note 16   177

Note 17   179

References   180

CHAPTER 7—Psychological Reactions to Body Stress   185

Birth defects: (a) reaction of parents; birth defects: (b) reaction of child; blind children; acute illness: (a) general reaction; acute illness: (b) specific reaction (i) burns; (ii) tonsillectomy; chronic illness: (a) general reaction; chronic illness: (b) specific reactions; the child's concept of death: child's response to parents' reaction to death; reaction of parents (a) rapid death; reaction of parents: (b) prolonged dying; sibling's reaction to death; physician's reaction to death; child's reaction to his own dying.

Note 18   201

References   205

Index   209

Chapter 1

PRIOR TO BIRTH

prenatal development

The psychological development of the child has its anteecdents during the prenatal period. It is known, for example, that the fetus can react to loud sounds by gross motor activity (Bernard and Sontag, 1947). Actual behavior conditioning of the fetus may even be possible, although this has not yet been convincingly demonstrated. Nevertheless, certain behavior does occur in the fetus (Hooker, 1952), including a sucking reflex at about 20 weeks. The important point here is that heredity and environment are already interacting, and that it is conceivable that future psychologically motivated behavior might be influenced by manipulating the genetic and environmental variables. In any case, from the beginning the new organism in its own right exerts an influence on the world. For example, the quickening movements of the fetus evoke a response in the mother, representing an early contribution of the child to the mother-child interaction. Throughout development the child will continue to influence his environment through his own activity.

prenatal environment

The environment of the prenatal child of course is intrauterine,

1

but even this relatively homeostatic environment is to some extent influenced by the mother's physical and emotional state. Malnutrition, illness, and drugs taken by the mother may seriously affect the development of the fetus. Once outside the womb the active infant encounters the mother more directly. The mother now constitutes what Hartmann has called the "average expectable environment" (Hartmann, 1939; see Note 1). It is the mutual relationship between infant and mother that enables the infant to survive and thrive. The personality of the mother continues to influence this relationship. More specifically, the impact of the events of pregnancy, labor, and birth of a live child upon the mother in turn causes her to influence her child in various ways.

mother's personality

Four major elements of the mother's attitude influence her relationship with her child: *First is the mother's personality prior to, during, and after the pregnancy.* Perhaps the single most important factor here is the nature and extent of the mother's own experience of being mothered. Persisting aspects of the mother's relationship with her own parents, her sense of feminine identification, and her relationship with the child's father are further variables to be considered. Many of these kinds of prevailing personality factors affect the mother's relationship to her child. Sometimes direct displacement of the mother's feelings and attitudes onto the child will occur. At other times the child will be used as a weapon (or battlefield) in a continuing struggle, say, with the husband. At all times the mother's particular perceptual capacities, mothering skills, and ability to develop during the phase of motherhood affect the mother-child relationship (Freud, A., 1955).

acceptance of pregnancy

The mother's specific attitudes toward the pregnancy. Besides the fear or pleasure she may have experienced, there may lie more or less hidden the complex motivations in getting pregnant. There may have been a wish to please the grandparents of the expected child. Sometimes a child is hastily conceived in an unrealistic wish to save a marriage. Occasionally, a mother wishes to have a child in an attempt to deal with anxiety about her own concerns about frigidity or sterility. Again, a mother may yearn for a child to reverse roles with the child and herself become the baby. Sometimes hostile attitudes toward the fetus are crystallized during a painful or physically traumatic labor.

reaction to pregnancy

The acute impact of the normal psychological reactions to pregnancy. During the normal crisis of pregnancy the woman first moves through a phase of enhanced preoccupation with herself ("cathexis of the self"), until quickening brings about a new person ("object") with whom the woman forms a complex relationship (Bibring, *et al.*, 1961). Moreover, this crisis in the mother usually continues beyond parturition, and may influence the nature of the mother-child relationship. Sometimes unresolved psychological reactions to pregnancy spill over and cause disturbances in the delicate balance of the earliest mother-child relationship. For example, the multiple stresses of childbirth may temporarily upset the mother's psychic equilibrium, producing any kind and degree of psychiatric disorder (Normand, 1967). The specificity of the disorder in part depends upon such factors as the previous level of emotional maturity, including the sense of femininity, and the presence of certain unresolved conflicts such as hostility toward the mother's own mother. Typically, the onset of clinical symptoms occurs during the puerperium. Perhaps the most common symptoms are depressive in nature. It should be said that many normal women experience postpartum blues (Markham, 1961). This depression may lead to some withdrawal, accompanied by partial rejection of the baby. This, in turn, may result in early feeding difficulties in the baby, leading to further rejection and the creation of a vicious cycle. In this way a psychological reaction to the pregnancy and labor may interfere with the normal development of the mother-child interaction. Attempts have been made to predict postpartum psychosis; the pregnant woman who is all "sweetness and kindness" was thought by Zilboorg to be at risk, while the woman who had an emotionally stormy pregnancy was thought least likely to develop a psychotic reaction (Zilboorg, 1957).

expectations of the child

The mother's latent expectations of the child. A child may come to be used by the mother to express her own conscious or unconscious wishes. Occasionally, she may have the fantasy that she can remake herself in the child, or at least "correct" (usually it is an over-correction) the bad ways in which she was brought up.

modifying factors

These influences become even more complex if either parent is absent through separation or divorce, illness or death. And the attitudes and expectations become more powerful when there are reinforcing reality factors such as adoption, difficult childbirth, brain damage, the fear of hereditary traits, illness, etc. Furthermore, none of these factors remains static: they are in a continuous state of flux. Some of these factors will be discussed later as they impinge on the child at different phases in his development. One point must still be emphasised; in any continuing conflict between the parent and child, the child continues to make a contribution of his own.

role of father

The mother, of course, is only part of the child's environment, albeit the most important part in the child's early years. What has been said so far about the mother could also be said about the father. While the father may not have concerns about bodily harm during the pregnancy, he may resent the change in focus of attention and displace this resentment onto the child. Hopefully, the father will love the child as a natural outcome of his love for the child's mother. But the father may not love the mother, or, more commonly, may feel ambivalent. He may lack the motivation or maturity for marriage and fatherhood. Occasionally, the father will become anxious at the prospect of increased responsibility, or the identification with his own father (Zilboorg, 1931). Sometimes the father's ideas of what a mother's role and a father's role should be are in conflict with the mother's ideas on the subject. Then again, if the father is insecure in his work, he may be unable to meet the needs of the mother and child.

grandparents and siblings

Grandparents, uncles and aunts, and siblings also form part of the child's environment. Without being exhaustive, it must be obvious that some grandparents are helpful while others are intrusive. Yet, it must also be said again that it takes two people to make a conflict, and usually a parent who is in conflict with a grandparent has either encouraged the conflict or has not been able, for various reasons, to take the necessary steps to resolve the conflict.

environmental variables

Many environmental variables may affect the fetus. Outstanding among these are the nutritional state of the mother, as well as the presence of illness, drugs and other toxic agents, and the vicissitudes of the birth process itself. For example, severe prematurity (birth weight less than $4\frac{1}{2}$ pounds), severe complications of pregnancy and/or delivery, and severe familial stress have been shown to make their contribution to behavior disorders in later life even when social class factors are held constant (Drillien, 1964). Overactivity and restlessness are the most common behavior problems that are related to severe prematurity, *i.e.* with a birth weight of 3 pounds or less. On the other hand, of course, complications of birth do not necessarily result in psychiatric disorder. In a study where the obstetric histories of 100 primary school children referred to a psychiatric department with reactive psychiatric disorders were compared with those of 100 matched controls, no significant differences were found between the two groups in maternal age, birth weight, factors suggestive of an abnormal fetus, complications of pregnancy, complications of delivery, or the postnatal conditions of the child (Wolff, 1967).

What is being suggested here is that the infant arrives in the world with an already complex development behind him, possessed with an array of functions operating in ways that are peculiar to him, and actively making a contribution of his own. Far from being a "tabula rasa," the infant at birth has certain behavioral characteristics, brought about even prenatally by the interaction of genes and the environment, which are unique to him. Furthermore, these functions operate in such a way that a state of partial adaptedness may be said to exist at birth. There is, of course, no evidence at present that anything like consciousness exists; at this stage an anencephalic infant at birth may show many of the behavioral characteristics of a normal infant (although, of course, in the case of an anencephalic there will be virtually no further development). Finally, at the point of birth it is possible to observe more directly the interaction between the infant's biological equipment and his environment.

anticipatory guidance

Attempts have been made to forestall some of the possible difficulties just described by means of "anticipatory guidance," a method first conceptualized by Milton Senn (1947; see Note 2). Success in this work is dependent upon the sensitivity and skill of the pediatrician on the one hand, and the capacity of the parent to change on the other hand. Unfortunately, many of the attitudes and fantasies just mentioned are often unconscious. Consequently, considerable resistance to any change is encountered in such parents.

In summary, most children are born into an environment that is more or less prepared for the child, an environment that is virtually never "ideal" but fortunately is at least a "good enough" environment, and an environment to which they have, in part, themselves contributed. Furthermore, the mental activity of the infant turns a "good-enough" environment ("the ordinary good mother is good enough") into a perfect environment (Winnicott, 1958).

NOTE 1

Hartmann, H., 1939. *Ego Psychology and the Problem of Adaptation.* New York: International Universities Press, 1958, (tr. D. Rapaport).

In his prologed helplessness the human child is dependent on the family, that is, on a social structure which fulfills here—as elsewhere—"biological" functions also....

The processes of adaptation are influenced both by the constitution and external environment, and more directly determined by the ontogenetic phase of the organism....

No instinctual drive in man guarantees adaptation in and of itself, yet on the average the whole ensemble of instinctual drives, ego functions, ego apparatuses, and the principles of regulation, as they meet the average expectable environmental conditions, do have survival value. Of these elements, the function of the ego apparatuses....is "objectively" the most purposive. The proposition that the external world "compels" the organism to adapt can be maintained only if one already takes man's survival tendencies and potentialities for granted....

A state of adaptedness exists before the intentional processes of adaptation begin....

NOTE 2

Senn, M. J. E., 1947. Anticipatory guidance of the pregnant woman and her husband for their roles as parents. In: *Problems of Early Infancy (Transactions of the First Conference)*. New York: Josiah Macy, Jr. Foundation, pp. 11-16.

At the New York Hospital pediatricians who are Fellows in Pediatric-Psychiatry, interviewed women at various periods of pregnancy....In the experiment as set up, the pediatrician who interviewed the parents prenatally was the physician who examined the baby in the newborn period, planned its feeding program, and provided general medical care. This pediatrician was also responsible for the care of the baby throughout infancy and early childhood.

This experiment at the New York Hospital has shown that both men and women approaching parenthood do desire to talk about the coming event, and are exceedingly pleased to have an opportunity to meet and talk with the pediatrician who will care for their baby through the early years of its life. In fact, many women who heard about the experiment demanded pediatric consultation before the birth of their baby. Unfortunately this could be done only for relatively few women, as the experiment was set up on a limited scale.

It was brought out that the pregnant woman often is actually more apprehensive about her role as a mother than her ability to deliver a viable infant. She is anxious about her own health and the life of the fetus and fearful of her ability to come through labor without too much discomfort or delivery without dying in the process. Even with such great anxiety about labor and delivery, however, it is significant and interesting to learn that she has an almost equally great apprehension that she may somehow fail in her role as a mother in the years when she is to care for and guide her child.

The father also was invited to meet with the pediatrician and in every case he came for a least one prenatal interview.

At each interview the prospective parent or parents are encouraged to talk about the pregnancy, about their feelings generally, and to ask any questions concerning the infant and its care. The pediatrician's role is a dual one—that of listener and adviser. He describes technic of baby care, breast feeding, breast care before and after birth of the baby, weaning, supplementary and complementary formula feeding, and the preparation of foods. Practical advice is given as to what to purchase in the way of equipment. The advantages of breast feeding are mentioned but there is no attempt made to "sell" breast feeding to the exclusion of bottle feeding, lest the parents be overcome with guilt or other adverse emotions in those instances where breast feeding is attempted and is unsuccessful. The psychological concomitants of infant feeding are stressed repeatedly. In the interviews talk about the baby and its care is purposely limited to the newborn period, that is, the first month of life, lest the parents become confused and confounded by the manifold material discussed.

As a result of the prenatal pediatric interviews, the incidence of breast feeding can be kept above 80%. Furthermore, the mother is able to prepare for the neonatal care well in advance, so that she can spend a good part of her time caring for the infant without feeling guilty about other duties which are neglected or taken over by substitutes. The mother has learned technics of infant care and thereby is relaxed in her relationship to the new baby, her husband and others in the household. Where there are other children, both parents have been prepared for the usual sibling rivalry feelings and can protect the siblings as much as possible from the trauma, incident to the birth of the new baby. The father is able to accept the role as mother-substitute and as housewife-substitute because he has been told what the reality situation would be like in the household after the birth of the new baby, and to act in a supportive way to his wife not only during the pregnancy, but also through the neonatal period when the mother and newborn return to the home. Where other persons in the family have to be considered, either physically or psychologically, the prospective parents are encouraged to make arrangements for their temporary care outside the family well in advance of the birth of the baby so that their presence does not influence adversely the convalescence of the mother or the early life of the baby.

In conclusion, the experiment of interviewing pregnant women and their husbands in terms of their function as parents has demonstrated to pediatricians that their role as physician-guide to the mother could best begin before the birth of the infant, through what may be called "anticipatory guidance," and that modern pediatrics should train physicians so that this role might be filled with optimum benefit to parent and child alike.

references

1. Bernard, J. and Sontag, L. W., 1947. Fetal reactivity and sound. *J. Genet. Psychol.*, 70:205–210.

2. Bibring, G. L., Dwyer, T. F., Huntington, D. S., and Valenstein, A. F., 1961. A study of the psychological processes in pregnancy and of the earliest mother-child relationship. *The Psychoanalytic Study of the Child*, 16:9–72.

3. Drillien, C. M., 1964. The effect of obstetrical hazard on the later development of the child. In: *Recent Advances in Paediatrics*, D. Gairdner (ed.). London: Churchill.

4. Freud, A., 1954. Safeguarding the emotional health of our children: an inquiry

into the concept of the rejecting mother. In: *National Conferences of Social Work: Casework Papers*. New York: Family Service Association of America, 1955, p. 5.

5. Hartmann, H., 1939. *Ego Psychology and the Problem of Adaptation*. New York: International Universities Press, 1958 (tr. D. Rapaport).

6. Hooker, D., 1952. *The Prenatal Origin of Behavior*. Laurence, Kansas: University of Kansas Press.

7. Markham, S., 1961. A comparative evaluation of psychotic and non-psychotic reactions to childbirth. *Amer. J. Orthopsychiat.*, 31:565.

8. Normand, W. C., 1967. Post-partum disorders. In: *Comprehensive Textbook of Psychiatry*, A. M. Freedman and H. I. Kaplan (eds.). Baltimore: The Williams & Wilkins Co., 1161–1163.

9. Senn, M. J. E., 1947. Anticipatory guidance of the pregnant woman and her husband for their roles as parents. In: *Problems of Early Infancy (Transactions of the First Conference)*. New York: Josiah Macy, Jr. Foundation, pp. 11–16.

10. Winnicott, D. W., 1958. Mind and its relation to the psychesoma. In: *Collected Papers Through Paediatrics to Psycho-Analysis*. London: Tavistock Publications Ltd., p. 245.

11. Wolff, S., 1967. The contribution of obstetric complications to the etiology of behavior disorders in childhood. *J. Child Psychol. and Psychiat.*, 8 (1):57–66.

12. Zilboorg, G., 1931. Depressive reactions related to parenthood. *Amer. J. Psychiat.*, 87:927.

13. ——, 1957. The clinical issues of post-partum psychopathological reactions. *Amer. J. Obst. and Gynec.*, 73:305.

Chapter 2

EARLY INFANCY— THE FIRST YEAR

concept of development

Development is a complex process (Escalona, 1969). The linear growth and emergence of specific capacities is usually referred to as maturation. The totality of full blossoming and multiple uses of emerging functions and skills, brought about by interaction between the individual and his environment, and to which the events of maturation contribute, is called development. In this way development is the resultant of the mutual influences of endowment, maturation, and environmental factors. Human development appears to follow what Erikson calls the "epigenetic principle," which states that anything that grows has a *ground plan,* and that out of this plan the *parts* arise, each part having its *time* of special ascendency until all parts have arisen to form a *functioning whole* (Erikson, 1959).

A number of abstract criteria for development have been postulated. There is, first of all, a constant order of succession from one stage to another. Each successive stage in normal development represents an advance from the previous stage. Moreover, each later stage supersedes all earlier stages in that an inferior stage becomes part of a superior stage. The change is qualitative as well as quantitative. Each stage in development involves progressive structuralization of the psychic apparatus (see page 24). Development can be viewed as a whole or as a sector of the whole, such as "cognitive development." There is, lastly, an inevitable thrust toward development, given an environment that is appropriately nurturing and stimulating.

critical period

Implicit in the stage concept of theories of human development is the concept of the "critical period," analogous to the critical period in embryogenesis wherein certain organs are irreversibly laid down only at specific times and can never be formed at other times. In a broad general way there are critical periods in psychological development, such as the importance of the first 2 years for the development of the capacity to form relationships. However, attempts at greater specificity for this concept have run into difficulties because of the multiple variables involved in the development of any given function, the unitary functioning of the individual as a whole, and the possibilities for at least partial reversibility. For example, it had previously been postulated that if a child does not learn to read during the critical formative school years he will have difficulty in learning to read at a later date. To some extent this is true. However, the important emphasis here is in the ease of learning to read. Some illiterate adults inducted into the armed services can be taught to read, although not to read well. Moreover, the factors that resulted in the illiteracy are multiple. And, lastly, the critical period, if any, for learning to read may be quite extensive, so that even a prolonged period of illiteracy may subsequently give way to the capacity to read when the conditions change.

The difficulties involved in the irreversibility aspect of the concept of the critical period, as well as the mutiple factors that are usually at work, have led to a modification of the concept to one in which the individual will, say, achieve or learn some things better, faster, or with less training at some times in his life cycle than at others. This modification has been called the concept of the "sensitive period" (Wolff and Feinbloom, 1969). Few functions exist in pure isolation, and most clinical phenomena have multiple determinants. For example, stimulus deprivation, somatic injury, malnutrition, and other factors at work during the sensitive period of the early years may produce an end result of a child who has failed to thrive and appears to be arrested at a retarded level. Yet, it is still often difficult to assess the relative contribution of each of these antecedent factors, and usually impossible to say whether the function that appears to be affected (*e.g.*, intellectual development) is affected critically or irreversibly.

maternal deprivation

The concept of "critical period" may still be useful, however, particularly in very early development when irreversibility may indeed be a factor. Perhaps the best example of the use of the critical period concept is in the studies of early separation of mother and child where irreversibility is a strong possibility. For example, Spitz (1945), using the baby tests worked out by Hertzer and Wolf (1928), essentially studied 130 children, 61 in a foundling home and 69 in a nursery. The significant differences between the two institutions were as follows: the foundling home had few toys, the children were isolated and virtually screened from the world, lying supine in the hollow of their mattresses, and lacked all human contact for most of the day, particularly from the age of 3 months onward. The nursery, on the other hand, provided each child with a mother who gave, and continued to give, the child everything a good mother does and has.

Spitz found that the Developmental Quotient of children in the foundling home dropped from 124 to 72 by the end of the first year of life, and the children showed seriously decreased resistance to disease and an appalling mortality. Children in the nursery not only maintained but gained slightly in their Developmental Quotient (101.5 to 105 by the end of the first year of life).

The rapid decline in the development of children in the foundling home occurred at approximately the same time that they were weaned, *i.e.* between the third and fourth month. At this time even the human contact they had during nursing stopped. Their perceptual world was emptied of human partners. All the other kinds of deprivation could be compensated for by adequate mother-child relations, the very stimulation the foundling home children lacked.

Spitz concluded that it was the deprivation of maternal care, maternal stimulation, and maternal love that produced the clear evidence of damage to the foundling home infants, and that even when put in a more favorable environment after age 15 months, the psychosomatic damage could not be repaired by normal measures (Spitz, 1946). That is to say, the absence of adequate mothering during this critical period of development to all intents and purposes led to irreversible damage.

It would appear that this study supports the concept of critical period. However, Spitz himself was also careful to state that "whether it [the psychosomatic damage] can be repaired by therapeutic measures remains to be investigated." The qualifications of degree of irreversibility and extent of therapeutic intervention therefore are further considerations in the definition of the concept of critical period.

A further example of the concept of a critical period can be seen in the special case of gender identification arising out of the development of object relations. Gender identification is generally irreversibly established by $2\frac{1}{2}$ years of age. Wrong assignment of sex in the case of infants with intersex problems cannot usually be changed after that age. (See page 55.)

With these concepts in mind, development will be described here from the standpoints of maturation, personality development, cognitive development, and psychosocial development.

maturation

One of the great services Arnold Gesell did for pediatrics was to document in an orderly and detailed manner the sequence of skills that can be observed in a child as he advances in age (see Note 3). His work was avidly seized upon by pediatricians eager to reassure mothers that their child was normal. Unfortunately, the details of each step of maturation were sometimes taken as inviolable. The development of the child came to be viewed by some as an unfolding flower that only had to be watered and fed. Further, the precision with which each detail of any given stage was regarded in this viewpoint was unwarranted, since it did not take into account the enormous variation from child to child at any given age, and from time to time in any given child. And, of course, it did not completely answer the question of why a child behaved as he did, and what factors influenced his behavior. That is to say, the whole question of motivation and stimulation against the background of the interaction between equipment and relationships was sidestepped.

Nevertheless, important general sequences and milestones were described for the normal child, in a normal environment, and these are well worth noting.

motor sequence

Gesell and Amatruda (1941) observed that most children creep, can be pulled to their feet, and have a crude prehensory release by the time they are 10 months old. Within the next 2 months they can walk with help, and can prehend a small pellet. By 2 years of age they are running with ease, although not with great skill.

adaptive sequence

Similarly, by 10 months of age a child can combine 2 cubes, and within 2 months he can release a cube in a cup. By 2 years of age he can build a tower of 6 cubes, and can imitate a circular motion with a crayon on paper.

language sequence

The sequence of emergence of actual sounds is broadly the same in all children everywhere (Lewis, 1963). Children vocalize and respond to sounds from birth, and possibly do both prenatally too. The child can be soothed specifically by the voice of his mother as early as the first few weeks. The early phonetic characteristics of discomfort-cries of the infant appear to be the vocal manifestations of his total reaction to discomfort, determined in part by the physiological contraction of his facial muscles. By about the sixth week, the infant begins to utter repetitive strings of sound called babbling. In doing so, he finds satisfaction in producing at will those sounds which at first have occurred involuntarily, acquires skills in making sounds, and imitates as best he can the sounds of others. The nearer the approximation of his sounds to those of his parents, the more marked will be the approval of his parents, and the greater will be his incentive to repeat sounds. In this way he acquires the phonetic pattern of his mother tongue. What is important here is that in these earliest weeks the frequency and variety of sounds already may be restricted through inadequate fostering by the caring adult. A full account of how children learn to speak has been described by Lewis (1959).

Most children at 10 months heed their name when called, and usually understand certain simple commands (although this may be more the tone with which, say, the command "No!" is said than the word itself). Often the child can say a word, as well as ma-ma and da-da. More words are added, until by age 2 years a child usually has two sentences and can say "I."

personal-social development

A 10-month-old child can feed himself a cracker (sloppily), play "peek-a-boo," "pat-a-cake," and "so-big." Within 12 months he is finger feeding and somewhat cooperative in dressing. By 2 years of age he is verbalizing his toilet needs and playing with elementary jig-saw puzzles, balls, and pull toys. He is picking things up, throwing them down, and imitating others.

role of activity

It is important to keep in mind, however, that while the sequence just outlined is accurate, the timetable is immensely variable. Moreover, the child contributes to his own velocity of development. First of all, children start off with different innate capacities; some are active, some quiet, and some highly unpredictable. Fries attempted to classify children into various congenital activity types, suggesting that there was a continuity of a general activity level for given individuals (Fries and Woolf, 1953). More than this, however, is the fact that the infant's level of activity is an important determinant in his own development. For example, babies who are constitutionally very active and mobile appear to suffer less from a period of understimulation during a hospital stay than do less active babies (Schaffer, 1966). Moreover, later in development the interaction between equipment factors, including motor activity and sensitivity to discomfort on the one hand, and environmental factors including stimulation and the ability to soothe the infant on the other hand, subtly contribute to the identification processes of the infant (Ritvo and Solnit, 1958).

role of stimulation

At the same time, the amount and kind of stimulation a child receives greatly affects the degree of development and use of any particular skill that may appear on schedule and in its rudimentary form. The amount of stimulation provided by the adults is one of the major determinants of the infant's behavior (Schaffer and Emerson, 1964).

stimulation and language development

Specific stimulation for language development mentioned earlier is a case in point. In a study of 75 family-reared children and 75 institutionalized infants, Provence and Lipton (1962) observed that the response of the parent contributes to the process of differentiation in the infant's mental functioning. The parent's repetition, labeling, and response to the baby's reactions to his environment, his feelings, his vocalizations, etc., are important to his recognition of himself, of other persons, and of his world. Further, such responses of others are essential to the development of meaningful speech. For example, one of the ways in which the mother appears to influence the development of speech is through a process of "mutual imitation." Moreover, the mother's speech is "both a carrier of the emotions and an organizing influence on the infant's mental apparatus." The mother, through her way of responding to the infant in action, and especially in speech, identifies or "labels" for him many things such as people, toys, himself, his feelings and actions and those of others. He comes to be able to identify many aspects of inner and outer reality because she provides the appropriate experiences.

On the other hand, for the institutionalized infant who is

placed in a family at the end of the first year, there is a much later period when the speech is predominantly used to express a need or to repeat in a literal way some phrase or sentence learned by rote or from imitation of the parent. ". . . . it takes much longer before the (institutionalized) children verbalize their fantasies, comment upon their play, ask questions that express a wish to learn about things or talk about feelings. . . . In these (institutionalized) children one can demonstrate on the tests during and after the second year a greater facility in the aspects of language that represents a concreteness of thought (*e.g.* ability to name objects or pictures) than in some of the speech that reflects a capacity for more abstract and flexible thought." The institutionalized child's understanding of the adult's language is also retarded.

stimulation and visual activity

Another example of specific stimulation enhancing development is the increased growth of visual attention that comes about after extra handling of institutionalized infants (White and Held, 1966). Korner and Grobstein (1966) have also observed that when a crying newborn is picked up and put to the shoulder, there is an increase in the frequency of eye opening, alertness and scanning, as well as the obvious soothing effect. Calibration of the degree of attention to both visual and auditory stimulation in the newborn is achieved by using changes in the heart rate, motor responsivity and other measurable responses (Lewis, *et al.*, 1966).

influence of infant upon the mother

At the same time, the infant does not simply develop in response to the environment. The infant always makes a contribution of his own. Indeed, maternal behavior seems initially to be under the control of the stimulus and reinforcing conditions provided by the young infant in such a way that at first the mother is shaped by the infant, and this later facilitates her shaping the behavior of the infant (Moss, 1967). For example, eye-to-eye contact seems to serve to foster positive maternal feelings (Robson, 1967). These feelings in the mother have something to do with "being recognized" in a highly personal and intimate way, and it is perhaps for this reason that mothers of blind children often feel rebuffed at first. Again, Bowlby (1958) believes that the smiling of an infant acts as a social releaser of instinctual responses in the mother, along with such other innate "releasers" as crying, following, clinging, and sucking. Lorenz (1966) has gone so far as to suggest that the human smile is also a ritualized form of aggression comparable to the "greeting" ceremonies which inhibit intraspecific fighting in many lower animals.

infant's needs

In any case the infant responds to an internal as well as external environment. Initially the internal life of the infant consists of felt needs. These needs seem to fall into two categories, one immediate and the other long-range. The immediate needs are for relief of hunger, relief of discomfort, for sleep, and a need to suck. The infant appears to have little tolerance if any of these needs are unsatisfied.

The long-range needs are for the warmth and security of a mothering person, adequate stimulation (an infant needs to be talked to), and graduated performance expectations. While the infant may appear to have greater tolerance if any of these long-range needs are not met, serious character defects may appear later as a result of significant early deprivation in any of these areas.

sleep

Sleep in the infant has certain interesting characteristics. During the first few weeks of life the infant sleeps two-thirds of the time, for approximately 50-minute periods. This sleep of the infant may represent a third state of being inasmuch as a major proportion of his sleep appears to be so-called "rapid eye movement (R.E.M.) sleep." The phenomenon of rapid eye movement associated with the periodic low voltage phase that occurs in a regular electroencephalographic sleep cycle was first described by Aserinsky and Kleitman (1953). This phase of sleep appeared to have a periodicity in adults of 90 minutes, and lasted about 20 minutes. When adult subjects were awakened during this phase of "rapid eye movement (R.E.M.) sleep," a high incidence of dream recall was noted. Aserinsky and Kleitman postulated a special inhibiting mechanism that blocked all motor movement except those of the eye and middle ear muscles, and occasional brief muscle twitchings. When R.E.M. sleep was interrupted and the subject was deprived of R.E.M. sleep, there followed an increase in the number of times R.E.M. sleep appeared, an increase in the actual amount of R.E.M. sleep, and an increase in the size and duration of the twitches. There was also a shift toward hyperexcitability in the behavior of the subject. Anxiety seems to be a naturally occurring phenomenon that possibly suppresses R.E.M. sleep.

The curious fact is that the infant seems to spend much of his sleep in the R.E.M. state (Dreyfus-Brisac, *et al.*, 1958), at a time in his life when there is unlikely to be much content to his dreams, if indeed he is dreaming at all. A 10-week premature infant has about 80% of his sleep in the R.E.M. state, and a full-term infant has about 50% of his sleep in the R.E.M. state. There is thereafter a steady decline in the percentage of sleep during the R.E.M. state, to the extent that at the end of the first year it is down to 35%, and by 5 years of age it is only 20%. A shift toward a night pattern of sleep occurs at about 16 weeks of age, although the infant at this state is still rarely awake for more than 3 hours at a time (Parmelee, *et al.*, 1964). A plausible hypothesis is that this R.E.M. state is regulated by as yet unknown biochemical mechanisms, and may well have important basic survival functions prior to any consequent hypothesized functions of dreaming. Whatever its function, an adequate amount of R.E.M. sleep is an important need for the infant.

modes of need satisfaction

Most of the needs just mentioned are met within the mutual adaptation that occurs between the infant, who is born with a certain degree of preadaptiveness (Hartmann, 1939), and the "ordinary devoted mother" (Winnicott, 1945) who creates a sense of "basic" trust in her child. This sense of trust is engendered by the mother's appropriate and reliable response to her sensitive and accurate perception of the baby's needs (Erikson, 1959; see Note 4). Furthermore, for the first year or two the situation of greatest exchange and intimacy is when the child is being fed, coinciding as it does with the primacy of the buccal mucosa as the organ of greatest sensitivity.

But there are other important modes of exchange and gratification that should not be neglected during this early period. These modes include visual, auditory, tactile and kinesthetic stimulation.

signs of unmet needs

If these needs are not met soon, signs of acute tension appear, and if there is a chronic deficiency of need fulfillment, signs of a disorder of development appear. The signs of acute tension in early infancy are diffuse, and may consist of restlessness, fretfulness, whining, crying, clinging, physical tenseness, and various visceral dysfunctions such as vomiting, diarrhea, or a sleep disturbance. The extent and duration of the deprivation are significant factors. For example, weaning that is attempted too early, or is performed too abruptly, may cause acute anxiety in the child.

More prolonged deprivations of one or more of the need-satisfying nutrients of this stage may influence the development of the child in the direction of a personality that remains clinging and dependent, or that craves food and drink to console himself in times of stress, or that strives aggressively to win love or is chronically envious. Inconsistent gratifications may influence the child in the direction of an untrusting personality. Massive chronic early deprivation is found in children who develop the syndrome of "affectionless characters" (Bowlby, 1951; see Note 5), or "failure to thrive" (Leonard, *et al.,* 1966), or in some cases of failure to grow in height. Complete loss of the mother in the second half of the first year without any replacement mothering gives rise to the syndrome of "anaclitic depression," the chief symptoms of which are a dejected expression and a reluctance for motility (Spitz, 1946).

early personality development and the sense of self

Implied in what has been said so far is that the rudiments of the personality are present in the earliest period of life, and that the development of the personality stems, in part, from the body and its needs. It is necessary now to examine further the process by which the personality develops.

The body, first of all, is an obvious source of gratification as well as discomfort for the infant. He actively touches his body frequently, at first through random movement, next through intentional action, *e.g.* thumb or finger in the mouth, sometimes as early as 3 to 6 weeks. Furthermore, he passively receives body comforts of a rich variety as he is fed, burped, diapered, cuddled, whirled in the air, etc. Indeed, the infant appears initially to perceive his environment only to the extent that it alters his body. Fingers and mouth are highly important to the infant at this stage, constituting the first autoerotic play activity (Freud, S., 1905), with visual images and auditory impressions supplementing the earliest beginnings of fantasy formation. In the early months he does not initially appear to discriminate between his own fingers and those of others, his own mouth and that of his mother's (often mistaken for a sign of altruism or generosity as he puts food into his mother's mouth instead of his own). Further, an external object exists for the infant, if it exists at all, only as long as it gratifies a need. To the extent that for the infant the external environment and his internal life are as one, the infant may be said at first to be in a state of "primary identification" (Freud, S., 1923). To the extent also that the infant is oblivious of the external world, he may be said to be in a normal autistic state (Mahler, 1968). The infant then gradually perceives a breast, or the mother's face, although it is thought that the image is not well formed initially. This image of the breast, or mother, comes to be associated in the infant's mind with the need-fulfilling properties he attributes to the breast or mother. Hence, this stage is often called the need-fulfilling (or part-object) stage of object relations. The further development of the infant's relationships with others (termed "object relations" in psychoanalytic theory) will be returned to shortly.

origins of reality testing

The infant next discerns that some stimuli and sources of gratification can only come from the outside, indicating that he is beginning to make a distinction between stimuli that come from within and stimuli that come from the outside—so-called "reality testing." This function of reality testing is continually reinforced by his widening experience that some things are present and some are not ("peek-a-boo" games); some feelings can be made to go away, others cannot. That is to say, he is becoming increasingly aware of the boundaries between himself and the external world, and in doing so becomes aware of himself as a separate person.

development of object relations

During the earliest period when the infant does not as yet have an image of a particular face, he is said to be at the pre-object, or part-object, stage of relations (Spitz, 1965). Experimental evidence has shown, however, that the infant can recognize a pattern at this time. For example, a smile response can be elicited at 3 to 6 months by a mask consisting specifically of a forehead, eyes, and nose, in motion to distinguish it from the background (Spitz, 1965; see Note 6).

stranger anxiety

By the second half of the first year there are clear signs that the infant is now aware of a person as a whole object. He begins to imitate the other person, and begins to show signs of anxiety when he is confronted with a person who is unfamiliar to him—so-called "stranger anxiety." This phenomenon was first described by Baldwin (1895) who called it "organic bashfulness," and has since then been the subject of continuous study (Rheingold, 1968). It is most prominent at about 8 months of age. Several inferences may be drawn from this phenomenon. First, since the infant can now differentiate between his mother's face and that of a stranger, he must by now have a better defined mental image of his mother which he can also retain, i.e. he has clearly made use of the function of memory. Furthermore, he has clearly endowed that mental representation with certain attributes, e.g. security. This quality, while first attributed to the external object (the mother), has now been taken in (introjected) and is now a part of the more or less constant internalized mental representation of the mother.

early object relations and object constancy

The fact that he now begins to relate to people as people—and not simply as need-fulfilling objects—is a further step in the development of his capacity for object relations. Moreover, the external object (person) becomes increasingly experienced by the infant as being quite firmly separate from himself. And the infant, as already stated, is now able to retain in his memory a constant image of this other person. At this point the infant is said to have reached, but not yet fully consolidated, the stage of object constancy. (See page 55.)

early defense mechanisms

The infant appears now to have also exercised at least two further processes, or mechanisms, those of projection of an internal state onto the external object, and the introjection of those projected attributes to form an internalized mental object. These two processes, or mechanisms, are now available to the infant and form the earliest "defense mechanisms" (Freud, S., 1926) by which the infant attempts to deal with anxiety.

All of these functions—the sense of self, the capacity for object relations, the ability to test reality, and the use of defense mechanisms—are relatively enduring and autonomous, and as such they are referred to as psychic "structures" and are subsumed under the general heading of the "ego."

beginning of thought

At the same time that these functions are developing, the infant begins to manifest certain further changes in his thought processes. Early primary process thinking, characterized by virtually no capacity to delay the urge for immediate gratification of a need, rapid shifting from activity to activity in search of gratification (e.g. crying, thumb sucking, mouthing, tongue protrusion, when trying to gratify hunger), and the use of such preverbal processes as visual and auditory impressions, is still quite prominent in the first year of life. However, he now begins to use language and exhibits a form of logic, and he is developing an increased capacity to tolerate delay and frustration. This subsequent form of thinking is referred to as secondary process.

In the first month of life the infant seems to exercise a function simply because it is there, but there are a few signs of coordinated activity. The infant learns to recognize the nipple, but he cannot coordinate his head and his hand when his thumb falls out of his mouth. While he seems to be a sucking, looking, listening and grasping individual, it is impossible to know of what he is aware. As mentioned earlier, he is said to be in a state of primary repression, in the sense that there is no evidence yet of conscious thought. However, within a few months the infant finds that a chance action leads to a pleasurable experience, and this may act as one of the earliest stimuli to repeat that action—a so-called "primary circular reaction" (Piaget, 1952). Thus, there is now evidence of thinking, and it would appear that motor activity is one of the primary sources from which thinking develops. Piaget has put heavy emphasis upon the necessity of action for cognitive growth.

The first 8 months or so are particularly important from the point of view of later perceptive and intellectual development, since it is during this period that the child constructs the foundations of his cognitive structures. The actual process by which reality data are treated or modified so as to become incorporated into the psychic structure is just as important as any intrinsic connections in the external stimuli, since the infant becomes aware of these intrinsic connections only to the extent that he can assimilate them by means of his existing schema or structures. The basic cognitive structure in Piaget's account of cognitive development is, in fact, the "schema." A particular object in the environment arouses a behavior pattern, or "schema," in the child. This schema is then applied to an increasing variety of objects. New objects that are similar to the first object become "assimilated" into the existing schema.

thumb sucking

Take once more, for example, the phenomenon of thumb sucking, this time looked at from the cognitive viewpoint. Fortuitous, accidental, or reflex thumb sucking may occur prenatally. However, sometimes as early as the second month a more systematic thumb sucking involving coordination of hand and mouth occurs, indicating an assimilation with a previously existing schema of the breast, or nipple. Another way to put this is to say that the infant's previous sucking experience (the schema of, say, a nipple) is now broadened to include a new, but similar, experience, the thumb. The thumb, more specifically the new motor act of bringing the thumb into the mouth and the new sensory experience of the thumb, has now been assimilated into the previous schema with which it was initially matched. Much later in development this same process is used to assimilate similar but new ideas.

If the new aspect of the environment encountered is too dissimilar from the existing schema, then the existing schema in turn "accommodates," *i.e.* the existing schema is modified. For example, an infant will encounter an animal which he will call, say, "doggie." The "schema" subsumed under the concept "doggie" will, for a while, "assimilate" all new and similar animals, so that all animals will temporarily be called "doggie." Eventually an encounter with an animal which is sufficiently different will stimulate the child to modify his "schema" of doggie. The new "schema" will have "doggie" as a concept with more specific features, while other animals will be subsumed under different names. This modification of the schema is what Piaget means by accommodation. Assimilation and accommodation are reciprocal mental operations.

It is important to note that Piaget's account of cognitive development is based upon the interaction between the individual and his environment; it is not a theory of simple innate maturation, nor does it follow a simple stimulus—contingency model. As a matter of fact, Piaget became interested in the reasoning process behind the wrong answers given by children while he was attempting a standardization of Cyril Burt's tests on children in Binet's Laboratory School in Paris. Then, for the first time, cognitive structure was studied as an internal organization of patterns of thought, fulfilling the abstract criteria of development previously mentioned.

Some time in the second half of the first year of life the infant enters what Piaget calls the sub-stage of "secondary circular reactions" when he begins to alter his environment intentionally to satisfy a need. He will, for example, shake a crib to produce movement in a mobile suspended above him. But he may also believe that any other movement he observes while shaking the crib is the result of his action. Moreover, he seems to believe that the very existence of objects, and their movements, is entirely dependent on his actions and his perceptions. What the infant at this stage cannot see does not, for him, exist. The qualitative cognitive change that occurs in the evolution of secondary circular reactions may also be associated with neurophysiological changes in the brain. Thus the change from primary to secondary circular reaction may be related to the way in which the slow delta activity seen in the EEG is interspersed with faster activity (Walter, 1956).

Toward the end of the first year an increasing coordination of schemata can be observed, and the child begins to be aware of the existence of unperceived objects. He may knock down a screen to get at a hidden toy, and he seems now to behave as though he were aware that objects may be moved by external forces. Moreover, he will now begin to explore an object more fully, and the beginnings of an experimental approach can be seen, with so-called "tertiary circular reactions" (see Note 7) appearing. In these reactions the child will seek or create new situations to which he can react. He is learning about spatial relations, and will start putting smaller objects in and out of larger ones. However, he is not yet able to understand that he has to rotate a long toy through a right angle in order to pull it through the bars of a play pen; he will try to pull it through as it is.

Curiously, it appears that perception often, if not usually, precedes action, at least after the foundations of the initial schemata. For example, a child will frequently discriminate sounds before he can articulate them (Berko and Brown, 1960), or will distinguish forms long before he can draw them (Ling, 1941).

infantile fantasy life

Just exactly what goes on in the infant's mind during the first 6 months is not known. It *looks* as though the infant is engaged in an active fantasy life, and evidence adduced during psychoanalysis of adults has led to *inferences* that this fantasy life may have certain general characteristics. However, we have no direct access to the infant's thoughts at this stage, and any attempt at description is limited by the boundaries of direct observation of infantile behavior; the inferential nature of reconstruction from material derived from adult and child analyses; the impossibility of recapturing a pure preverbal state; and the handicap of sophisticated adult language.

Nevertheless, the urge to understand the infant has led to speculations about this early fantasy life. For example, Klein (1960) has suggested that in the first 3 or 4 months of life the infant is filled with omnipotent fantasies. Omnipotent fantasies are fostered by the repeated gratifications that follow an infant's active demands. For example, he may scream with hunger, and a nipple immediately and consistently is placed in his mouth. At the same time, every discomfort is thought to be experienced by the infant as inflicted by the outside, as though he were being persecuted. This attack gives rise to anxiety, which Klein has called "persecutory anxiety." Further consequences of the fantasy of being persecuted include the creation and welling up of revengeful destructive fantasies. Since the infant also highly values what he perceives as the attacking object (the "nipple" or "breast"), he meanwhile strives to preserve his source of gratification. He is said to accomplish this by splitting off his feelings of love from his feelings of hate. Some of the hate, which was first projected onto the "breast," is now turned inward and introjected, and the "breast" is preserved. The infant retains a feeling of gratitude, but sometimes experiences envy and often experiences greed. This whole speculative complex Klein calls the paranoid-schizoid position.

At about 5 to 6 months of age the infant, Klein postulates, becomes frightened of the harm his destructive impulses (some of which have been turned inward) and his enormous greed might do, and this gives rise to a depressive anxiety—the so-called depressive position. The infant then tries to placate his mother and make reparations by trying to please.

infantile anxiety

What can be said with some degree of certainty is that the infant does appear to manifest signs of tension or anxiety, and the commonest danger situation which seems to evoke anxiety during the first 18 months is the threat of losing the mother. Anxiety initially seems to develop automatically whenever the psychic apparatus is overwhelmed by an influx of stimuli, whether internal or external, too great to be mastered or discharged. As the ego develops, anxiety is produced in anticipation of such a danger. This anticipatory anxiety seems to act as a signal to activate whatever mechanisms are available to the infant to reduce or inhibit the danger situation. The advantage of signal anxiety over automatic anxiety is that it is less massive, does not incapacitate, and is far more economical and adaptive.

The findings and concepts just described have significance for normal child-rearing practices and for the understanding of certain pathological states. One of the goals of normal child rearing, for example, is to promote the development of a strong ego. Some of the factors that contribute to this development may be derived from a knowledge of child development. Thus, each of the ego functions mentioned earlier (page 24) requires specific conditions for optimum development; a few of the minimal requirements follow.

The sense of self requires consistent, gratifying responses from the adult, appropriate labeling of feelings and body parts, opportunities for body play and exploration, stimulation from the environment, and protection from states of overwhelming anxiety.

The development of object relations requires the reliable presence of a mother or mothering person who can perceive and respond to the infant's needs in an appropriate manner. Reliable presence implies at the very least the absence of prolonged separations, especially during the critical period of psychic representation formation that becomes prominent during the second 6 months of life and proceeds to object constancy during the period approximately 8 months to 3 or 4 years of age. Prolonged separation may still be a hazard after that age, but is less likely to be as crippling to the development of object relations than separation inevitably is during these early years. Reliable presence also implies a continuity of care, affection, and appropriate responsiveness.

The notion of the mother perceiving and responding in an appropriate manner should not be construed as meaning that the mother must precisely understand every need of her child and meet each need exactly. This would be an impossible task, and in any case would not promote development. The child learns what his needs are through the mother's approximate responses, and also learns to tolerate minor frustrations through the mother's unavoidable inexact or incomplete responses. However, it does imply that the mother protects the child from intolerable unpleasure and anxiety, and responds with appropriate measures to meet most of the child's needs; *i.e.*, if the child is crying from hunger, he is fed, and if he is crying from physical discomfort, he may require diapering.

The development of the ability to test reality requires an environment that labels events correctly for the child, provides appropriate visual, auditory, tactile, and kinesthetic stimulation, and reasonably gratifies the child.

The development of capacity to tolerate frustrations, and later mobilize defenses against anxiety, depends in part on the kind and degree of frustration to which the child is exposed.

Frustration experiences within the infant's current capacity for delay can be increasingly tolerated. Frustration that is real and rational, and not created artificially, is better tolerated by the infant, and also facilitates reality testing. Since the infant may interpret reality frustrations as hostile attacks upon him, explanations of the actuality of the frustration may minimize the tendency to form such frightening fantasies; may reduce the anxiety that such fantasies arouse; and may promote the use of secondary process logic in dealing with anxiety. However, the young child's ego usually requires additional support when the frustration exceeds the child's tolerance. For example, if separation from mother is for too long a period of time, a substitute mothering person or aspects of the mother is required.

The findings and concepts described earlier are also helpful in understanding certain pathological states. For example, sometimes there is an intrinsic internal failure to make meaningful patterns out of sensory stimuli, with a consequent handicap in dealing with the demands of the environment. The condition of early childhood autism is an extreme example of this kind of failure.

infantile autism

 The syndrome, first described by Kanner (1943), occurs in 2

or 3 per 10,000 children, with boys affected 3 times as often as girls. While there may be an onset as late as the second, third, or fourth years of life, many cases can be diagnosed within the first year of life. At first the child may appear to have normal developmental milestones, at least grossly. However, closer observation might reveal that speech is either not developing at all or is replete with such disorders as echolalia, disordered naming, fragmentation, altered order, portmanteauisms, etc. Speech in these children is an important prognostic factor: children in whom speech does not develop by the age of 5 years have a poor prognosis. The child may also manifest difficulty in developing such normal routines as sleeping, feeding, and eliminating. He may also show no anticipatory or adaptive posturing, seems unresponsive, and has a desire for sameness. He avoids looking you straight in the eye, and seems happiest indeed when left alone or when whirled. Furthermore, he shows a preference for inanimate things. He may strum his fingers toward the periphery of his gaze, but he is not blind. He may ignore loud sounds, but he is not deaf. Sometimes he is excessively quiet; at other times he may scream, rock, and bang his head.

The cause of this syndrome is not known. Environmentalists such as Kanner (1943), Rank (1955), Despert (1947), and Putnam (1955) have considered the primary disorder to be in the mother. Bender (1953), on the other hand, has taken an exclusively biological viewpoint, asserting that the pathological condition strikes at the substratum of integrative functioning be it vegetative, motor, perceptual, intellectual, emotional, or social. Because mixed clinical pictures occur, it is unlikely that either position alone would explain all cases, yet the clinical pictures are not clear enough to say which may be caused by the mother (if any), and which by organic causes. This has led others to invoke Freud's theory of the complemental series (Freud, 1905)[1] and look to see how both possible causes might interact with each other to cause the various clinical

1. "The constitutional factor must await experiences before it can make itself felt; the accidental factor must have a constitutional basis in order to come into operation. To cover the majority of cases we can picture what has been described as a 'complemental series', in which the diminishing intensity of one factor is balanced by the increasing intensity of the other."

pictures. In milder types, a state of "unusual sensitivity" has been postulated (Bergman and Escalona, 1949). In these cases the children appear to be easily hurt, easily stimulated, and unevenly precocious. The hypothesis is that these infants, who are not sufficiently protected from stimuli either because of a "thin protective barrier or because of the failure of maternal protection," may have to resort for such protection to premature formation of an ego. When this premature ego breaks down, possibly as a consequence of a trauma, the psychotic manifestations are thought to set in.

Margaret Mahler (1952) similarly hypothesized that the essential factor is a deficiency in the infant which interferes with the infant's capacity to utilize his mother for homeostasis. In this view it is the type of interaction between mother and child rather than the pathological condition of the mother that is important, and it is the infant's constitutional deficiency that leads to the pathogenic mother-child interaction. When psychosis does become manifest, the mother then is almost forced to give up her normal mothering function, and the infant remains fixated at the normal autistic phase.

The likelihood of a basic brain abnormality is high (Wing, 1966). Signs of brain damage or organic abnormalities are found with a greater frequency than in the normal population, and the characteristic perceptual and speech difficulties seem to be specific for this condition. In many cases there have been complications during the pregnancy.

In many, though not all, cases the manifestation of the constitutional deficiency within the child gives rise to an abnormal relationship between mother and child. A child in the normal autistic phase enjoys a social symbiosis between himself and his mother, with the infant utilizing the mother's capacity to serve as an external, auxiliary ego. If this is disturbed because of a primary disorder within the child, normal social biological adaptation fails to occur, with a subsequent failure in maturation, cognition, and ego development. Secondary reactions on the part of parents who have to deal day in and day out with a child who is emotionally draining and unresponsive further add to the child's difficulties, and further confuse the clinical picture.

Unfortunately, the prognosis in these children is guarded (Eisenberg, 1956). The majority have a poor outcome. Half of one group of 63 children studied remained in full-time residential settings, and 30 out of the same initial group of 63 remained mute. Only 3 of the 63 who had reached age 9 years could be said to function well academically and socially.

The syndrome of early childhood autism just described represents an extreme example of a primary intrinsic failure in the infant interacting with his environment. On the other hand, a number of other childhood syndromes primarily related to states of acute material insufficiency can also lead to disorders of early development. For example, the failure-to-thrive syndrome in infants and the syndrome of accidental poisoning in childhood are typical results of a breakdown in mothering which may have occurred for a variety of reasons. Certain cases of child abuse also fall into this category, as do children who present themselves frequently with injuries, sometimes quite consciously self-inflicted. The resources of the mothers in these families are often markedly depleted, and such mothers often feel unsupported and overwhelmed. Complete absence of any mothering at all of course leads to the syndrome of anaclitic depression, seen in some institutionalized infants.

maternal insufficiency

Failure to thrive in infants may have many causes, one of which is a disturbance in the mother-child relationship (Patton and Gardner, 1962). In one study of 13 infants ranging in age from 10 weeks to 27 months, who had fallen progressively below the third percentile in weight, Leonard, *et al.*, (1966) found multiple problems in each of their families. None of the mothers reported receiving dependable and appropriate nurturing during their own childhood, and many expressed current feelings of inadequacy. The fathers in these families were often absent, uninvolved in family life, and unsupportive. The infants themselves showed a wide range of abnormal behavior, ranging from unusual watchfulness and an unsmiling expression in the youngest infants, through to absence of any stranger anxiety in the 4- to 10-month-old infants, and superficial personal-social relationships in the older infants. Leonard postulated that the selection of the particular child who failed to thrive might have been brought about by multiple factors, including the psychological impact upon the mother of the complications of pregnancy that frequently occurred, the dissonance between the infant's temperament and the mother's personality, and the added burden that the infant represented to an already depleted mother. All of these factors contain a component that represents the infant's role in shaping the very environmental factors that are so detrimental to his own development. What is of further interest in this study is the view of motherhood as an unfolding developmental plan which is activated by pregnancy and the birth of a child. The mothers in this study fell into the category of what Anna Freud has called "unwilling mothers" (Freud, A., 1955), although this alone did not answer the question of exactly which are the most significant psychological factors that interfere with the normal, mutual thriving of mother and infant.

social deprivation

Maternal deprivation must also be seen in its social context. It has long been known that mothers in the lower socio-economic bracket have an increased incidence of complications of pregnancy and birth (Baird, 1959). Indeed, in some respects the disparity between the risks for the disadvantaged and the advantaged appears to be increasing over the years. For example, in the United States in 1930 twice as many non-white mothers died in childbirth as did white mothers; by 1960, 4 times as many non-white mothers died in childbirth as did white mothers (Baumgartner, 1965). The risks consequent upon the increased incidence of complications of pregnancy and labor (themselves due to multiple causes), and the increased incidence of postnatal pathology (such as iron deficiency anemia), expose infants who are economically and socially disadvantaged or who are in an ethnic group exposed to discrimination to massively excessive risks for maldevelopment (Birch, 1968). For example, malnutrition alone reduces the child's responsiveness to stimulation, and this reduced responsiveness itself can induce apathy in the adult who is caring for the child. In this sense, the child adds to his own disadvantaged environment. This underlying, mutual apathy may later result in an impairment of the capacity for satisfying object relations and, later still, learning (Cravioto, et al., 1966).

Children reared in the lower socio-economic group also seem to have a greater exposure to external dangers. For example, there appears to be a greater incidence of burns and other accidents in children in the lower socio-economic group (Spence, et al., 1954). Moreover, many mothers in the lower socio-economic group are often young and inexperienced and offer a different kind of mothering to an infant. Marked class differences have also been found in child-rearing methods, although the research findings are conflicting. For example, Sears found that middle class mothers are more permissive than those of the lower class (Sears, et al., 1957), while Davis concluded that middle class mothers are more restrictive (Davis and Havighurst, 1947). Whiting and Child (1953) went so far as to claim that children of the American middle class are among the most restricted anywhere in the world. In socially and culturally deprived homes there is usually little space and few toys or books. Parents are often preoccupied with their own problems and may have little energy to invest in their children's achievements (Wolff, 1969).

In summary, physical, socio-economic, cultural and educational factors in our society clearly have a significant impact upon the development of the child, and no study of the development of an individual is complete without an understanding of these factors (Eisenberg, 1968; N.I.C.H.D., 1969).

NOTE 3

Gesell, A. and Amatruda, C. S., 1941. *Developmental Diagnosis,* 2nd Edition (1964). New York: Paul B. Hoeber Medical Division, Harper & Row, Pub., pp. 8–14.

Stages and Sequences of Development.

Before describing diagnostic procedures it will be profitable to take a bird's-eye view of the territory which is to be explored by the developmental examination. Development is a continuous process. Beginning with conception it proceeds stage by stage in orderly sequence, each stage representing a degree or level of maturity. There are so many such levels that we must select a few which will serve best as a frame of reference for purposes of diagnosis. We have determined upon the following Key Ages: 4, 16, 28, 40 weeks; 12, 18, 24, 36 months.

To appreciate the developmental significance of these key ages it is well to examine their position in the early cycle of human growth. This cycle is depicted in the five charts which follow. The first chart gives a comprehensive view of the entire scope of development; it includes the fetal period, to indicate the continuity of the growth cycle.

The organization of behavior begins long before birth; and the general direction of this organization is from head to foot, from proximal to distal segments. Lips and tongue lead, eye muscles follow, then neck, shoulder, arms, hands, fingers, trunk, legs, feet. The chart reflects this law of developmental direction; it also suggests that the four distinguishable fields of behavior develop conjointly in close co-ordination.

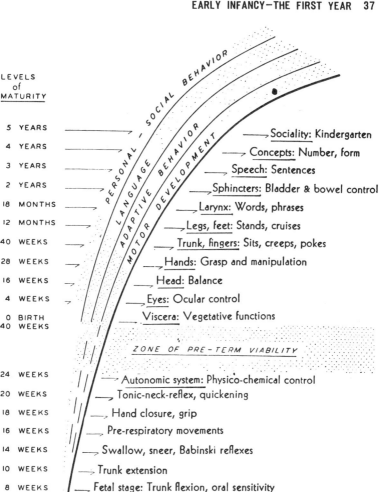

Fig. 1. The development of behavior in the four major fields.

In terse terms the trends of behavior development are as follows.

In the first quarter of the first year the infant gains control of his twelve oculo-motor muscles.

In the second quarter (16–28 weeks) he comes into command of the muscles which support his head and move his arms. He reaches out for things.

In the third quarter (28–40 weeks) he gains command of his trunk and hands. He sits. He grasps, transfers and manipulates objects.

In the fourth quarter (40–52 weeks) he extends command to his legs and feet; to his forefingers and thumb. He pokes and plucks.

In the second year he walks and runs; articulates words and phrases; acquires bowel and bladder control; attains a rudimentary sense of personal identity and of personal possession.

In the third year he speaks in sentences, using words as tools of thought; he shows a positive propensity to understand his environment and to comply with cultural demands. He is no longer a mere infant.

In the fourth year he asks innumerable questions, perceives analogies, displays an active tendency to conceptualize and generalize. He is nearly self-dependent in routines of home life.

At five he is well matured in motor control. He hops and skips. He talks without infantile articulation. He can narrate a long tale. He prefers associative play; he feels socialized pride in clothes and accomplishment. He is a self-assured, conforming citizen in his small world.

The remaining four charts diagram the sequences of development in Motor, Adaptive, Language, and Personal-Social fields of behavior. These four fields develop interdependently; and an adequate estimate of behavior maturity demands an appraisal of each major field. Each chart shows selected behavior patterns which illustrate the progressions of normal development. These patterns give a preliminary suggestion of the practical application of behavior norms.

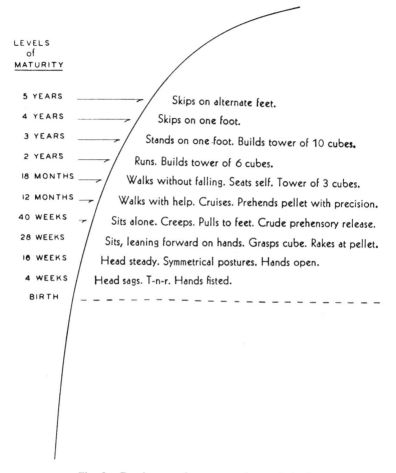

LEVELS
of
MATURITY

5 YEARS ——————————→   Skips on alternate feet.

4 YEARS ——————————→   Skips on one foot.

3 YEARS ——————————→   Stands on one foot. Builds tower of 10 cubes.

2 YEARS ——————————→   Runs. Builds tower of 6 cubes.

18 MONTHS ——————→   Walks without falling. Seats self. Tower of 3 cubes.

12 MONTHS ——————→   Walks with help. Cruises. Prehends pellet with precision.

40 WEEKS ————→   Sits alone. Creeps. Pulls to feet. Crude prehensory release.

28 WEEKS   Sits, leaning forward on hands. Grasps cube. Rakes at pellet.

16 WEEKS   Head steady. Symmetrical postures. Hands open.

4 WEEKS   Head sags. T-n-r. Hands fisted.

BIRTH

Fig. 2.   Developmental sequences of motor behavior.

The items on this chart include both gross motor and fine motor behavior patterns. To ascertain the maturity of postural control we institute formal postural tests which reveal the repertoire of the infant's behavior: supine, prone, sitting, and standing.

Fine motor control is evaluated in a similar manner. Small objects such as cubes, pellet and string elicit patterns of fine manual control.

Such tests illustrate the principles which also underlie the developmental diagnosis of behavior in the adaptive, language, and personal-social fields.

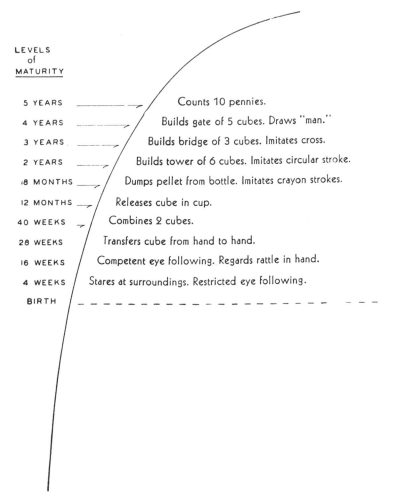

LEVELS
of
MATURITY

5 YEARS	Counts 10 pennies.
4 YEARS	Builds gate of 5 cubes. Draws "man."
3 YEARS	Builds bridge of 3 cubes. Imitates cross.
2 YEARS	Builds tower of 6 cubes. Imitates circular stroke.
18 MONTHS	Dumps pellet from bottle. Imitates crayon strokes.
12 MONTHS	Releases cube in cup.
40 WEEKS	Combines 2 cubes.
28 WEEKS	Transfers cube from hand to hand.
16 WEEKS	Competent eye following. Regards rattle in hand.
4 WEEKS	Stares at surroundings. Restricted eye following.
BIRTH	

Fig. 3.   Developmental sequences of adaptive behavior.

To determine how the infant uses his motor equipment to exploit the environment we present him with a variety of simple objects. The small red cubes serve not only to test motor co-ordination, they reveal the child's capacity to put his motor equipment to constructive and adaptive ends. The cube tests create an objective opportunity for the examiner to observe adaptivity in action—motor co-ordination combined with judgment.

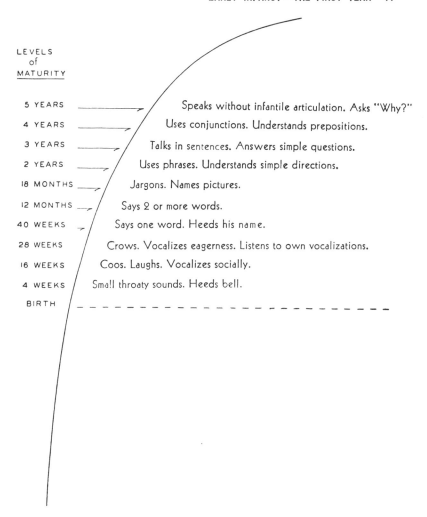

Fig. 4.   Developmental sequences of language behavior.

Language maturity is estimated in terms of articulation, vocabulary, adaptive use and comprehension. During the course of a developmental examination spontaneous and responsive language behavior is observed. Valuable supplementary information may also be secured by questioning the adult familiar with the child's everyday behavior at home.

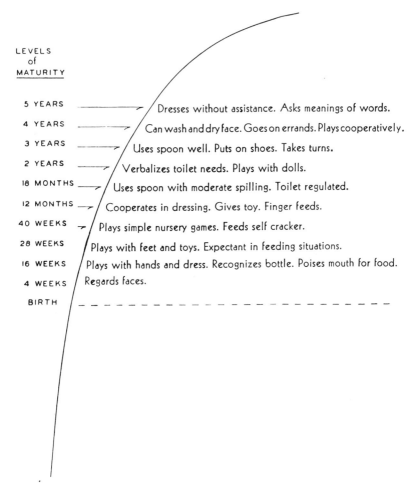

LEVELS
of
MATURITY

5 YEARS	Dresses without assistance. Asks meanings of words.
4 YEARS	Can wash and dry face. Goes on errands. Plays cooperatively.
3 YEARS	Uses spoon well. Puts on shoes. Takes turns.
2 YEARS	Verbalizes toilet needs. Plays with dolls.
18 MONTHS	Uses spoon with moderate spilling. Toilet regulated.
12 MONTHS	Cooperates in dressing. Gives toy. Finger feeds.
40 WEEKS	Plays simple nursery games. Feeds self cracker.
28 WEEKS	Plays with feet and toys. Expectant in feeding situations.
16 WEEKS	Plays with hands and dress. Recognizes bottle. Poises mouth for food.
4 WEEKS	Regards faces.
BIRTH	

Fig. 5.   Developmental sequences of personal-social behavior.

Personal-social behavior is greatly affected by the temperament of the child
and by the kind of home in which he is reared. The range of individual variation
is wide. Nevertheless maturity factors play a primary role in the socialization of
the child. His social conduct is ascertained by incidental observation and by
inquiry. The chart illustrates types of behavior which may be considered in
evaluating the interaction of environmental influences and developmental readiness.

NOTE 4

Erikson, E. H., 1959. *Identity and the Life Cycle. Psychological Issues 1 (1).* New York: International Universities Press, pp. 55–61.

Basic Trust versus Basic Mistrust

I

For the first component of a healthy personality I nominate a sense of *basic trust,* which I think is an attitude toward oneself and the world derived from the experiences of the first year of life. By "trust" I mean what is commonly implied in reasonable trustfulness as far as others are concerned and a simple sense of trustworthiness as far as oneself is concerned. When I say "basic," I mean that neither this component nor any of those that follow are, either in childhood or in adulthood, especially conscious. In fact, all of these criteria, when developed in childhood and when integrated in adulthood, blend into the total personality. Their crises in childhood, however, and their impairment in adulthood are clearly circumscribed.

In describing this growth and its crises as a development of a series of alternative basic methods, we take recourse to the term "a sense of." Like a "sense of health" or a "sense of not being well," such "senses" pervade surface and depth, consciousness and the unconscious. They are ways of conscious *experience,* accessible to introspection (where it develops); ways of *behaving,* observable by others; and unconscious *inner states* determinable by test and analysis. It is important to keep these three dimensions in mind, as we proceed.

In *adults* the impairment of basic trust is expressed in a *basic mistrust.* It characterizes individuals who withdraw into themselves in particular ways when at odds with themselves and with others. These ways, which often are not obvious, are more strikingly represented by individuals who regress into psychotic states in which they sometimes close up, refusing food and comfort, and becoming oblivious to companionship. In so far as we like to assist them with psychotherapy, we must try to reach them again in specific ways in order to convince them that they can trust the world and that they can trust themselves. . . . .

As the newborn infant is separated from his symbiosis with the mother's body, his inborn and more or less coordinated ability to take in by mouth meets the mother's more or less coordinated ability and intention to feed him and to welcome him. At this point he lives through, and loves with, his mouth; and the mother lives through, and loves with, her breasts.

For the mother this is a late and complicated accomplishment, highly dependent on her development as a woman; on her unconscious attitude toward the child; on the way she has lived through pregnancy and delivery; on her and her community's attitude toward the act of nursing—and on the response of the newborn. To him the mouth is the focus of a general first approach to life—the incorporative approach. In psychoanalysis this stage is usually referred to as the "oral" stage. . . . .

During the "second oral" stage the ability and the pleasure in a more active and more directed incorporative approach ripen. The teeth develop and with them the pleasure in biting on hard things, in biting *through* things, and in biting *off* things. This active-incorporative mode characterizes a variety of other activities (as did the first incorporative mode). The eyes, first part of a passive system of accepting impressions as they come along, have now learned to focus, to isolate, to "grasp" objects from the vaguer background and to follow them. The organs of hearing similarly have learned to discern significant sounds, to localize them, and to guide an appropriate change in position (lifting and turning the head, lifting and turning the upper body). The arms have learned to reach out determinedly and the hands to grasp firmly. We are more interested here in the overall *configuration and final integration* of developing approaches to the world than *in the first appearances of specific abilities* which are so well described in the child development literature. . . . .

The crisis of the oral stage (during the second part of the first year) is difficult to assess and more difficult to verify. It seems to consist of the co-incidence in time of three developments: (1) a physiological one: the general tension associated with a more violent drive to incorporate, appropriate, and observe more actively (a tension to which is added the discomfort of "teething" and other changes in the oral machinery); (2) a psychological one: the infant's increasing awareness of himself as a distinct person; and (3) an environmental one: the mother's apparent turning away from the baby toward pursuits which she had given up during late pregnancy and postnatal care. . . .

What the child acquires at a given stage is a certain ratio between the positive and the negative which, if the balance is toward the positive, will help him to meet later crises with a better chance for unimpaired total development. The idea that at any stage a *goodness* is achieved which is impervious to new conflicts within and changes without is a projection on child development of that success ideology which so dangerously pervades our private and public daydreams and can make us inept in the face of a heightened struggle for a meaningful existence in our time. . . .

NOTE 5

Bowlby, J., 1951. Maternal care and mental health. World Health Organization, Monograph #2. Quoted in *Child Care and the Growth of Love,* edited by M. Fry. London: Penguin Books Ltd., 1953.

Prolonged breaks (in the mother-child relationship) during the first three years of life leave a characteristic impression on the child's personality. Such children appear emotionally withdrawn and isolated. They fail to develop loving ties with other children or with adults and consequently have no friendships worth the name. It is true that they are sometimes sociable in a superficial sense, but if this is scrutinised we find that there are no feelings, no roots in these relationships. This, I think, more than anything else, is the cause of their hard-boiledness. Parents and school teachers complain that nothing you say or do has any effect on the child. If you thrash him he cries for a bit, but there is no emotional response to being out of favour, such as is normal to the ordinary child. It appears to be of no essential consequence to these lost souls whether they are in favour or not. Since they are unable to make genuine emotional relations, the condition of relationship at a given moment lacks all significance for them . . . . During the last few years I have seen some sixteen cases of this affectionless type of persistent pilferer and in only two was a prolonged break absent. In all the others gross breaches of the mother-child relation had occurred during the first three years, and the child had become a persistent pilferer.

NOTE 6

Spitz, R. A., 1965. *The First Year of Life.* New York: International Universities Press, Inc., pp. 89–90.

An extremely simple experiment can be performed to show that what triggers the smile is a sign Gestalt which consists of a circumscribed part of the face. In this experiment contact is made with a three-month-old by smiling at him and nodding one's head; the infant will react by smiling, by becoming active and by wriggling.

One now turns one's head into profile, continuing to smile and to nod; the infant will stop smiling, his expression becomes bewildered. Developmentally advanced infants frequently seem to search with their glance somewhere in the region of the experimenter's ear, as if searching for the eye which disappeared; sensitive children appear to respond with a kind of shock, and it takes time to re-establish contact. This experiment shows that the three-month-old is still unable to recognize the human face in profile; in other words, the infant has not recognized the human partner at all; he has only perceived the sign Gestalt of forehead, eyes, and nose. When this Gestalt is modified through turning into profile, the percept is no longer recognized; it has lost its tenuous objectal quality.

NOTE 7

Piaget, J., 1952. *The Origins of Intelligence in Children.* New York: International Universities Press, Inc., pp. 266–269.

Tertiary circular reaction is quite different: if it also arises by way of differentiation, from the secondary circular schemata, this differentiation is no longer imposed by the environment but is, so to speak, accepted and even desired in itself. In effect, not succeeding in assimilating certain objects or situations to the schemata hitherto examined, the child manifests an unexpected behavior pattern: he tries, through a sort of experimentation, to find out in which respect the object or the event is new. In other words, he will not only submit to but even provoke new results instead of being satisfied merely to reproduce them once they have been revealed fortuitously. The child discovers in this way that which has been called in scientific language the "experiment in order to see." But, of course, the new result, though sought after for its own sake, demands to be reproduced and the initial experiment is immediately accompanied by circular reaction. But, there too, a difference contrasts these "tertiary" reactions to the "secondary" reactions. When the child repeats the movements which led him to the interesting result, he no longer repeats them just as they are but gradates and varies them, in such a way as to discover fluctuations in the result. The "experiment in order to see," consequently, from the very beginning, has the tendency to extend to the conquest of the external environment. . . . .

Observation 141.—This first example will make us understand the transition between secondary and "tertiary" reactions: that of the well-known behavior pattern by means of which the child explores distant space and constructs his representation of movement, the behavior pattern of letting go or throwing objects in order subsequently to pick them up.

One recalls . . . . how, at 0:10 (2) Laurent discovered in "exploring" a case of soap, the possibility of throwing this object and letting it fall. Now, what interested him at first was not the objective phenomenon of the fall—that is to say, the object's trajectory—but the very act of letting go. He therefore limited himself, at the beginning, merely to reproducing the result observed fortuitously, which still constitutes a "secondary" reaction, "derived," it is true, but of typical structure.

On the other hand, at 0;10 (10) the reaction changes and becomes "tertiary." That day Laurent manipulates a small piece of bread (without any alimentary interest: he has never eaten any and has no thought of tasting it) and lets it go continually. He even breaks off fragments which he lets drop. Now, in contra-distinction to what has happened on the preceding days, he pays no attention to the act of letting go whereas he watches with great interest the body in motion; in particular, he looks at it for a long time when it has fallen, and picks it up when he can.

At 0;10(11) Laurent is lying on his back but nevertheless resumes his experiments of the day before. He grasps in succession a celluloid swan, a box, etc., stretches out his arm and lets them fall. He distinctly varies the positions of the fall. Sometimes he stretches out his arm vertically, sometimes he holds it obliquely, in front of or behind his eyes, etc. When the object falls in a new position (for example on his pillow), he lets it fall two or three times more on the same place, as though to study the spatial relations; then he modifies the situation. At a certain moment the swan falls near his mouth: now, he does not suck it (even though this object habitually serves this purpose), but drops it three times more while merely making the gesture of opening his mouth. . . . .

Observation 146.—At 1; 2 (8) Jacqueline holds in her hands an object which is new to her; a round, flat box which she turns all over, shakes, rubs against the bassinet, etc. She lets it go and tries to pick it up. But she only succeeds in touching it with her index finger, without grasping it. She nevertheless makes an attempt and presses on the edge. The box then tilts up and falls again. Jacqueline, very much interested in this fortuitous result, immediately applies herself to studying it . . . . Hitherto it is only a question of an attempt at assimilation . . . . and of the fortuitous discovery of a new result, but this discovery, instead of giving rise to a simple circular reaction, is at once extended to "experiments in order to see."

In effect, Jacqueline immediately rests the box on the ground and pushes it as far as possible (it is noteworthy that care is taken to push the box far away in order to reproduce the same conditions as in the first attempt, as though this were a necessary condition for obtaining the result). Afterward Jacqueline puts her finger on the box and presses it. But as she places her finger on the center of the box she simply displaces it and makes it slide instead of tilting it up. She amuses herself with this game and keeps it up (resumes it after intervals, etc.) for several minutes. Then, changing the point of contact, she finally again places her finger on the edge of the box, which tilts it up. She repeats this many times, varying the conditions, but keeping track of her discovery: now she only presses on the edge!

references

1. Aserinsky, E. AND Klietman, N., 1953. Regularly occurring periods of eye motility, and concomitant phenomena, during sleep. *Science*, 118:273–274.

2. Baird, D., 1959. The contribution of obstetric factors to serious physical and mental handicap in children. *J. Obst. and Gynec.*, 66:743.

3. Baldwin, J. M., 1895, *Mental Development in the Child and the Race*. New York: Macmillan.

4. Baumgartner, L., 1965. Health and ethnic minorities in the sixties. *Amer. J. Public Health*, 55:495.

5. Bender, L., 1953. Childhood schizophrenia. *Psychiat. Quart.*, 27:663.

6. Bergman, P. and Escalona, S., 1949. Unusual sensitivities in very young children. *The Psychoanalytic Study of the Child*, 3/4:333–352.

7. Berko, J. and Brown, R., 1960. Psycholinguistic research methods. In: *Handbook of Research Methods in Child Development*. P. Mussen (ed.). New York: Wiley.

8. Birch, H. G., 1968. Health and the education of socially disadvantaged children. *Developmental Medicine and Child Neurology*, 10:580–599.

9. Bowlby, J., 1951. Maternal care and mental health. *World Health Organization*, Geneva.

10. —, 1958. The nature of a child's tie to his mother. *Int. J. Psychoanal.*, 39:350–373.

11. Cravioto, J., DeLicardi, E. R., and Birch, H. G., 1966. Nutrition, growth and neuro-integrative development: an experimental and ecologic study. *Pediatrics*, 38:319.

12. Davis, A. and Havighurst, R. J., 1947. *Father of the Man*. Boston: Houghton Mifflin Company.

13. Despert, J. L., 1947. The early recognition of childhood schizophrenia. *Med. Cl. N. Amer.*, May, p. 680.

14. Dreyfus-Brisac, C., Samson, D., Blanc, C. and Monod, N., 1958. L'electroencephalogramme de l'enfant normal domoins de 3 ans. *Etudes Neo-Natales*, 7:143.

15. Eisenberg, L., 1956. The autistic child in adolescence. *Amer. J. Psychiat.*, 112:607.

16. —, 1968. Racism, the family and society: a crisis in values. *Mental Hygiene*, 52(4):512–520.

17. Erikson, E. H., 1959. *Identity and the Life Cycle. Psychological Issues, 1(1)*. New York: International Universities Press, Inc., pp. 55–61.

18. Escalona, S. K., 1969. *The Roots of Individuality: Normal Patterns of Development in Infancy*. Chicago: Aldine Publishing Company, p. 547.

19. Freud, A., 1955. Safeguarding the emotional health of our children: an inquiry into the concept of the rejecting mother. *National Conferences of Social Work: Casework Papers*, 1956. New York: Family Service Association of America, p. 9.

20. Freud, S., 1905. *Three Essays on Sexuality*. Standard Edition 7, (1953). London: The Hogarth Press, p. 168.

21. —, 1923. *The Ego and the Id*. Standard Edition 19 (1961), pp. 12–59. London: The Hogarth Press.

22. —, 1926. *Inhibitions, Symptoms and Anxiety*. Standard Edition 20 (1959). London: The Hogarth Press, pp. 87–172.

23. Fries, M. E. and Woolf, F. J., 1953. Some hypotheses on the role of the congenital activity type in personality development. *The Psychoanalytic Study of the Child*, 8:48–62.

24. Gesell, A. and Amatruda, C. S., 1941. *Developmental Diagnosis*. 11th Edition, 1964. New York: Paul B. Hoeber Medical Division, Harper & Row, Pub. pp. 8–14.

25. Hartmann, H., 1939. *Ego Psychology and the Problem of Adaptation*. New York: International Universities Press, Inc.

26. Hertzer, H. and Wolf, K., 1928. Baby tests. *Zeitschrift fur Psychologie*, p. 107.

27. Kanner, L., 1943. Autistic disturbances of affective contact. *Nervous Child*, 2:217.

28. Klein, M., 1960. Our adult world and its roots in infancy. London: *Tavistock Pamphlet No. 2, Tavistock Publications*, p. 15.

29. Korner, A. F. and Grobstein, R., 1966. Visual alertness as related to soothing in neonates: implications for maternal stimulation and early deprivation. *Child Development*, 37:867–876.

30. Leonard, M. F., Rhymes, J. P., and Solnit, A. J., 1966. Failure to thrive in infants. *Amer. J. Dis. Children*, 3:600–612.

31. Lewis, M. M., 1959. *How Children Learn to Speak*. New York: Basic Books, Inc.

32. —, 1963. *Language Thought and Personality in Infancy and Childhood*. New York: Basic Books, pp. 15–24.

33. Lewis, M., Kagan, J., Campbell, H. and Kalafat, J., 1966. The cardiac response as a correlate of attention in infants. *Child Development*, 37:63–72.

34. Ling, B. C., 1941. Form discrimination as a learning cue in infants. *Comp. Psychol. Monogr.*, 17:2.

35. Lorenz, K., 1966. *On Aggression* (tr. M. Wilson). New York: Harcourt, Brace and World.

36. Mahler, M. S., 1952. On child psychosis and schizophrenia: autistic and symbiotic infantile psychosis. *The Psychoanalytic Study of the Child*, 7:286–305.

37. Moss, H. A., 1967. Sex, age and state as determinants of mother-infant interaction. *Merrill-Palmer Quart. of Behavior and Development*, 13(1):19–36.

38. N.I.C.H.D., 1969. *Perspectives on Human Deprivation: Biological, Psychological and Sociological*. U.S. Department of Health, Education, and Welfare. Public Health Service, National Institute of Health, National Institute of Child Health and Human Development. U.S. Government Printing Office, Washington, D.C.

39. Parmelee, A. H., Wenner, W. H., and Schulz, H. R., 1964. Infant sleep patterns: from birth to 16 weeks of age. *J. Pediat.*, 65:576.

40. Patton, R. G. and Gardner, L. I., 1962. Influence of family environment on growth: the syndrome of maternal deprivation. *Pediatrics*, 30:957–962.

41. Piaget, J., 1953. *The Origins of Intelligence in Children*. New York: International Universities Press, Inc.

42. Provence, S. and Lipton, R., 1962. *Infants in Institutions*. New York: International Universities Press, Inc.

43. Putnam, M. C., 1955. Some observations on psychosis in early childhood. In: *Emotional Problems of Early Childhood*, G. Caplan (ed.). New York: Basic Books, pp. 519–526.

44. Rank, B., 1955. Intensive study and treatment of preschool children who show marked personality deviations or "atypical development" and their parents. In: *Emotional Problems of Early Childhood*, G. Caplan (ed.). New York: Basic Books, p. 491.

45. Rheingold, H. L., 1968. The effect of a strange environment on the behavior of infants. In: *Determinations of Infant Behavior: IV*. B. M. Foss (ed.). London: Methuen.

46. Ritvo, S. and Solnit, A. J., 1958. Influences of early mother-child interaction on identification processes. *The Psychoanalytic Study of the Child*, Vol. XII, p. 64.

47. Robson, K. S., 1967. The role of eye-to-eye contact in maternal-infant behavior. *J. Child Psychol. and Psychiat.*, 8(1):13–25.

48. Schaffer, H. R., 1966. Activity level as a constitutional determinant of infantile reaction to deprivation. *Child Development,* 37:595.

49. Schaffer, H. R. and Emerson, P. E., 1964. The development of social attachments in infancy. *Monogr. Soc. Res. Child Development, 29,* No. 3, Serial #94.

50. Sears, R. R., Maccoby, E. E., and Levin, H., 1957. *Patterns of Child Rearing.* Illinois and New York: Row, Peterson Co.

51. Spence, J., Walton, W. S., Miller, F. J. W., and Courts, D. M., 1954. *A Thousand Families in Newcastle Upon Tyne.* London: Oxford University Press.

52. Spitz, R. A., 1945. Hospitalism: an inquiry into the genesis of psychiatric conditions in early childhood. *The Psychoanalytic Study of the Child,* 1, 53–74.

53. —, 1946. Hospitalism: a follow-up report. *The Psychoanalytic Study of the Child,* II, 113–117.

54. —, 1946. Anaclitic depression: an inquiry into the genesis of psychiatric conditions in early childhood. *The Psychoanalytic Study of the Child,* II, 313–342.

55. —, 1965. *The First Year of Life.* New York: International Universities Press, Inc.

56. Walter, G., 1956. Electro-encephalographic development of children. In: *Discussions on Child Development,* J. M. Tanner and B. Inhelder (eds.). London: Tavistock Publications Ltd., p. 146.

57. White, B. L. and Held, R. M., 1966. Plasticity of sensori-motor development in the human infant. In: *The Causes of Behavior: Readings in Child Development and Educational Psychology,* J. R. Rosenblith and W. Allinsmith (eds.). Boston: Allyn & Bacon (2nd Edition), pp. 783–866.

58. Whiting, J. W. M. and Child, I. L., 1953. *Child Training and Personality: A Cross-Cultural Study.* New Haven: Yale University Press.

59. Wing, J. K., 1966. *Early Childhood Autism.* Pergamon Press.

60. Winnicott, D. W., 1945. Primitive emotional development. *Collected Papers.* New York: Basic Books, 1958.

61. Wolff, P. H. and Feinbloom, R. I., 1969. Critical periods and cognitive development in the first 2 years. *Pediatrics,* 44(6):999–1006.

62. Wolff, S., 1969. *Children Under Stress.* London: Penguin Press, p. 143.

Chapter 3

INFANCY—1-3 YEARS

motor sequence

A steady increase in motor skills can be observed in most children, so that by age 3 years a child can stand on one foot, dance and jump. He is also more dexterous, and can build a tower of 10 cubes. Ambidexterity also gives way to lateralization some time during the third year, although the establishment of handedness may not be really firm for several years. "Leggedness," "eyedness," and "earedness" may also not become firmly established until the seventh, eighth, or ninth year, or even later. This will have some significance when reading difficulties in the third grade of school are considered.

adaptive sequence

At 18 months the child can usually imitate a crayon stroke. By age 2 he is imitating a circular stroke, and by age 3 years he can imitate a cross. He is also capable at 3 years of age of constructing a bridge with 3 cubes.

language sequence

Most children talk fairly well by the age of 3 years. They can talk in sentences, although the tenses of the verbs are not always correct and conjunctions are often missing. Nevertheless, a 3-year-old is usually quite capable, within the limits of his vocabulary and experience, of telling a simple story. He can now also clearly communicate through verbal language.

personal-social behavior

By the age of 3 years, most children can take themselves to the toilet, feed themselves, and begin to dress themselves.

fantasy life and play

This maturation sequence, described by Gesell (1941), once again can only be considered the barest skeleton of the child's psychological development during these years. Fantasy life, for example, is more complex by the time the child is 2 years of age. Glimpses of the child's fantasies can be observed indirectly as they are expressed in his play. The play style is initially repetitious, with few variations. There is little risk, no climax and no real plot. The play materials are usually stuffed animals, balls, push toys, and elementary puzzles. By the end of the first year the child has usually acquired a transitional object (Winnicott, 1951; see Note 8), which often consists of a piece of rag, or pillow, or blanket, to which he has become very attached and to which he returns when he wishes to comfort himself. Such times may be at bed time or following any stress, such as a separation. The transitional object seems to represent a halfway step between attachment to himself (say, his thumb) and attachment to the outside world (the mother). Often when he holds his "transitional object" close to his nose, or cheek, or mouth, he also manages to insert a finger into his nostril or mouth.

The play sometimes has as its underlying motif a working through of anxiety evoked by a fantasy or fear that he will lose his mother's love. From about 18 months to 2½ or 3 years of age this represents the most important and commonest danger situation for the infant. As the child's ego develops, other basic danger situations are perceived by the child, and each will be mentioned in sequence later.

manifest object relations

By the end of the second year, the manifestations of ambivalent behavior can be clearly seen in the child. For example, he may attempt to control his mother through clinging, sometimes demanding, behavior that can be desperately trying to the parent. A child who feels secure about his parents' presence and love now also feels quite free to turn his aggression onto the external world. As the child feels more autonomous, negativistic behavior increases during this period. At the same time, while he can more or less feed himself, he still feels free to wet and soil unless his mother interferes.

peer relations

As much as others are perceived at all, the young infant perceives others as disturbers of his relationship with his mother or father. He next relates to other children more or less as lifeless objects to be used, and only gradually becomes aware that they are alive and have feelings of their own. At first he uses other children simply as playmates, limiting the partnership to the period of time needed to perform a particular task. By the time he is $2\frac{1}{2}$ to 3 years of age, however, he is beginning to share with others, a task he will be helped to master in nursery school. The role of nursery school in education is discussed later. (See page 125.)

Even by the end of the third year the child still plays mostly within the confines of his own fantasies. While he may want others to play with him, the play is rarely truly or continuously shared at this time. When a group of children at this age are observed playing in a room, the activities of each child seem still to be more or less isolated. However, a tendency toward progressive social involvement can be observed. Thus a shift from solitary, independent play to parallel activity in which children play alongside but not with each other, occurs during this period. Later, play in which there is common activity, with sharing and taking turns, occurs, culminating in cooperative play in which there is a common goal, with each child playing a specified role (Parten, 1933).

parent development

The child's ambivalent behavior at this stage requires a shift in the mother's attitude to her child. She must now set limits for the child, at the same time as she must deal with the strong feelings that are now evoked in her. The two-way street aspect of the dyadic relationship between mother-child is now much more obvious and much more demanding. Parents too are in a state of continuous development. Past unresolved feelings are continuously re-evoked at each stage of development of the child, while the parents are themselves currently developing and experiencing life differently as they grow older. Sometimes a mother fails to thrive herself, and the consequent failure to thrive of her infant may add to her feelings of inadequacy or guilt. This may lead to inadequate or inconsistent limit setting. Problems of poor impulse control in children often have their origins in this period, when internalization of controls firmly set from without should be occurring.

body image

During the second and third years the child's concept of his body begins to take recognizable shape. He often has a passionate interest in Band-Aids. He may become quite upset at a small graze, and want to cover up the wound with a Band-Aid—as if to hide the wound and prevent the loss of body fluid. It would appear that his idea of his body at this time is that it is a kind of sac filled with fluid which sometimes oozes out. Occasionally, he may have some idea of internal organs, such as a heart (usually in the shape of a valentine).

Further evidence of his developing sense of his body and his feelings can be seen in other typical play activity at this time. For example, toys that can be filled and emptied, opened and shut, fitted in, messed and cleaned, seem to reflect in part an interest in his body parts and their functions. Movable toys seem to help him master with pleasure his increased motility. Toys that can be built up and then knocked down nicely serve as instruments for the expression of ambivalent feelings. He will also hoard toys or throw them out at this time, as he "holds on" and "lets go," say, of his bowel movements.

gender identification

Early gender identification as well as body image formation occurs during this period. In a study of 76 hermaphroditic patients,

Money, *et al.* (1955) showed that one cannot attribute psychological maleness or femaleness to the chromosomal sex, gonadal sex, hormonal sex, internal accessory reproductive organs, or external genital morphology. Sex assignment and rearing is the crucial variable in the determination of gender role and orientation. Gender imprinting begins by the first birthday, and the critical period is reached by about the age of 18 months. By the age of $2\frac{1}{2}$ years, gender role is already established in normal children. However, abnormal attitudes in the parents and certain specific external stresses may contribute toward deviant sexual identity problems, such as transvestitism (Stoller, 1967). The full meaning of maleness and femaleness does not reach maturity until after adolescence.

sense of self

Literally standing now on his own two feet, the child delineates "I" and "you," and increasingly expresses his sense of individuality and autonomy. The process by which the child achieves a feeling of individuality and autonomy is not well understood. Mahler (1967) has attempted to delineate a series of phases during the first 3 years of life, starting with a "normal autistic phase" during the first 2 months of life. From about 2 months onward, a normal, undifferentiated, "symbiotic phase" begins. This is a phase "in which the infant behaves as though he and his mother were an omnipotent system—a dual unity within one common boundary." This phase is said to reach its height around 4 to 5 months. From about 9 months and onward, what Mahler calls the "separation-individuation" process takes place. This process consists essentially of the child's achievement of separate functioning in the presence and emotional availability of the mother. By about 18 months of age the child appears to be at the peak of his belief in his own magic omnipotence. During the second 18 months of life individuation proceeds, culminating in the attainment of stable, object constancy and a sense of autonomy.

object constancy

The term "object constancy" as used here is a psychoanalytic concept formulated by Hartmann (1952), connoting the ability to maintain constant relations with a person ("object") regardless of the state of need in the infant. In this sense, object constancy is different from Piaget's term "object permanence," which connotes the infant's responding toward items in his environment as if they possessed some permanence, a development that occurs perhaps around 5 or 6 months of age. A prerequisite for the development of object constancy is a lessening in the strength of the infant's needs, or greater ego control of the needs, that will enable the infant to retain a relationship with a person instead of shifting immediately to another person in search of immediate satisfaction (Freud, A., 1957). Anna Freud has noted that the very young infant is so exclusively dominated by his needs (the domination of the pleasure principle) that he cannot maintain his attachment to a non-satisfying object for more than a given period that may vary from several hours to several days. Separation between approximately 5 months and 2 years of age, therefore, causes extreme distress. As the ego matures, however, and as the pleasure principle gives way to the reality principle (see page 62), children gradually develop the ability to retain attachments to and investments in the absent love object during separation of increasing length.

sense of autonomy

At this stage the child also increasingly experiences a sense of individuality and self-control that leads to a feeling of achievement and pride, contrasting with a sense of shame and self-doubt when he has an "accident" and loses control (Erikson, 1959). Erikson has also stated in this context that it is really necessary to "be firm and tolerant" with the child at this stage in order for him to be firm and tolerant with himself. "He will (then) feel pride in being an autonomous person; he will grant autonomy to others; and now and again he will even let himself get away with something."

cognitive development

As long as the child feels that his thoughts are omnipotent, he will also believe that others can do the same. Fraiberg (1959) described a 2-year-old girl who, on seeing the sun disappear after a spectacular sunset, turned to her father and said, "Do it again, Daddy!" However, by the end of the second year some symbolic representation also emerges. The child can now use mental trial and error instead of action trial and error. He looks now for external causes of movements he sees, and he of course quite clearly distinguishes between himself and an object. Piaget has called this whole first period of cognitive functioning, lasting until about 2 years of age, the sensori-motor stage, and describes the infant's state during this first two years as "egocentric." "Egocentrism" is used here not in the common sense but as a term meaning that initially the boundaries between objects and self are not differentiated; the child has little or no self-perception; and by virtue of that fact he does not at first see his place in relation to the universe, which at that time has no existence for the infant (Piaget, 1954). Piaget uses the term egocentric then in a purely epistemological sense, without any affective or moral connotation. To the extent that children consider their own point of view as the only possible one, then to that extent they are egocentric. Indeed, the child who is egocentric is unaware that the other person has a point of view at all, and for this reason he is incapable of putting himself in someone else's place. A young child, for example, may make up his words and assume that everyone knows exactly what he means by that word. He cannot conceive that the other person does not know what he understands by the new word. Egocentrism will be referred to again when adolescence is considered.

Gradually the infant moves into a symbolic, pre-conceptual stage, so that by age 3 years or so there is evidence of some attempts at verbal reasoning, as well as symbolic activity in make-believe play. However, the child still tends to endow inanimate objects, such as thunderstorms, clouds, the moon, etc., with feeling—so-called "animism" (Piaget, 1929), and he cannot yet understand the meaning of "I promise."

Toward the end of the sensori-motor stage, and as he moves into the symbolic, pre-conceptual stage, the child can solve problems by inventiveness. For example, he will now rotate a stick through 90° to bring it through the bars of his crib, and he will use one toy as an instrument to get another.

developmental tasks

Some time between 1½ and 3 years of age it becomes clear that a child is tackling several developmental tasks. He is, first of all, achieving greater physical independence. The maturation of his muscle system is central also to his feeling of self-worth; he has now made a shift from a passive position to an active position. Furthermore, he can now think more adequately, using a language with symbols and concepts. Whereas earlier the child used the few words he had in the service of direct discharge of feelings (primary process), language comes now to be used independently in the service of conflict-free ego activities (secondary process). [At times, however, language is reinstinctualized, as in certain cases of stuttering (Bergman, 1968) or, later, hysterical aphonia.] Along with this development, definite attitudes toward people are formed, especially toward those who set limits. It is toward such persons that the child behaves in a negativistic manner; *e.g.,* "I don't want to," and "no!" are frequently used expressions when the parent makes a request or sets a limit. It is as though the child were once more defining his autonomy through his oppositional behavior. However, in some instances the behavior may be a manifestation of anxiety as the child struggles against a regressive pull. In other instances the behavior seems to represent a direct discharge of aggression against the parent, especially in those cases where there is an ambivalent mother-child relationship.

aggression

It might be useful to digress for a moment and consider at this point certain broader aspects of the psychoanalytic concept of aggression and its overall role in the total development of the individual. Such a digression might be helpful in putting into context the particular stage of development now being considered. Each maturing function has been conceptualized in psychoanalytic theory as being derived, in part, from a source of energy termed the aggressive drive. This aggressive drive is said to serve the adaptive needs and functions of the child at the same time as it finds an avenue for discharge through those functions. In the very young infant, for example, changes in attention states in response to environmental changes are thought to derive in part from aggressive energy, which also is believed to enable the infant to perform such adaptive reflex behavioral reactions as anticipatory posturing. Subsequent motor activities such as crawling, climbing, standing, walking, running; increased skills with hand, thumb, and forefinger; coordinated balancing skills, etc., similarly are believed to require an amount of aggressive energy to function and each activity in turn is thought to act as a motor pathway for the discharge of aggression as well as serve the adaptive efforts of the infant. Later, play, symbolic language and intellectual development serve similar purposes. Aggression is thought by some to have at all times direction, in that it is primarily object-seeking (Fairbairn, 1952). The concept of "amount" and "direction" are implied when the term "cathexis" is used in psychoanalytic theory.

Aggressive tension may be heightened by frustration, leading to certain behavioral reactions that are often accompanied by the affects of rage and hate. The young infant may turn his aggression inward (e.g. head banging) or outward (e.g. temper tantrums, destructive behavior). When the 2- or 3-year-old child is able to manipulate his bowel and bladder functions, these, too, may be used in the service of discharging aggression outwardly; albeit in such indirect forms as soiling and wetting. Later, the child may discharge his aggression in more subtle forms. He may, for example, manage not to hear the request of an adult, whether parent or teacher. His aggression also may be disguised by slyness, or covered by such reaction formations as shyness and embarrassment. Occasionally, a child will remove himself from any situation that invites his own aggression, or he may deny to himself as well as others that he has ever had an aggressive wish. At other times, the child may cunningly stick to the letter of a rule—he will do something which is allowed in one situation but which in the present context is clearly an aggressive act. In the young school age child, aggression may be dealt with by the child by being turned into its opposite—the child who is too sweet or too good.

As more defense mechanisms become available to the child, conflict over aggression may be dealt with by other processes including repression, displacement, projection, and various reaction formations, particularly guilt. A child, for example, may feel guilt about an aggressive wish, then blame another person for his aggressive behavior, and subsequently identify with that person. Or he may attempt to rationalize his actions. A 7- or 8-year-old child may begin to attempt to exercise his capacity for moral judgment to help control his aggression.

Aggression is also fused with the sexual drive (Hartmann, *et al.*, 1949), although this may only be seen clearly when it is a later phenomenon. Yet, there is some evidence for fusion in early childhood. For example, the intrusive, inquisitive, and invading curiosity of the 3- to 6-year-old child may be combined with his preoccupation with the anatomical differences between the sexes and the making of babies, and merge with his strong love for both parents. In some ways the development of the aggressive drive parallels the development of the sexual drive, although the theory of aggressive drive development has not been well thought out.

Aggression is said to be "neutralized" when it serves conflict-free, adaptive ends, notably in intellectual functioning. Sublimation, say through artistic work, is perhaps a special case of the general process of neutralization by which unbound aggression is modified and used to serve higher purposes.

If a mature love relationship, gratifying sexual intercourse, and child bearing are some of the ends of sexuality, it should also be possible to postulate certain ends, or aims, for aggressive drive development. In the context of Western society, it would appear that the goal of aggressive drive development is the successful neutralization of aggression toward achieving the efficient functioning of those activities that provide for continuing autonomy within the context of relationships with others; expanding intellectual activity relatively free from intrusive impulses; and a capacity to satisfy urges in creative and adaptive ways. These aims are not, of course, fully achieved during childhood. On the contrary, demanding, biting, and torturing behavior is normal during infancy. Signs of aggression and symptom formations occur throughout childhood, and outright aggressive behavior, directed outward or inward, occurs in the period of imbalance and turmoil during adolescence. Even during adulthood the role of aggression and its control is not fully understood.

⊕ toilet training

Returning now to the adaptive tasks and developmental achievements of the child between 1 and 3 years of age, it becomes clear that while the child is adapting to his environment, his environment is at the same time changing its attitudes and expectations of the child. Questions of discipline arise, particularly in relation to the aggressive behavior of the child. Conflicts between parents and child now become more apparent. The task of toilet training may become one of the many possible foci of conflicts at this time. Beyond a child, a mother, and a toilet, there are three requirements for toilet training. First of all, a child must be physiologically capable of controlling his anal sphincter. The timing of this varies with each child from, say, 14 to 15 months to $2\frac{1}{2}$ or more years. It often coincides with the maturation of the child's skill in walking. Equally important, the child must be psychologically capable of postponing the urge to let go of his stool as soon as he feels the impulse. That is to say, some capacity to delay must be available, as well as a wish to please his parents. Thirdly, since initially the child usually needs assistance, it is helpful if he can give a warning signal, and have this signal properly read by a parent who is prepared to assist. Later, of course, he will be able to dispense with this assistance and get to the bathroom on his own.

Several outcomes may arise during the toilet training process. Children who have an understanding and satisfactory relationship with their parents usually have a strong wish to please their parents and conform with their expectation and pleasure in the child's achievement of bowel control. Sometimes the child will identify with the parents in their own reaction formations, such as disgust. Occasionally, a child will conform out of fear. In such cases there is often an underlying rage and resentment which may be expressed as negativism, refusal to eat, or crying. Lastly, he may object for a variety of reasons, and develop the syndrome of encopresis, to be described shortly.

difficulties in the parents

Some of the problems in toilet training arise from the parent. A mother may experience anxiety or a strong feeling of disgust when she sees the child gratify a forbidden impulse. She may try to rush the child, or punish him, or simply frustrate the child too much. Sometimes a mother wishes to show off how clean, or precocious, her child is, and will try to master her child's fumbling early attempts. Or a mother may express her hostility toward the child through early forceful training. Occasionally, a mother may simply be ignorant of the requirements for toilet training, or will be trying to follow a cultural or family pattern.

difficulties in the child

The child for his part may not understand what his parents want, particularly if they themselves do not know what they want. Even when the parents are clear in their minds, the child may be confused by their behavior—first they praise him for his beautiful BM, then they promptly flush it down the toilet. In some cases the child may use bowel training as the issue with which he expresses his earlier hostility toward his parents. Hostility is sometimes induced specifically in relation to toilet training. A sibling may be in the offing around the time the child is being toilet trained. The child may then experience a sense of loss of love, or pending loss, and expresses this in a reluctance to train. Occasionally, actual separation and real loss may cause a relapse of previous progress. An important factor is the child's ability to give up a pleasure for the sake of a greater social gain. That is to say, the child may not yet be able to give up the narcissistic gratification the creation of a BM offers. Sometimes, too, a child is unwilling or unready to take this next step in development. From a psychoanalytic point of view it requires, essentially, a shift from the pleasure principle to the reality principle.

pleasure principle ; reality principle

The pleasure principle (Freud, 1911) under which the infant first operates allows, in fact compels, the infant to press toward immediate gratification, regardless of any consequences. On the other hand, when the infant begins to heed reality, and consequently learns to delay and restrain the urge toward immediate discharge, he is said to be operating under the reality principle. Bernard Shaw stated the difference succinctly: "to be able to choose the line of greatest advantage instead of yielding in the direction of least resistance" (Shaw, 1903).

separation

Several types of external stress may influence the course of development at this stage. Among these stresses is separation, to which partial reference has already been made in relation to toilet training. It is necessary now to examine further the various impacts of separation. Separation from parents during early childhood is not a simple phenomenon (Yarrow, 1964). However, some general observations that have clinical significance can be made. During the first six months of life, if substitute mothering is provided, the child may experience little more upset than would be expected from the change in routine. However, from the second half of the first year onward, after the child has made a significant attachment to the individual person who is his mother, more serious reactions occur. Indeed, the stronger the love tie, the greater the anxiety that is produced. Other factors that influence the reaction to separation are the degree and duration, the way in which the separation is managed, the child's previous experiences of separation, the presence of additional stresses such as illness, pain, sibling birth, etc., the child's innate individual tolerance, and subsequent experiences which may reinforce or mitigate the initial trauma.

Separation during these early years is usually accompanied by a short, but significant, period of grief (Freud and Burlingham, 1943; see Note 9). The child seems to experience the absence as a confirmation, or punishment, even a consequence, of his negative wishes. He may feel guilt, and sometimes tries momentarily to be extra good. He will also try to deal with his feelings and fantasies through his play, and at times his level of behavior will regress and symptoms may appear. If the separation is prolonged, more or less complete, and without substitute, the child may, after a "stage of protest" (Bowlby, 1961) sink into a state of despair and may eventually become and remain depressed.

separation and reaction to hospital

Separations, of course, are sometimes inevitable; a child may have to go into the hospital. The reaction to separation during hospitalization is difficult to assess. The stress of body illness is itself a major factor and will be discussed in more detail in Chapter 7. However, even in the well child the hospital setting, with its unfamiliarity and its threat to bodily integrity by medical and surgical procedures, produces a reaction, particularly in relation to certain phase-specific anxieties; *e.g.* castration anxiety, and this reaction may be reinforced when there is also a separation, particularly in the young child. Children between 7 and 12 months of age hospitalized for less than 2 weeks show marked anxiety toward strangers, desperate clinging to their mothers, and loud crying when their mothers depart (Schaffer and Callender, 1959). Children 2 to 3 years of age show fear and anger at the time of their parents' departure, are acutely anxious with strangers, and manifest depressive behavior such as crying and withdrawal from people; restlessness, hyperactivity, and rhythmic rocking; regressive behavior such as soiling and a refusal to chew solid food; and physical disturbances such as diarrhea and vomiting (Prugh, *et al.*, 1953; see Note 16). Follow-up studies of children who had been hospitalized have shown that long-term effects are frequently seen, particularly the recurrent fear that their parents would leave them.

Rarely, separation may promote development. Lewis (1954) noted that children exposed to hostile mothers gained if they were placed into the care of sensitive substitute mothers (although ordinarily one would first attempt to help the hostile mother resolve her destructive tendencies). Langford (1948) observed that many sick children in the hospital develop "constructive compensations" and come out more mature than they were before they were sick. This constructive growth experience was more likely to occur if the parent-child relationship was healthy and if the illness was well handled by parents, nurses, and physicians. A particular way in which a parent can help the child experience the hospitalization as a constructive experience has been beautifully documented by Robertson (1956). Further recent studies have confirmed the possibility of some positive effects from hospitalization in older children (Solnit, 1960).

Many of the adverse reactions just described may be mitigated by specific measures. Parent living-in, particularly for children under the age of 4 years, avoids, of course, any separation at all. Adequate preparation that offers the child explanations and opportunities for expressive play is helpful (Plank, *et al.*, 1959). Pre-admission visits to become acquainted with the ward and the nurse, and the elimination of unnecessary admission routines, are also useful. The child is also comforted if he can bring with him something familiar from home, and if the daily routine, *e.g.* bathing, feeding, elimination, sleeping, etc., are adjusted as far as possible to those to which he is accustomed. If the mother can not live in, frequent visits with active participation in the care of the child allay the child's anxiety. And the assignment to one nurse the responsibility for the major care and attention to the child is often reassuring and comforting for the child.

separation and maternal depression

Psychological separation may occur without the actual physical separation that occurs when a child enters hospital. For example, a sense of separation and loss may be brought about in the child when the mother withdraws into herself during, say, a state of mourning and grief following a loss she has experienced, such as the loss of her husband through separation, divorce, illness or death. Normally the mother will recover from her grief, find a new love object, and will then re-invest her child with her maternal care. Less commonly she may attempt to substitute a child for her lost husband, with disastrous results for the child.

However, if the mother's grief continues as a state of depression, the child may be forced to deal with this state. Many children at this stage cannot at the time deal completely with the loss that they feel. Instead, a child may deny the feelings initially, and then deal with them subsequently on a "piecemeal" basis as he encounters future developmental tasks that require the presence of a mother. The adequacy with which a child deals with loss at this stage is dependent on such factors as his developmental state; the relationship that previously existed with the lost mother; and the support available from the environment.

If the mother's depression is chronic, a characteristic phenomenon may occur. The child may attempt to deal with his loss through identification with his concept of the depressed mother. The child, so to speak, internalizes his impressions of what he considers to be certain aspects and attributes of his mother. This identification may form the basis of a true depression in which the child feels a sense of blame and emptiness, and at the same time experiences feelings of guilt and anxiety as his rage and aggression are turned inward against the now "introjected" mother. The child may attempt to ward off such feelings by increased motor activity and self-punitive behavior. Occasionally, the child exhibits a pseudo-depression as he identifies with the outer characteristics of the depressed mother without the internalization of aggression.

At all events, the young child does not appear to mourn adequately, in part because his need for a full loving relationship is vital at this stage and the interruption of continuity of affection and care, even though partial, may be too great an obstacle to overcome. Anna Freud (1965) has noted that "in the young child the capacity for outgoing love is still bound up inextricably with the reliable presence of the person who has been instrumental in calling forth this emotion and in interchange with whom it has developed." If the continuity of care and affection is broken, damage is "done to the personality by the loss of function and destruction of capacities which follow invariably on the emotional upheavals brought about by separation from, death or disappearance of the child's first love-objects."

Tolerance for the break in continuity and the consequent deprivation is low at this age, and an alternate mother is not usually available under the circumstances of, say, a mourning mother. This kind of experience of loss often permanently colors the child's future love relationships.

crucial developmental tasks

Perhaps the crux of this period of development is the child's move toward greater separation, independence, and autonomy at a time when he is capable of being demanding, intrusive, and negativistic. The extent to which the child can successfully emerge from this stage is dependent on many factors, not the least of which are, on the one hand, the child's state of preparedness for the specific tasks just mentioned, and on the other hand the degree to which the parents facilitate or hamper the child's progress.

❧ symbiotic psychosis

A special case of the impact of inadequate preparedness in the child for the specific task of separation and emergence of autonomy can be seen in the so-called "symbiotic psychosis" syndrome described by Mahler and referred to earlier.

Clinically the child with symbiotic psychosis (Mahler, 1952) presents with panic-stricken behavior some time between age 2 and 5 years, with perhaps a peak in the fourth year. Severe temper tantrums occur, and the child may feverishly attempt to restore within himself the feeling of infantile omnipotence. In an attempt to deal with this massive anxiety, the child will resort to a retreat into an autistic state, accompanied at times by additional secondary symptoms such as a preoccupation and pleasure in being whirled around. Later, certain so-called tertiary symptoms appear as other mechanisms of defense, such as repression, isolation, and reaction formations are brought into play. Auto-aggressive and active aggressive behavior may occur. In the older group of children a more benign form seems to occur, with more neurotic symptoms in evidence. The form of these neurotic symptoms may be phobias, compulsions, conversion symptoms, and hypochondriasis.

A careful analysis of the behavior and history of these children led Mahler to postulate that the onset of acute and massive anxiety occurs at a time when they encounter a separation from the mother for which they are inadequately prepared in terms of their intrapsychic development. In some cases maturational growth itself might have inadvertently enabled them to separate physically prematurely, in the sense that the child is able to move away from the mother physically when he is even less emotionally prepared to do so than is usual at this age. In other cases an external environmental event, such as illness, prematurely places a separation stress upon the child.

Thus it seems as though children who suffer a symbiotic psychosis are emotionally at the level still of the need-satisfying, part-object stage of development, and either remain fixated at or regress to the symbiotic phase that normally gives way to the separation-individuation phase toward the end of the first year (Mahler, 1967). These symptoms do not appear until the second, third, or fourth year because the symbiosis has not been threatened until then.

inadequate parenting

Sometimes the quality of the mothering and fathering interferes with the tasks of acquiring impulse control and achieving an harmonious state of independence and autonomy, especially in cases in which a state of chronic maternal inadequacy exists. Because there is a weak love relationship, the preschool child in this position may have little wish to please.

accidental poisoning in children

A prototypical syndrome resulting from such a failure of synchronization and mutual development between mother and child is the event of so-called accidental poisoning in children. The poisoning event in early childhood can be viewed as the result of an interaction between certain developmental characteristics of the child and certain qualities in the mothering person. For example, in one study (Lewis, et al., 1966) it was clear that in children under 18 months of age the child's increased maturational ability for motor exploratory behavior appeared to be uncurtailed and uncontrolled, giving the impression of a heightening level of motor activity. At the same time, a state of maternal depletion existed in the mothers, who were unable to cope without the expected support of their husbands or their own mothers.

In children between approximately 18 and 30 months of age in that study, the developmental characteristics of negativism in the child was an important factor. The negativism seemed heightened in these children, perhaps because the child experienced frustration and the relative deprivation he endured while in the care of his depleted mother. This now heightened negativism seemed to combine with the apparent increased motor activity that followed from poor internalization of controls to produce a situation in which the child could now deliberately do what he also knew he was not supposed to, namely, swallow a forbidden substance. It was as though the child's wish and capacity to defy his mother was now greater than his wish to please her. Furthermore, there was in these children little incentive to delay the impulsive urge to imbibe the forbidden substance. Another interesting aspect of this group of children was the developmental characteristic of imitation, which often expressed itself in the imitation of an older sibling. In some of these children the increased motor activity also seemed to be in the service of the ego in the sense that through such motor activity the child was attempting to ward off a depression that resulted from the maternal deprivation.

Children over about 30 months of age seemed to ingest poison more specifically as a reaction to loss. The poisoning act seemed to have a symbolic meaning of replenishment to the feeling of loss.

A 43-month-old girl ingested an antibacterial powder that was used for washing the diapers of her 9-month-old sister. This powder was unattractive visually, texturally, and to taste. In order to acquire her sister's special powder, the child had to climb, open a cupboard door, and unscrew a cap. The home was well organized and the family was apparently functioning well. The parents appeared to be clear and consistent in teaching the child what was safe and what was dangerous, what was acceptable and unacceptable, and what the boundaries were in regard to safety in motility and behavior. Investigation revealed that a crucial factor in this poisoning event was the mother's reaction to her own mother moving out of the home in order to take a job and to establish a life of her own. This loss, in addition to the birth of a second child, depleted the mother's resources of loving attention for the older child. The father, incidentally, was unused to being of help, since he had regularly retired to his hobby room after supper, leaving his mother-in-law to help his wife. The child reacted with increased negativism and what appeared to be a fierce determination to get what her infant sister had received.

A sense of loss appeared to be felt when there was a diminution in the mother's capacity to love and attend her child, perhaps because of illness, separation, or the birth of another child. The state of maternal depletion also interfered with the mother's capacity to organize a safe environment for the child.

Another consequence of a weakened love tie is the possibility that the child will have less incentive to control his body as well as his impulses. Clinically this may express itself through such symptoms as enuresis and encopresis, or as an impairment in the child's capacity to play adequately with other children, or in a tendency toward destructive behavior.

encopresis

A case of encopresis will be considered as a paradigm in this context, bearing in mind, of course, that this is a single case with its own peculiar characteristics and that, like all clinical cases, it is not purely a case of encopresis.

Mrs. D., a high school graduate, married for 14 years, was a depressed, ineffective, and somewhat confused woman. Her depression had worsened considerably at the time of her mother's illness and subsequent death which occurred when Harvey, her middle child, was in his first year of life. Mrs. D. had never been able to cope well, and a visiting nurse once described the home as sparsely furnished and poorly kept. Mrs. D. was unable to discipline her children, and the nurse noted at the time of her visit that both Harvey (by that time age 5) and his younger sister, Esther, were both noticeably understimulated. Mrs. D. rarely interacted in any loving way with her children, and seemed at times to be uninvolved. None of her children seemed at all eager to obey or please her; indeed, at times it looked as though her son Harvey wished to tease and provoke her.

Mr. and Mrs. D. communicated very little with each other. Mr. D. held two jobs, but did not offer Mrs. D. much help in the rearing of the children.

When Harvey was 2 years of age it was noted that he was constipated, and suppositories were used freely. At the age of 2 years, 5 months, Harvey was hospitalized for a tonsillectomy and adenoidectomy. At this time Harvey was still constipated, with straining at stool, holding himself rigid, soiling, and screaming. He would not sit on the toilet; instead he would stand up, stiffen and grow red in the face in an effort to hold back his feces. When he was $2\frac{1}{2}$, his sister was born. Mrs. D. was depressed at the time and could not prepare him for this event, to which Harvey reacted with intense jealousy and rage. At the age of 4 years, Harvey was still constipated and his parents were now concerned that he might be retarded because his behavior was uncontrolled, immature, and babyish, and his speech was infantile and unclear. He would also cling a great deal to his mother in a demanding, almost torturing way.

On psychological testing Harvey was shy and did not really participate actively. He had an I.Q. of 83, with very poor performance on verbal items. There was no sign of organicity.

This case illustrates, among other things, the impact upon the child of a depression in the mother. Mrs. D. was unable to provide the protective and facilitating function needed for optimum development of her child. Thus Harvey was exposed to his mother's withdrawal, repeated enemas, a tonsillectomy, the birth of his sister (for which he was inadequately prepared), and repeated medical workups including barium enemas, all before he was 5 years of age. Furthermore, each of these stresses, *i.e.* repeated enemas, tonsillectomy, sibling birth, has a potential for trauma in its own right. Finally, it should be said that no case is ever pure and simple: the father of this encopretic boy ran a diaper service. The ready availability of laundry service was used by the father as an excuse to avoid any confrontation with his son or his wife.

perennial developmental tasks, environmental stresses, and individual characteristics

It could probably be said that throughout development the individual is remolding certain major perennial tasks. Outstanding among these tasks are those of control of his body and impulses, achieving a sense of individual self, and the evolution and resolution of his feelings toward his family and toward others. Furthermore, the vicissitudes of life are such that there is no shortage of events which serve to sharpen and shape the conflicts involved in each of these and many other developmental tasks. Separation and loss, particularly separation and loss during the age period 1 to 3 years, are perhaps the most poignant, and have already been mentioned. However, it sometimes happens that a particular characteristic of the child places him in the position of experiencing a seemingly normal environment as one that is adverse, and his development and resolution of any of the perennial tasks just mentioned suffers as a consequence of the vicissitudes that follow. The child who is mentally retarded, for example, may find himself in such a position.

The psychological aspects of mental retardation are being considered particularly at this point in development to underscore the clinical need for early diagnosis. In general, the concept of mental retardation may be defined as "significantly sub-average intellectual functioning, manifested during the developmental period, and associated with distinct impairment in adaptive be-havior" (Dybwad, 1968). While the level of intellectual function can be "measured" [e.g. the Intelligence Quotient (I.Q.) is usually below 70], the degree of social performance is less easy to define. However, even a "measurement" of I.Q. is a doubtful criterion, since the I.Q. is by no means a measure of personality, and in any case the I.Q. can change when social conditions change. In a study carried out by Skeels (quoted by Luce, 1968) 13 retarded orphans were placed as "houseguests" in a state institution at a very early age. Three of them were categorized as imbeciles. Eleven of the children so profited from the extra play and care that they became "normally" intelligent, were put up for adoption, and later became self-supporting middle class adults. A control group of children the same age, who were initially of normal intelligence, were left in an orphanage in which the infants received little individual attention. One child, who began with a rating of good average intelligence, had become an imbecile by age 19, after a life in the orphanage. After a number of years both groups were tested. The supposedly retarded children who were placed as "houseguests" had gained in I.Q. The normal children within the orphanage lost I.Q. points. Thus the impact of environment on intelligence was dramatically demonstrated.

Many conditions are associated with mental retardation (Masland, et al., 1958; Bavin, 1968). Yannet (1956), for example, reported that mental retardation was an important symptom in more than a hundred syndromes. Among the many causes is that of a genetic endowment which places the individual at the lower part of the normal distribution curve for intelligence (Penrose, 1963). Such children are said to have "familial retardation." What particularly sets many of these children apart is not some postulated inherent defect or even their limited intellect, but rather the unfortunate socialization process they undergo in the course of their development. Even their low score on an intelligence test is a result of many factors, and perhaps the most important of these factors again is the child's social adjustment (Heber, 1962).

What is being emphasized here is that both intellective and non-intellective factors play a role in the wide range of final socialization patterns achieved by retarded children. Among the non-intellective factors, personality, motivational, and environmental factors seem to be the most significant (Zigler and Harter, 1969). For example, the retarded child may continuously experience failure, which may lead to a lower performance than that which would occur if he had repeated success experiences. This occurs partly because he comes to distrust his own solutions to problems and relies instead on others. He may also have experienced considerable deprivation in or out of an institution, leading to an exaggerated dependency. Curiously, retarded children in institutions take longer to solve concept-formation problems in a social setting with a warm, supportive experimenter than they do in a setting in which the experimenter is out of view (Harter, 1967). It would appear that the opportunity of meeting a need for warmth and support competes with the child's attention to a task, leading to a lowered performance.

The child, of course, is especially prey to his parents' attitudes and feelings. Parents of a child who is retarded for no obvious organic cause only slowly, and painfully, become aware of their child's limitations. Every childbirth entails a risk, and the risk of a child born with a potential at the lower end of the normal distribution curve for what we choose to call intelligence is a real one. Three types of parental reactions have been observed (Kanner, 1953). In one type the parents exhibit a mature reaction, in which feelings of loss, defeat, resentment, and guilt are experienced and worked through (Solnit and Stark, 1961). In a second type there is recognition, but not acceptance. Parents in this group often engage in a pursuit of the "culprit." The third type is when the parents completely deny the defectiveness of their child.

While no amount of optimizing the social adaptation of the retarded child will transform him into an individual with superior or even average intelligence, the difference in intelligence still should have nothing to do with the rights of the child as a human being in all its dimensions (Zigler and Harter, 1969). Certainly the compounding of a retarded child's difficulties by the failure on the part of society to make a partial adaptation to the child is neither necessary nor morally defensible.

NOTE 8

Winnicott, D. W., 1951. Transitional objects and transitional phenomena.* In: *Collected Papers.* London: Tavistock Publications Ltd., 1958, pp. 229–242.

. . . . . I have introduced the terms "transitional object" and "transitional phenomena" for designation of the intermediate area of experience, between the thumb and the teddy bear, between the oral erotism and true object relationship, between primary creative activity and projection of what has already been introjected, between primary unawareness of indebtedness and the acknowledgement of indebtedness. . . .

By this definition an infant's babbling or the way an older child goes over a repertoire of songs and tunes while preparing for sleep comes within the intermediate area as transitional phenomena, along with the use made of objects that are not part of the infant's body yet are not fully recognized as belonging to external reality. . . .

. . . .there is the third part of the life of a human being, a part that we cannot ignore, an intermediate area of experiencing, to which inner reality and external life both contribute. It is an area which is not challenged, because no claim is made on its behalf except that it shall exist as a resting-place for the individual engaged in the perpetual human task of keeping inner and outer reality separate yet interrelated. . . .

In the case of some infants the thumb is placed in the mouth while fingers are made to caress the face by pronation and supination movements of the forearm. The mouth is then active in relation to the thumb, but not in relation to the fingers. The fingers caressing the upper lip, or some other part, may be or may become more important than the thumb engaging the mouth. Moreover this caressing activity may be found alone, without the more direct thumb-mouth union. (Freud, 1905, Hoffer, 1949.)

In common experience one of the following occurs, complicating an autoerotic experience such as thumb-sucking:

1. with the other hand the baby takes an external object, say a part of a sheet or blanket, into the mouth along with the fingers; or

2. somehow or other the bit of cloth[2] is held and sucked, or not actually sucked. The objects used naturally include napkins and (later) handkerchiefs, and this depends on what is readily and reliably available; or

3. the baby starts from early months to pluck wool and to collect it and to use it

---

1. Based on a paper read before the British Psycho-Analytical Society on 30th May, 1951. *Int. J. Psycho-Anal.,* Vol. XXXIV, 1953.

2. A recent example is the blanket-doll of the child in the film A Two-Year-Old Goes to Hospital by James Robertson (Tavistock Clinic. cf. also Robertson et al. (1952).

for the caressing part of the activity.[3] Less commonly, the wool is swallowed, even causing trouble; or

4. mouthing, accompanied by sounds of "mum-mum", babbling, anal noises, the first musical notes and so on. . . .

All these things I am calling *transitional phenomena*. Also, out of all this (if we study any one infant) there may emerge some thing or some phenomenon—perhaps a bundle of wool or the corner of a blanket or eiderdown, or a word or tune, or a mannerism, which becomes vitally important to the infant for use at the time of going to sleep, and is a defence against anxiety, especially anxiety of depressive types. (Illingworth, 1951). Perhaps some soft object or cot cover has been found and used by the infant, and this then becomes what I am calling a *transitional object*. This object goes on being important. The parents get to know its value and carry it round when travelling. The mother lets it get dirty and even smelly, knowing that by washing it she introduces a break in continuity in the infant's experience, a break that may destroy the meaning and value of the object to the infant.

I suggest that the pattern of transitional phenomena begins to show at about 4-6-8-12 months. Purposely I leave room for wide variations.

Patterns set in infancy may persist into childhood, so that the original soft object continues to be absolutely necessary at bed-time or at time of loneliness or when a depressed mood threatens. In health, however, there is a gradual extension of range of interest, and eventually the extended range is maintained, even when depressive anxiety is near. A need for a specific object or a behavior pattern that started at a very early date may reappear at a later age when deprivation threatens.

This first possession is used in conjunction with special techniques derived from very early infancy, which can include or exist apart from the more direct autoerotic activities. Gradually in the life of an infant teddies and dolls and hard toys are acquired. Boys to some extent tend to go over to use hard objects, whereas girls tend to proceed right ahead to the acquisition of a family. It is important to note, however, that *there is no noticeable difference between boy and girl in their use of the original Not-Me possession*, which I am calling the transitional object.

As the infant starts to use organized sounds (mum, ta, da) there may appear a "word" for the transitional object. The name given by the infant to these earliest objects is often significant, and it usually has a word used by the adults partly incorporated in it. For instance, "baa" may be the name, and the "b" may have come from the adult's use of the word "baby" or "bear". . . .

It is true that the piece of blanket (or whatever it is) is symbolical of some part-object, such as the breast. Nevertheless the point of it is not its symbolic value so much as its actuality. Its not being the breast (or the mother) is as important as the fact that it stands for the breast (or mother).

When symbolism is employed the infant is already clearly distinguishing between fantasy and fact, between inner objects and external objects, between primary creativity and perception. But the term transitional object, according to my sugges-

---

3. Here there could possibly be an explanation for the use of the term "wool-gathering", which means: inhabiting the transitional or intermediate area.

tion, gives room for the process of becoming able to accept difference and similarity. I think there is use for a term for the root of symbolism in time, a term that describes the infant's journey from the purely subjective to objectivity; and it seems to me that the transitional object (piece of blanket, etc.) is what we see of this journey of progress towards experiencing....

There are certain comments that can be made on the basis of accepted psychoanalytic theory.

1. The transitional object stands for the breast, or the object of the first relationship.

2. The transitional object antedates established reality-testing.

3. In relation to the transitional object the infant passes from (magical) omnipotent control to control by manipulation (involving muscle erotism and co-ordination pleasure).

4. The transitional object may eventually develop into a fetish object and so persist as a characteristic of the adult sexual life. (See Wulff's development of the theme.)

5. The transitional object may, because of anal-erotic organization, stand for faeces (but it is not for this reason that it may become smelly and remain unwashed....)

The mother, at the beginning, by an almost 100 per cent adaptation affords the infant the opportunity for the *illusion* that her breast is part of the infant. It is, as it were, under magical control. The same can be said in terms of infant care in general, in the quiet times between excitements. Omnipotence is nearly a fact of experience. The mother's eventual task is gradually to disillusion the infant, but she has no hope of success unless at first she has been able to give sufficient opportunity for illusion....

....The transitional phenomena represent the early stages of the use of illusion, without which there is no meaning for the human being in the idea of a relationship with an object that is perceived by others as external to that being.

The idea illustrated in Fig. 19 is this: that at some theoretical point early in the development of every human individual an infant in a certain setting provided by the mother is capable of conceiving of the idea of something which would meet the growing need which arises out of instinctual tension. The infant cannot be said to know at first what is to be created. At this point in time the mother presents herself. In the ordinary way she gives her breast and her potential feeding urge. The mother's adaptation to the infant's needs, when good enough, gives the infant the *illusion* that there is an external reality that corresponds to the infant's own capacity to create. In other words, there is an overlap between what the mother supplies and what the child might conceive of. To the observer the child perceives what the mother actually presents, but this is not the whole truth. The infant perceives the breast only in so far as a breast could be created just there and then. There is no interchange between the mother and the infant. Psychologically the infant takes from a breast that is part of the infant, and the mother gives milk to an infant that is part of herself. In psychology, the idea of interchange is based on an illusion.

In Fig. 20 a shape is given to the area of illusion, to illustrate what I consider to be the main function of the transitional object and of transitional phenomena. The transitional object and the transitional phenomena start each human being off with what will always be important for them, *i.e.* a neutral area of experience which will not be challenged.

FIG. 19   FIG. 20

 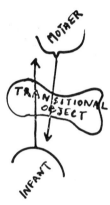

.... It is assumed here that the task of reality-acceptance is never completed, that no human being is free from the strain of relating inner and outer reality, and that relief from this strain is provided by an intermediate area of experience which is not challenged (arts, religion, etc.). (cf. Riviere, 1936). This immediate area is in direct continuity with the play area of the small child who is "lost" in play.

In infancy this intermediate area is necessary for the initiation of a relationship between the child and the world, and is made possible by good enough mothering at the early critical phase. Essential to all this is continuity (in time) of the external emotional environment and of particular elements in the physical environment such as the transitional object or objects.

The transitional phenomena are allowable to the infant because of the parents' intuitive recognition of the strain inherent in objective perception, and we do not challenge the infant in regard to subjectivity or objectivity just here where there is the transitional object....

. . . . I do consider that transitional phenomena are healthy and universal.

references

1. Freud, Sigmund (1905). 'Three Essays on the Theory of Sexuality.' Complete Psychological Works of Sigmund Freud. Vol. VII. London: Hogarth Press.

2. Hoffer, W. (1949). 'Mouth, Hand, and Ego-Integration.' *Psychoanal. Study Child,* Vol. III-IV. London: Imago.

3. Illingworth, R. S. (1951). 'Sleep Disturbances in Young Children.' *Brit. Med.J.*

4. Riviere, J. (1936). 'On the Genesis of Psychical Conflict in Earliest Infancy.' *Int. J. Psycho-Anal.,* Vol. XVII.

5. Robertson, J., Bowlby, J. and Rosenblith, Dina (1952). 'A Two-Year-Old Goes to Hospital.' *Psychoanal. Study Child,* Vol. VII. London: Imago.

6. Wulff, M. (1946). 'Fetishism and Object Choice in Early Childhood.' *Psychoanal. Quart.,* Vol. XV.

NOTE 9

Freud, A. and Burlingham, D., *War and Children,* edited by P. R. Lehrman. Medical War Books, 1943, pp. 50–54. "Freud-Burlingham Reports," Foster Parents' Plan for War Children.

Reactions to parting . . . . (during the phase from about 6 months to 2 years of age) . . . . are particularly violent. The child feels suddenly deserted by all the known persons in its world to whom it has learned to attach importance. Its new ability to love finds itself deprived of the accustomed objects, and its greed for affection remains unsatisfied. Its longing for its mother becomes intolerable and throws it into states of despair which are very similar to the despair and distress shown by babies who are hungry and whose food does not appear at the accustomed time. For several hours, the "hunger" for its mother, may over-ride all bodily sensations.

There are some children of this age who will refuse to eat or sleep. Very many of them will refuse to be handled or comforted by strangers. The children cling to some object or to some form of expression which means to them, at that moment, memory of the material presence of the mother. Some will cling to a toy which the mother has put into their hands at the moment of parting; others to some item of bedding or clothing which they have brought from home.

Some will monotonously repeat the word by which they are used to call their mothers, as for instance, Christine, seventeen months old, who said: "mum, mum, mum, mum, mum" . . . .

She repeated it continually in a deep voice for at least three days.

Observers seldom appreciate the depth and seriousness of this grief in a small child. Their judgement of it is misled for one main reason. This childish grief is short-lived. Mourning of equal intensity in an adult person would have to run its course throughout a year; the same process in the child between one and two years will normally be over in thirty-six to forty-eight hours. The difference in duration is due to certain psychological differences between the state of childhood and adultness . . . .

. . . . A love object who does not give it immediate satisfaction is no good to it. Its memories of the past are spoilt by the disappointment which it feels at the present moment. It has no outlook into the future and it would be of no help to it if it had. Its needs are so urgent that they need immediate gratification; promises of pleasure are no help.

The little child will therefore, after a short while, turn away from the mother image in its mind and, though at first unwillingly, will accept the comfort which is offered. In some cases acceptance may come in slow stages. Christine, for instance, would at first only let herself be fondled or held by an unseen person. She would sit on somebody's lap, turn her head away, enjoy the familiar sensation of being held, and probably add to it in her own mind the imaginary picture of her own mother. Whenever she looked at the face of the person who held her she began to cry.

There are other children who are spared these violent reactions. They seem placid, dazed, and more or less indifferent. It takes a few days or even a week before this placidity is disturbed by a realisation of the fact that they are among strangers; all sorts of slighter depressive reactions and problems of behavior will then result. All children of this age, those with violent reactions as well as those where reaction is delayed, will show a tendency to fall ill under the new conditions; they will develop colds, sore throats, or slight intestinal troubles.

That the shock of parting at this stage is really serious is further proven by the observation that a number of these children fail to recognise their mothers when they are visited after they have "settled down" in their new surroundings. The mothers themselves realise that this lack of recognition is not due to any limitations of the faculty of memory as such. The same child who looks at its mother's face with stony indifference as if she were a complete stranger, will have no difficulty in recognising lifeless objects which have belonged to its past. When taken home again it will recognise the rooms, the position of the beds and will remember the contents of cupboards, etc.

. . . . The mother has disappointed the child and left its longing for her unsatisfied; so it turns against her with resentment and rejects the memory of her person from its consciousness.

references

1. Bavin, J. T. R., 1968. The genetics of mental deficiency. In: *Foundations of Child Psychiatry*, E. Miller (ed.). Oxford: Pergamon Press, 457–488.

2. Bergman, R., 1968. A case of stuttering. *J. Amer. Acad. Ch. Psychiat.*, 7(1):13–30.

3. Bowlby, J., 1961. Separation anxiety: a critical review of the literature. *J. Child. Psychol. and Psychiat.*, 1:251–269.

4. Dybwad, G., 1968. Who are the mentally retarded? *Children*, 15(2):43–48.

5. Erikson, E. H., 1959. *Identity and the Life Cycle. Psychological Issues*, Vol. 1, No. 1. New York: International Universities Press, Inc., pp. 65–74.

6. Fairbairn, W. R. D., 1952. *An Object-Relations Theory of the Personality*. New York: Basic Books, Inc., p. 176.

7. Fraiberg, S. H., 1959. *The Magic Years*. New York: Charles Scribners Sons, p. 305.

8. Freud, A., 1957. The mutual influences in the development of ego and id. *The Psychoanalytic Study of the Child*, 7:42–50.

9. ——, 1965. Continuity in theory from practice. In: *The Family and the Law*, J. Goldstein and J. Katz (eds.). New York: The Free Press, p. 1053.

10. Freud, A. and Burlingham, D., 1943. *War and Children*. New York: International Universities Press, Inc.

11. Freud, S., 1911. *Formulations on the Two Principles of Mental Functioning*. Standard Edition (1958), Vol. 12, 213–226. London: The Hogarth Press.

12. Gesell, A. and Amatruda, C. S., 1941. *Developmental Diagnosis*. New York: Paul B. Hoeber Medical Division, Harper & Row, Pub., 2nd Edition (1964).

13. Harter, S., 1967. Mental age, I.Q., and motivational factors in the discrimition learning set performances of normal and retarded children. *J. Experimental Child Psychol.*, 5:123–141.

14. Hartmann, H., 1952. The mutual influences in the development of ego and id. *The Psychoanalytic Study of the Child*, 7:7–70.

15. ——, 1956. Notes on the reality principle. In: *Essays on Ego Psychology* (1964). New York: International Universities Press, Inc., pp. 241–264.

16. Hartmann, H., Kris, E., Lowenstein, R. M., 1949. Notes on the theory of aggression. *The Psychoanalytic Study of the Child*, 3/4:9–36.

17. Heber, R. F., 1962. Mental retardation: concept and classification. In: *Readings on the Exceptional Child*, P. E. Trapp and P. Himelstein (eds.). New York: Appleton-Century-Crofts, pp. 69–81.

18. Kanner, L., 1953. Parents' feelings about retarded children. *Amer. J. Ment. Def.*, 57:375–383.

19. Langford, W. S., 1948. Physical illness and convalescence: their meaning to the child. *J. Pediat.*, 33:242–250.

20. Lewis, H., 1954. *Deprived Children*. London: Oxford University Press.

21. Lewis, M., Solnit. A. J., Stark, M. H., Gabrielson, I. W., and Klatskin, E. H., 1966. An exploratory study of accidental ingestion of poison in young children. *J. Amer. Acad. Child Psychiat.*, 5:255–271.

22. Luce, G., 1968. The physiological imprint of learning. In: *Mental Health Program Reports No. 2*. U. S. Dept. of Health, Education and Welfare. P.H.S. Publication No. 1743, 91–92.

23. Mahler, M. S., 1952. On child psychosis and schizophrenia: autistic and symbiotic infantile psychoses. *The Psychoanalytic Study of the Child*, 7:286–305.

24. ——, 1967. On human symbiosis and the vicissitudes of individuation. *Amer. Psychoanal. Assoc.*, 15:710–762.

25. Masland, R. I., Sarason, S. B., Gladwin, T., 1958. *Mental Subnormality. Biological, Psychological and Cultural Factors*. New York: Basic Books, Inc.

26. Money, J., Hampson, J. G., and Hampson, J. L., 1955. An examination of some basic sexual concepts: the evidence of human hermaphroditism. *The Johns Hopkins Hosp. Bulletin*, 97:301–319.

27. Parten, M. B., 1933. Social play among preschool children. *J. Abnorm. Soc. Psychol.*, 28:136–147.

28. Penrose, S. L., 1963. *The Biology of Mental Defect*. London: Sidgwick and Jackson.

29. Piaget, J., 1929. *The Child's Conception of the World*. New York: Harcourt, Brace & World, Inc.

30. ——, 1954. *The Construction of Reality in the Child*. New York: Basic Books, Inc., p. XII.

31. Plank, E. N., Caughey, P., and Lipson, M. J., 1959. A general hospital child-care program to counteract hospitalism. *Amer. J. Orthopsychiat.*, 29:94–101.

32. Prugh, D. G., Staub, E., Sands, H., Kirshbaum, R., and Lenihan, E., 1953. A study of the emotional reaction of children and families to hospitalization and illness. *Amer. J. Orthopsychiat.*, 23:70–106.

33. Robertson, J., 1956. A mother's observations on the tonsillectomy of her four-year-old daughter, with comments by Anna Freud. *The Psychoanalytic Study of the Child*, 11:410–433.

34. Schaffer, H. R. and Callender, W. M., 1959. Psychologic effects of hospitalization in infancy. *Pediatrics*, 24:528–539.

35. Shaw, G. B., 1903. *Man and Superman*, Act III.

36. Solnit, A. J., 1960. Hospitalization: an aid to physical and psychological health in childhood. *Am. J. Dis. Children*, 9:153–163.

37. Solnit, A. J. and Stark, M. H., 1961. Mourning and the birth of a defective child. *The Psychoanalytic Study of the Child*, 16:523–537.

38. Stoller, R. J., 1967. Transvestites' Women. *Amer. J. Psychiat.*, 124(3):333–339.

39. Winnicott, D. W., 1951. Transitional objects and transitional phenomena. In: *Collected Papers*. London: Tavistock Publications Ltd., 1958, pp. 229–242.

40. Yannet, H., 1956. Classification and etiological factors in mental retardation. In: *Mental Retardation, Readings and Resources,* J. H. Rothstein (ed.). New York: Holt, Rhinehart & Winston, Inc., 1961.

41. Yarrow, L. J., 1964. Separation from parents during early childhood. In: *Review of Child Development Research.* New York: Russell Sage Foundation, Vol. I.

42. Zigler, E. F. and Harter, S., 1969. The socialization of the mentally retarded. In: *Handbook of Socialization Theory and Research,* D. A. Goslin (ed.). Chicago: Rand McNally and Company, pp. 1965–1102.

Chapter 4

EARLY CHILDHOOD—3-6 YEARS

maturation

Children become increasingly agile as they grow and develop during this period, learning, for example, to skip on alternate feet. Their perceptual-motor skills also improve at this time: a child at 2 years of age can copy a circle, and at 3 years can copy a cross; by 5 years of age he can copy a square, and at 7 years a diamond. His memory is improving, such that by age 6 years he can count five digits forward and three digits backward. The use of language is, of course, extensive at this point, and he learns during this period to dress himself without assistance and wash himself.

childhood sexual theories

At the same time, fantasy is now much more elaborate, and is influenced by such factors as the child's growing awareness of sexual differences, pregnancy, childbirth and death; his life experiences; and the persisting magical quality of his thinking capacity. Childhood sexual theories begin to emerge (Freud, S., 1908). For example, the child at this stage attempts to solve the problem of conception by postulating the idea that something is swallowed. The child also seems to view what takes place between mother and father as an act of violence. Most children initially believe that the delivery route is via the rectum, and later think that the baby comes out through the navel.

manifestation of sexual theories in food attitudes

Some of these theories may manifest themselves in certain irrational attitudes toward food. Avoidance of all food, or the fear of being poisoned, is sometimes related to a fear of pregnancy in the later years of this stage, when pregnancy is associated with oral intake. Occasionally, avoidance is based on the association of fatness with pregnancy, especially if the child is told that a baby grows in the mother's stomach. More specific food aversions, such as sausages or the yolk of an egg, often have more specific fantasies attached to them. That is to say, like all neurotic symptoms they may represent the forbidden wish as well as the defense against the wish, and may therefore be part of a reaction formation such as disgust. They may represent an attempt to avoid direct expression of sadistic or cannibalistic fantasies such as swallowing a penis or engulfing a newborn baby.

family romance

Every child also appears to develop some form of a family romance fantasy (Freud, S., 1909a). As the child becomes increasingly aware of the discrepancy between his idealized image of his parents and the actuality of his parents, he becomes increasingly disillusioned with his parents. Part of the process of dealing with the disillusionment is the elaboration of a fantasy that his present set of parents are not really his parents, but that he "really" comes from, say, a royal family. This fantasied family, of course, can and does freely possess all the idealized characteristics he had previously attributed to his parents. At the same time, this splitting also serves to lessen the guilt he feels about his incestuous fantasies toward his parents at this time.

oedipal fantasies

Fantasies also now appear to be more sex differentiated. The initial systematic description of these fantasies by Freud (1900) were subsequently augmented in numerous case studies [*e.g.* Freud,

1905, 1909b, 1909c, 1918; Brunswick, 1940; Bornstein, 1949 (see Note 11), 1953.] From these case studies it would appear that a characteristic grouping of drives, unconscious and conscious fantasies, and personal relationships occur in both boys and girls.

prototypical fantasies of boys

Boys, for example, tend to begin feeling toward their mothers the way they imagine their fathers do. But in doing so, a boy feels that his father is not only his rival but an enemy who he fears will hurt him. The form of the harm that he imagines might befall him is, in part, determined by his current preoccupation with the anatomical differences between boys and girls and, in part, by any actual threats that may have been made. He observes that girls do not have a penis and, believing that they once had a penis that was removed, he fears the same fate may befall him.

In order to avoid that fate, the boy normally gives up his active love for his mother and identifies with his father, thus terminating his oedipal conflict. However, occasionally he retains his active love for his mother and even goes so far as to accept a "castrated" position with respect to his father. In such cases the boy virtually offers himself to the father as a love object. This position has been called the "passive oedipus conflict" (Brunswick, 1940).

A 19-year-old student recalled during treatment that when he was 6 years old he used to take a bath with his sister. He remembered that he used to think that she had a penis once and it had been cut off. His current behavior was largely directed at giving others the impression that he was powerless, helpless, and a threat to no one. The two "events" were linked together in his mind, as though he were saying, "leave me alone, you can pass me by. I've been done already." At the same time, he also yearned for physical contact with men.

Mothers, obviously, by and large, do not treat the boy as they do the father. The boy often feels resentful and feels some degree of inadequacy—a sense that is reinforced, of course, by his actual physical inferiority.

In order to reassure himself and at the same time attract the attention of his mother, he may even under normal circumstances become self-conscious about his penis—or he may have a strong wish to exhibit his penis. Sometimes this takes a pathological form, particularly if the parents heighten the conflict by their own behavior.

> A 4-year-old boy was brought to the emergency room at 4:00 a.m. in an acute agitated state. For the previous 4 hours he had said there were spiders under his pajamas and there were shadows inside of him. While in the waiting room he screamed as his aunt attempted to keep a coat over his completely nude body. He refused to wear any clothes at all, and remained unashamedly naked!
>
> On further study it was found that the boy and his mother slept together. There was a serious marital difficulty, which included a severe sexual problem and violent behavior between the parents, who slept apart.
>
> Later it was learned that the boy's mother would often allow him to sit on her lap. He would feel her pelvis and ask her why she did not have the same feeling his father had. He would also be allowed to fondle his mother's breasts, and his mother noted that he would get an erection at the slightest touch—her touch. It became clear that this boy's fears about wearing his clothes were his way of reassuring himself and allaying his anxiety by keeping his genitalia always in sight. For example, in a progressive play sequence the boy first exhibited his fear of spiders crawling on his skin, then touched his thigh, and subsequently his penis, and finally wanted to look inside his trousers in search of his penis.

prototypical fantasies of girls

Girls during this period tend to turn their love away from their mothers, at least to some extent, and direct their attention increasingly to their fathers. Some shift has to occur since the girl, unlike the boy, eventually has to make a complete shift in the sex of her love object. However, this shift is difficult to achieve, in part because of the strength of the tie to the mother. Probably the active strivings toward the mother are never really given up, but instead find their expression later when the girl is able to complete her identification with her active mother at the time she herself is able to become a mother to a child of her own. In the meantime, however, the wish to have a baby cannot be realized, and the girl seems to vacillate between loving her mother and loving her father, between wanting to be a girl and wanting to be a boy. She may envy the penis as a token of power, and act upon her envy by becoming a tomboy. Sometimes this tomboy behavior represents an attempt at denial of her femininity. Occasionally, a girl will try to demean the boy in attempts at ridicule, making him feel stupid or repulsive. In some girls the disappointment in the female genitalia may lead to a partial repudiation of the mother and a tendency instead to identify with the father. In others, the penis may be regarded as abnormal growth on the body. There are several circumstances that may lead to this fantasy. First, a girl may feel so secure about her femininity that it is the boy who looks odd. Second, the view of the penis as a growth may represent a special case of the girl's wish to downgrade the boy's possession of a penis. Third, in some families women may dominate and may encourage the girl to view the male as defective.

The girl's vacillation is reinforced by the disappointment she experiences at not getting a baby from her father on the one hand, and not getting a penis from her mother on the other hand. Yet throughout, the young girl is still, of course, dependent on her mother for the satisfaction of her daily needs, so that any jealousy of the mother because of mother's place beside father is accompanied usually by anxiety. Thus, any disapproval by the mother at this stage is acutely felt by the young girl, the more so because her thinking still lacks logic and she still tends to imbue the mother with magically omnipotent and dangerous power. Furthermore, in a sense any "punishment" is "immanently" justified, since the unconscious crime of a hostile wish against the mother has indeed been committed, and the line between a wish and an act performed is not always clear to the child's mind at this stage. This vacillation of feelings leads to a characteristic ambivalence, found especially in women who have not adequately resolved their feelings toward their parents.

Both boys and girls feel guilty about their destructive wishes, and they are afraid of retaliation; boys at this stage more often fear physical injury, girls mostly seem to fear abandonment. According to Jones, the fear of abandonment in girls may be related to an earlier fear of a loss of the personality itself and the annihilation of all capacity to be gratified—a condition for which the term "aphánisis" has been coined (Jones, 1929). Both boys and girls often seek, therefore, to reassure themselves. One common behavior pattern that serves this purpose is that of entering the parents' bedroom. In doing this, they are not only near the person they love, but can also be reassured that the rival is still alive. Further, by preventing intercourse they may be attempting to prevent the arrival of another sibling, although more probably they are acting out their own fantasies of union with a parent, and defending against the prevalent fantasy at this age that parents are damaging each other during intercourse.

consolidation of the superego

Resolution of the oedipal feelings appears to require some degree of identification with the parent of the same sex, and some degree of internalization of the good and bad, loving and beloved, praising and forbidding, rewarding and punishing aspects of both parents, a process that takes place over a period of time and which consolidates the formation of what Freud conceptualized as the superego (Freud, S., 1924). In addition, a repression of direct sexual and aggressive fantasies in relation to either parent occurs, to the extent of an amnesia for these first few years of life. In spite of evidence of excellent memory functioning during these years, in later life few people can remember much from their first three or four years of life. Sometimes a displacement of sexual and aggressive impulses occurs. A girl or a boy may discharge their feelings onto another family member. Usually some sublimation occurs, as seen for example in boys who engage in competitive, but less dangerous, activities with their peers. This will be discussed further in the next chapter (see Note 13).

factors influencing oedipal fantasies and feelings

The oedipal situation and its resolution just outlined represent the prototypical course (Freud, S., 1905; see Note 10). In actual life there are hundreds of variations brought about by a host of factors. Parts of four major clusters of factors affect almost every child. First, of course, is the state of the preoedipal organization of the child. If the child has failed to achieve, say, a sense of self or a feeling of trust, he is obviously that much less prepared to resolve the problems and tasks of this period of his life.

Sibling relationships clearly affect the child's feelings. Sibling rivalry is almost always caused by the way parents relate to their children, but once it exists it is a force in its own right (Levy, 1937; Hawkins, 1946).

Parents themselves are an obvious factor. The kinds of responses a parent makes to a child are determined in part by the state of the marital relationship; the specific relationship between a parent and a particular child; the development and changing roles demanded of parents as the child develops and as they themselves grow older; and the, at times, unwelcomed resurgence of previously dormant conflicts, now activated by the child at a particular stage in his development.

Lastly, there is the wide range of chance encounters that may befall a child, including illness, separations, births, deaths, seduction, divorce, etc., each with its characteristic impact.

special situations

There are, at the same time, specific situations which have fairly well defined impacts upon the oedipal conflict and its resolution. Two outstanding situations that have been carefully studied are the oedipal conflict in the adopted child and the oedipal conflict in the one-parent child. While the impacts of these situations have certain characteristics, the outcome is still dependent on the balance of all the other variables just mentioned.

adoption

Adoption can act as a powerful reality that reinforces the phase-specific fantasies just described. The adopted child finds it difficult then to deal with the heightened fantasy, and tends toward an action-oriented, repetitive behavior pattern that in effect plays out the child's fantasies. Unfortunately, the result is often one ·of multiple psychological difficulties for the child.

Extrafamilial adoptees in the United States below the age of 18 years constitute about 2 % of the population (Brieland, 1965). However, a higher proportion of these children are referred for psychiatric help than would ordinarily be expected (Toussieng, 1966). The range of diagnostic categories of these children is broad, with perhaps a preponderance of children who tend to act out aggressively and sexually. The most powerful fantasies in the children are often woven around a search for the biological parent, leading at times to actual explorations. This occurs in part because the psychological presence of two sets of parents alters the superego structure of the child. The adopted child may continue to split the two sets of parents into "good" parents and "bad" parents, in either direction.

Many other factors, however, contribute to the psychological problems of the adopted child. For example, the parents of the adopted child continuously have to deal with their own reactions to their infertility and their own fantasies about the adopted child, who is often an illegitimate child. The continuous presence and behavior of the adopted child stimulates these fantasies in the parents, and these fantasies further interfere with the rearing skills of the parents (Schechter, *et al.*, 1964). For example, the idea of "the bad seed" is a prevalent shared fantasy, and often leads to prophecy-fulfilling behavior in the child. The way in which a child is told about his adoption can be both an indicator of existing psychological problems and part of the etiology of future psychological difficulties.

Some of the difficulties in telling a child about his adoption stem from emotional conflicts in the parents. On the other hand, it is also true that there are unresolved conceptual problems regarding the best approach. Kirk (1964), for example, holds the view that the adoptive parents must face their own feelings and attitudes, especially those around the issue of being unable to produce children, and that they should discuss this openly with the child along with the subject of the child's illegitimate birth. Peller (1961; 1963), on the other hand, feels this should be a private matter within the family, and "adoption day" should not be a matter of public pronouncement. Again, many workers feel that the child should be told about his adopted status very early so that the child, as it were, grows up with this knowledge, allowing the child and his parents to deal with the many different aspects of the problem as the child's development proceeds. In this view, telling a child about his adoption is a continuous process, having different meanings at different stages of development. Wittenborn (1957), for example, found that children who were told of their adoption early tended to have a higher I.Q., to speak better, and to appear less clumsy than those who were not told early. However, as Lewis noted, the parents who felt comfortable telling their child of his adoption early were also parents who had many good qualities, a factor that may have been more significant than the mere fact of early telling (Lewis, 1965). Other workers favor postponing telling the child about his adoption until he has consolidated some of the major tasks of development and a period of relative emotional stability has been achieved, *e.g.* between, say, 6 and 10 years of age.

Neither method is simple, and many variables, such as the age and status of the siblings and the socio-cultural environment, need to be considered. Moreover, much depends upon the degree of comfort in the parents with the position they have taken in the matter of talking with the child they have adopted, and their understanding of the kinds of problems that can arise.

the one-parent child

The problem of the one-parent child is another example of a complication in reality that hampers the child's resolution of the oedipal conflict. In a detailed survey of 10 reported cases of an absent parent during the oedipal period, the pathogenic impact upon sexual identification and superego formation was impressive (Neubauer, 1960). For example, homosexuality occurred, with either a harsh, sadistic superego or a deficient superego which allowed incestuous acting out. However, it was not possible to distinguish between the effect of the parent's absence and the pathological condition of the remaining parent, who often appeared to be seductive. Furthermore, the timing of the loss, and the sex of the missing parent in relation to the child's sex, were significant variables that could not be adequately controlled in the reported studies. Herzog and Sudia (1968) recently emphasized that the effect of fatherlessness *in itself* is difficult to evaluate. Besides the attitudes and role of the mother in the fatherless home, the extent to which other male models influence the child is another important variable. Nevertheless, in almost every case reported by Neubauer, the absent parent was either "immensely idealised or endowed with terribly sadistic attributes." Idealization is a process by which the child denies what is disappointing without withdrawing from the object (in this case the absent parent), in contrast to pure fantasy in which the child simply turns disappointing parents into satisfactory ones (Hoffer, 1949). Since both parents are necessary for the full richness of the oedipal experience, children with one parent have difficulty in achieving a satisfactory oedipal and postoedipal organization.

However, it simply cannot be said that if, say, a boy is born illegitimately, has no father for the first 5 years of his life, and is exposed to his mother's seductions, then that boy will become a homosexual. He may, as did Leonardo da Vinci; but who would say that to produce a genius you must be born illegitimately, have no father, and be open to your mother's seductions? The subject of some of the origins of homosexuality will be discussed shortly.

play characteristics

Some of the fantasies of this period and the psychological mechanisms invoked to cope with them are represented in the normal play of the child at this stage. The play is quite spontaneous in style as the child uses a wide range of feelings and fantasy themes. Role playing is highly characteristic, with a rich use of dolls, props, dress, etc. Time sequences and duration, however, are largely disregarded. Some sharing of fantadsies occurs, at least implicitly in the common activities of the children involved. Much of the play at this stage is clearly an attempt to copy adults, sometimes with envy, sometimes out of anger or fear. Occasionally, the play seems to be an attempt at self-reassurance as the child performs big and powerful roles (mothers and fathers, doctors and nurses), or clearly expresses a family romance. In any event, the play leads to a widening experience of the world, and as such dilutes the child's sense of sexual urgency in the child's relationships with his parents. At the same time, it provides for the first attempts at preparation for needed adult skills.

functions of play

It becomes clear that play is an essential occupation of childhood (Waelder, 1933). The pleasure in functioning and achieving in itself motivates the child toward further exploration as well as it provides him with a sense of well-being. The term "function pleasure" was first used by the Buhlers (1930) to describe the pleasure observed in infants on mastering simple motoric tasks. The child can now also actively repeat for himself a gratifying experience. The representational aspect of play has already been mentioned. Erikson has described three spheres of activity in the child: the macrosphere, the autosphere, and the microsphere (Erikson, 1940). The macrosphere is the world at large in the child's experience, e.g. a visit to the dentist. The autosphere is the internal fantasy life of the child, e.g., "I am being attacked and will be hurt and mutilated." The microsphere is the play world that the child creates for himself—small, compact, manageable and encompassadle, e.g. the child may play at being a dentist: in this way he turns a passive situation into one of active mastery, he can discharge some of his own revengeful aggressive fantasies, he can make it come out differently in the end—and he can repeat it all at his bidding. Here, play is seen performing a defense function (turning passivity into activity); a discharge function (aggressive drive discharge); and there is, too, some suggestion of a movement toward sublimation.

There is a further important aspect of play as a developmental step. Play can be viewed as an intermediary step in the development of thought. If thought is conceptualized as a trial of action through controlled reason, it can be seen how the play of the child might facilitate that process. After all, play for the child is a process in which different solutions are tried out in controlled action in the world of play before being executed in modified form in the world at large. Gradually this kind of "play" becomes internalized, and the process is entirely carried out at the mental level.

cognitive development

A more detailed account of the structure of thought at this stage is seen in the studies of Piaget (1926). (See also Flavell, 1963). Piaget attempted to study how the child progressively understands such concepts as space, time, object and causality; spatial and numerical relations, conservation of length, area and volume, and the necessary processes that enable the child to understand how to classify, etc. At this stage, between 2 and 7 years of age (called by

Piaget the preoperational stage), the child is, of course, aware of himself as a separate person. He is also aware that persons and things have a separate existence, and are moved by forces other than himself. He is quite capable of permanent intrapsychic representation of objects that are not perceptually present. In this symbolic and preconceptual period of preoperational thought (approximately $1\frac{1}{2}$ to 4 years of age), the child can engage in symbolic activity in make-believe play and can also make attempts at verbal reasoning. Yet he may still tend to endow inanimate objects with feeling (the "animisms" mentioned earlier).

Some time during the second half of this so-called preoperational stage, Piaget describes what he calls an "intuitive stage" (approximately age 4 to 7 years), in which there is an increased accommodation to reality (although the child is still bound to some extent to spatial relationships), a categorizing capacity that makes use of one characteristic of an object, and an inclination on the part of the child to follow his own line of thought when he talks to another child, with very little actual exchange of information. The child can add, say $6 + 4 = 10$, but is not capable of reversible thinking that will later enable him also to say $10 - 4 = 6$. Several other characteristics of the child's thinking at this stage have been noted by Piaget. For example, the child increasingly tries to verify his statements by trials of action, accommodating to what he then observes. The process of assimilation becomes in this way increasingly "decentered" from the child's interests, although he still tends to see things from his point of view only. To the extent that he does this and finds it still hard to take the view of another person, he is still "egocentric."

At this stage, too, the child appears to think along the lines of "immanent justice." That is, the child believes that punishment for wrong deeds is inevitable, and inherent in the universe—a sort of early Hollywood-type level of thought. An interesting clinical aspect of this kind of thinking is its persisting quality (hence the popularity of certain early Hollywood-type films?) and its impact upon the child who is striving to deal not only with conscious but also unconscious, real or imagined, misdeeds. Any punishment, or rather any event that is seen by the child as a punishment, is almost expected, sometimes welcomed, and frequently guilt-relieving. The child may observe this sense of relief and develop a behavior pattern that then actively seeks punishment, since it is so relieving. Indeed, the child, so to speak, gets off the hook very easily since he no longer has to suffer his guilt.

signs of anxiety

Neither boys nor girls may be entirely successful in the resolution of their oedipal conflicts, and may show signs of anxiety through a conduct disorder or by suffering from excessive guilt (see page 97), especially about masturbation (see page 100). Perhaps the commonest conduct disturbance is a heightened aggressivity in play, in which a child may threaten others or hurt himself. Occasionally severe reaction formations against the wish to exhibit occur, with excessive shyness and withdrawal. Early learning difficulties may present themselves as the child imposes upon himself an inhibition against discovering forbidden knowledge. Nail biting, tics and other "nervous symptoms," such as nose picking, sniffing, and coughing, may also appear. Fears of the dark, of animals, of injury, of doctors and death, may also occur, representing in part an underlying fear of being overwhelmed by the current thrust of unacceptable wishes and impulses. More persistent phase-specific symptoms, such as enuresis (page 104), encopresis, and such sleep disorders as nightmares, night terrors, and bad dreams may occur (see below), suggesting a failure to cope with one or more of the tasks mentioned earlier.

nightmares, night terrors, and bad dreams

In nightmares the child wakes up afraid, the episode is fleeting, and the child can often remember the dream the next day. In night terrors he does not awaken completely, looks horrified, perspires, cries out, and often cannot be aroused from his state for 10 to 15 minutes. He frequently has no memory for this event when he is finally awakened.

dreams and R.E.M. sleep

A further distinction should perhaps be made between a bad

dream and a nightmare. Bad dreams occurring during R.E.M. sleep are a normal, recurring psychic event, present from infancy onward, and appear to represent controlled anxiety. Nightmares triggered in Stage IV sleep, on the other hand, are less common, and appear to represent uncontrolled anxiety. Since there seem to be moments in which the ego's capacity to deal with anxiety breaks down, true nightmares are more like an encapsulated psychotic episode (Fisher, 1970).

While the nightmare is triggered in Stage IV sleep, the nightmare itself is experienced in an aroused though not fully alert mental state. The child appears panicked and hallucinating until he is fully alert and has regained contact with his environment. Fisher states that it is possible that emotional conflicts may be released during deepest sleep when the "risk" that the victim will remember the dream is minimal and protective barriers are lowered.

The bad dreams of children at this stage often take the form of a monster who is, say, coming in through the window and is about to attack the child, whereupon the child suddenly wakes up, often with a pounding heart. A common underlying dream process (part of the "dream work") in such dreams is the projection and displacement of the child's own unacceptable aggressive fantasies onto the monster, who then turns around and threatens to attack the child.

The concept of "dream work" is a crucial one in psychoanalytic theory. Indeed, Freud regarded his "The Interpretation of Dreams" as his most important work, stating that "insight such as this falls to one's lot but once in a lifetime" (Freud, S., 1900). Essentially it proposes a series of psychological processes and mechanisms by which the individual deals with psychological conflicts about forbidden wishes that arise during the sleeping state. The theory is too complex to be dealt with adequately in this context and should be studied separately.

child's concept of dreams

During the early part of this period, dreams themselves still tend to be conceptualized by the child as external events, a process that Piaget calls "realism" (Piaget, 1951). However, the child soon begins to understand that dreams are not real external events. By the fifth birthday, most American middle-class children recognize that their dreams are not real events, and shortly afterwards understand that dreams cannot be seen by others. By age 6 years, children are aware that dreams take place inside them, and by age 7 years they are clearly aware that dreams are thoughts caused by themselves (Kohlberg, 1968).

✦ guilt

Guilt was mentioned earlier (page 95) as another consequence of unresolved oedipal conflicts. In fact, guilt is a powerful affect at this stage even with normal resolution of conflicts. If castration danger was the prototypical danger situation in the third and fourth years of life, guilt seems to be the overriding danger situation from about the fourth or fifth year onward, in greater or lesser degree. Erikson, for example, has described the developmental crisis at this state as "initiative versus guilt" (Erikson, 1959). The child's imagination is exuberant to the point where at times he can frighten himself as he believes that a particular fantasy was virtually a committed crime. He then feels guilty. He feels guilty even for mere thoughts, let alone for deeds which nobody may have seen. Rapaport (1967) tells the story of the little boy who goes toward a candy jar. Before he can lay a hand on the jar he hears a great clap of thunder. He is momentarily taken aback, looks up, and says: "Good God, isn't one even permitted to think of it?" Yet, at the same time, he is learning quickly, desirous of sharing in obligations and being disciplined, and seems altogether more of an integrated child.

✦ origin of guilt

The origin of the emergence of such a strong affect of guilt is still to be explained. Children in their first year of life obey the commands of adults only for the duration of the command; there is very little carry-over to the next time the same situation arises (*e.g.* parents have repeatedly to say to a child, "Stay away from the plug," as well as placing covers over all electric outlets and physically intervening when necessary). Gradually the child internalizes these prohibitions, and one can observe 2-year-old children repeating to themselves the same prohibition they have heard repeatedly from their parents, occasionally seeking reinforcement from their parents by provocative behavior and questions, or by inviting their parents to see how good they have been.

purpose of guilt

Guilt, like anxiety, is an affect, and like all affects it serves a purpose. The purpose, it would seem, is to provide a signal that a punishment will occur if certain behavior is persisted in, or committed at all. The stimulus for the child's response is the internalized real and imagined prohibitions of the parents (the "superego" described on page 88). Thus, guilt arises essentially when there is a conflict between the child's wishes and his conscience. Like all affects, guilt may become acutely uncomfortable, causing the child to mobilize further defenses to ward off the guilt. Thus, defenses may act against affects as well as against drives. Sometimes rage may be mobilized to deal with guilt. A multiple layering of such affects may thus occur.

The child's conscience requires reinforcement from the environment. The environment usually provides this reinforcing nutriment in the form of such social sanctions as marriage, parenthood, and normal social expectations in regard to ethics and morals, etc. If this nutriment is lacking, or faulty, the superego becomes corruptible. If the parents themselves have faulty values, not only will the child internalize these values complete with their faults, (cf. "superego lacunae"; Johnson, 1949), but the child's values will become further corruptible for lack of adequate nutriments in the form of appropriate parental sanctions. On the other hand, certain strong moral attributes can be transmitted, particularly through specific family myths (Musto, 1969).

It would appear that these early prohibitions are in part internalizations of the child's perception of the parents' prohibitions, especially those that have been spoken aloud and heard by the child. However, in part they are also reinternalizations of the attributes and strictness that the child has previously externalized and projected onto the parents. Along with the spoken prohibitions of the parents is the implied threat of loss of the parents' love if the child disobeys. This threat is often conveyed by a glance, a change in receptivity, a gruffness, etc., in the parents' relationship with the child at that moment. The child feels, or should feel, a consistency and firmness in the parents' command, and a sense of guilt about disobedience. If there is inconsistency, the child will sense the double message and disobey. The parents will then feel nonplussed by the child's "naughtiness," and, not recognizing their own inconsistency, may begin to punish the child, often through spankings.

Guilt is often expressed in a form of behavior which constantly provokes punishment. It is as though the punishment will be a just retribution for the forbidden unconscious crime. Through this punishment the child is relieved, temporarily, of the onerous feeling of guilt. Physical punishment administered at this time usually fits in with the child's fantasies and needs.

guilt and socialization

The internal problem of guilt is perhaps central to the external socialization of the child. In order to avoid the feeling of excessive guilt, the child may, for example, try to behave in accordance with accepted social rules of conduct. However, even this solution is tempered by intrapsychic, environmental and developmental factors. Internally, the child's ability to postpone the urge for immediate gratification; his self-esteem; his ability to empathize with the feelings of others; as well as his intelligence and his capacity for judgment, may all modify the child's tolerance for guilt.

External modifying factors include the varying impact of parental, peer, and societal sanctions; the child's experiences of gratification or deprivation; and the child's assessments, insofar as he can make such judgment, of the risk of detection, the effort and ingenuity required, and the possible consequences versus the possible gains when, say, he experiences the urge to cheat, lie, steal, or perform some other forbidden act.

From a cognitive-developmental point of view, the child's increasing ability to make a moral judgment parallels in part his level of cognitive development. For example, no matter what environmental influences are at work, a gradual shift takes place from making a judgment in terms of immediate external physical consequences to judging in terms of subjective or internal purposes, norms or values (Kohlberg, 1964). Most children have an understanding of the basic moral rules of society by the time they start first grade (Hartshorne and May, 1930). However, which particular way they will make a moral judgment is dependent upon the degree to which specific moral values have been internalized.

masturbation

An almost universal source of guilt in the child is the urge to masturbate and the fantasies connected with masturbation. Although the term masturbation in its ordinary sense is understood to represent self-stimulation of the genitalia, in its technical sense it means the gratification of the sexual drive by the self or an extension of the self. Since the sexual drive seems to have a sequence of development (Freud, S., 1905; see Note 10) in much the same way that there is a sequence of development in thinking, motility, speech, etc., the self-gratification of the earliest manifestations of the sexual drive, while not genital, should also be considered as masturbation. Thus, the mouthing behavior of the infant can be considered a rudimentary form of masturbation in that it is a manifestation of autoerotic activity in which the primitive, oral stage, sexual drive is being gratified by the self. The pleasures involved later in having a bowel movement may also have a masturbatory component.

At the same time penile erections do occur in infancy, both spontaneously and in response to manipulation. Spontaneous early penile erections appear to be associated with R.E.M. sleep (Fischer, et al., 1965). It is therefore plausible that such erections may represent a physiological change as well as a psychic event.

Direct manipulation of the genitalia reaches its first peak somewhere between 3 and 4 years of age, although accidental touching of the genitals may occur in very young infants. An interesting observation is that foundling home infants deprived of object relations do not play with their genitals even in their fourth year, while family raised infants with good object relations play with their genitals toward the end of the first year (Spitz, 1962). More disguised masturbation takes place in the course of "horse play" when the child contrives to rub his or her genital area against, say, the knee of an adult.

Another interesting detail is the fact that girls appear to masturbate mostly through pressure of the thighs rather than direct fingering of the genitalia. A possible hypothesis for this phenomenon is that the girl wishes to avoid exact tactile localization that might arouse anxiety about the absence of a penis (Brunswick, 1940). On the other hand, many girls masturbate by inserting foreign objects into the vagina. Later, during adolescence, it would appear that girls probably derive sexual gratification by stimulation in the region of the clitoris rather than the vagina, and this remains true of adult women who achieve orgasm most regularly from stimulation in the region of the clitoris. In fact, it appears that in adults there is no such thing as a vaginal orgasm distinct from a clitoral orgasm (Sherfey, 1966). That is to say, clitoral and vaginal orgasms are not separate biologic entities, and regardless of where the female body is stimulated, there is absolutely no difference in the responses of the pelvic viscera, provided the sexual stimulation is effective (Masters and Johnson, 1966.)

origins of masturbation

Several hypotheses have been offered about the origins of masturbation activities and fantasies in the child. Brunswick (1940), for example, asserted that the early physical care of the child by the mother, a care that inevitably involves touching the genitals and that seems to be experienced by the child as a pleasurable seduction, constitutes a significant component of the basis for early childhood masturbation. Another stimulus to masturbate lies in the intense and jealous interest of the child in the sexual life of the parents, which the child may have seen or about which he may have elaborated fantasies.

masturbation fantasies

During the act of masturbation the child may envisage what he fantasies takes place between the parents. He may, for example, in keeping with his sexual theories, envisage either parent being suckled by the other, or his suckling either parent, or his being suckled himself. Such fantasies may be displaced especially in girls, onto the imagery of suckling a doll. Occasionally, the child may fantasy a mutual touching of the genitals, much along the lines of his own experience of pleasure in touching his own genitals or having his genitals touched, especially by the mother. Sometimes, in keeping with the child's sexual theory of sexual intercourse as a sadomasochistic interaction, he may have accompanying fantasies of violence, often disguised, say, as rockets blasting off, cars crashing into each other, or wars between armies.

masturbation and fantasies of being beaten

Sometimes a specific fantasy of being beaten occurs during masturbation (Freud, 1919). According to Freud the fantasy first occurs before the fifth or sixth year, and is accompanied by feelings of pleasure having a masturbatory quality. Freud thought that the fantasies arose from the oedipal fantasies of the child and underwent a complicated series of changes. In boys, for example, the beating fantasy was thought to be passive from the very beginning, and derived from a feminine attitude to the father. The sequence of changes in the fantasy that Freud reconstructed were: "I am loved by my father," leading to the unconscious fantasy, "I am being beaten by my father," which resulted finally in the conscious masochistic fantasy, "I am being beaten by my mother." In girls the first conscious form of the fantasy appeared to be sadistic, *e.g.* "A teacher is beating a number of boys," but the satisfaction was still thought to be essentially masochistic. In both boys and girls the fantasies appeared in part to be attempts to deal with their wish to be loved by their father.

masturbation and social rules

Masturbation is a normal, even necessary phenomenon, such that children of all ages need the opportunity to masturbate in private. But, like eating habits and bowel training, the practice of masturbation is also usually subject to normal social rules in the interests of social relationships. It has even been suggested, although without supporting evidence, that cultures which permit the unrestricted gratification of the sexual urge during the elementary school years and early puberty have a large proportion of their people whose level of personality development and intellectual functioning is lowered (Spitz, 1962). Compulsive masturbation is usually regarded as a sign of tension or disorder whose sources require resolution before the masturbation itself is contained. Occasionally, a child will become addicted to masturbatory stimulation. Extreme anxiety and guilt are often engendered when the child is threatened with punishment or spanked for his masturbation activities.

spankings

Spankings, however, do not usually correct this or any other situation. They may appear to have an effect at the time, but the parent usually finds that he has to spank the child for the same misdeed over and over again. Even when it does seem to have a more lasting effect it is often because of fear and a strong repression of the rage in the child. In that case the long-term psychological results may be equally unhappy, resulting sometimes in a personality disorder. Occasionally, as a result of learning to control his impulses only through the mobilization of fear of a strong external punishment, the child may repeatedly seek such punishment in order to dissipate any rising anxiety brought about by a threatened breakthrough of an impulse believed to be dangerous. Spankings may also reinforce the wish and the opportunities for the child to put his feelings into actions. This comes about partially through identification with the parent model of hitting when desperate that which he sees before him.

Sometimes the spanking event is sexually exciting. Parents report that they try to hold themselves back, feel provoked, and then suddenly let go. After the discharge through physical activity, they then report how calm and loving is their relationship with the child. But this is usually short-lived, and the whole cycle starts again. And the parent, in spite of seeing how useless it is for purposes of discipline, persists in this activity. The cycle of rising excitement, climax, discharge, and period of calm is suspiciously like a sexual gratification, which in some families seems to be the true aim of the spanking.

Even this does not exhaust the reasons spanking is often the very opposite of being really useful to the child in the long run. (It often seems to be administered because it is more "useful" for the parents than it is for the child.) For example, instead of the child feeling guilty and learning for himself internal ways to delay and divert the direct discharge of his impulses, a child may simply be let off the hook by a spanking: the child is immediately relieved of his guilt and can continue repeating his activity, provided he feels the external price he has to pay is not too high. That is to say, the child can reason that stealing an apple is worth the risk of a spanking, so he is free to continue to steal. No internalization has occurred; wrong learning has taken place.

bed wetting

Mention was made earlier of enuresis as a symptom of anxiety related to the conflicts prevalent at this stage of development (page 95). Enuresis may be defined here as involuntary wetting of the bed past the age at which most children remain dry (Green and Richmond, 1954). Most normal children establish daytime control by $2\frac{1}{2}$ years, and nighttime control by $3\frac{1}{2}$ to 4 years of age, with perhaps an age range of between 3 and 7 years (Harper, 1962). Some observers have stated that normal maturation in some children may not occur until puberty (Campbell, 1951).

Control usually comes about as a result of the interaction between this neuromuscular maturation and the psychological ability to postpone the urge to void. The psychological capacity to delay an impulse is in turn part of the total psychological development of the child and is derived from many sources. Some of these sources include all those factors that contribute toward such ego functions as object relationships, motivation, and the capacity to deal with conflict.

Furthermore, since the total psychological development of the child is integrally related to his environment, such factors in the environment as the attitudes of the child's parents and the hazards of illness, separation, seduction, etc., in turn again play a vital role in developing the capacity for impulse control.

Given this complex interaction of factors, it is not surprising that enuresis is a common symptom in early childhood, perhaps amounting to at least 4% of children after the age of 4 years (Lemkau, 1955).

Bed wetting of course can be a symptom of many different kinds of organic disorders. Several clinical points suggest the possibility of an organic cause. The wetting may be diurnal as well as nocturnal. There may never have been a significant "dry" period. Symptoms of an infection may be present. Bed wetting may also occur in children who have unusually small bladders (so-called "primary" enuresis), or as a result of a sleep disorder. For example, enuretic boys age 5 to 9 years seem to skip the first R.E.M. cycles of sleep and wet in the deepest stage of sleep, State IV (Pierce, *et al.*, 1961). Wetting occurs generally just before a dream episode, and least frequently in R.E.M. periods (Gastaut and Broughton, 1964; Hawkins, *et al.*, 1965). Enuresis does seem to occur in children who are sleeping heavily and are hard to awaken. However, the causes of the sleep patterning are unknown at present. While bed wetting, sleep walking, and nightmare attacks occur during sudden intense arousal from slow-wave (Stage IV) sleep, other "nervous" signs, such as teeth grinding, occur during R.E.M. sleep (Reding, *at al.*, 1964).

Nevertheless, there is still a large number of enuretic children who do not have an organic basis for their symptom. Among these children it is possible to discern the following groupings:

I. Developmental delay
   1. Slow maturation
   2. Inadequate training
   3. Insufficient stimulation
II. Psychological conflict
   1. Temporary regressive phenomena
   2. Relatively stable neurotic symptom formation

In Group I, the primary causes of the enuresis tend to be extrapsychic or reactive in nature. (This is not to say, of course, that secondary anxiety may not arise; it usually does.)

In Group II, the primary causes of the enuresis tend to be

intrapsychic and internalized in nature. Enuresis as a regressive phenomenon, for example, commonly occurs when a stress (such as illness, birth of a sibling, separation and loss) is experienced before autonomous bladder control has been fully established. Enuresis as the expression of an internalized intrapsychic conflict tends to occur when fantasies common during this period of development, *i.e.* phase-specific fantasies, have been heightened by the interaction between internal and external events and produce anxiety of a degree that requires neurotic symptom formation (Katan, 1946).

For example, a common fantasy during this period of development is the fear of harm from persons of the opposite sex. This fear may arise as a fantasied consequence of destructive wishes toward the rival parent, or it may arise from an overwhelming sexual experience, which in many instances consists of a hostile seduction by the parent who takes charge of the child at night by handling the child's penis in the bathroom as the stream of urine is directed into the toilet. In the case of a boy, the fear of the mother may lead to a passive compliance in which urination is not within his control. In the case of the girl, her fear of the father as an aggressor may lead to a passive relinquishing of control (Gerard, 1939). In both instances the bed wetting also has a passive-aggressive revenge component. Furthermore, in many children who wet the bed the symptom is brought about by the same mechanisms that produce a conversion symptom, so that the child's wishes and his defense against his wishes are represented symbolically in the outpouring of urine. The conflict, as it were, leaks out through the symptom!

What can be seen here is the interaction between a phase-specific fantasy and an external reality that is consonant with that fantasy, resulting in a conflict which expresses itself through a symptom in which all the factors are represented.

major developmental thrusts

Several major developmental thrusts seem to be occurring during this stage of the child's life. The child's relationships are now much more centered on identified people and bear witness to the exciting and anxiety-arousing fantasy life just described. Thus, in the child's manifest behavior, possessiveness of the parent of the opposite sex, and jealousy and rivalry with the parent of the same sex can be observed. The child is also at times protective, curious, exhibitionistic, seeking compliments and, in the case of girls, changing toward a somewhat masculine relationship with the mother. Children now begin to see other children as fellow children with feelings, wishes, and rights of their own.

The child's increasing ability to take directions is matched by his increased internal controls system. His play and his interaction with other children shifts from parallel play to cooperative play. Language and concept development reach a new level as he observes and imitates others and learns a sense of time. Curiosity about anatomical differences, pregnancy, childbirth and death, abounds, and masturbation is at its peak. During this state the child strives to resolve his individual complex, oedipal feelings with the early formation of a superego, and he learns to accept his own gender and his sex role.

phobic organization

At the same time, there appears to be a general tendency toward a phobic organization manifest in the numerous fears, *e.g.* fear of the dark, that occur at this stage. The phobic nature of the defense organization at this time seems to be determined in part by a number of factors. One factor is the level of cognitive development, which may not yet permit more sophisticated mechanisms such as intellectualization. Another factor is the general maturation and development of the psychic apparatus, which may not yet have provided the individual with a very wide range of autonomous defense functions. A third factor is the degree to which the child experiences a heightening of anxiety common at this developmental stage by virtue of a current event which is close to the prevailing fantasy. For example, tonsillectomy in a child who is concerned about mutilation of his body may heighten castration anxiety and stimulate specific defense mechanisms (Lipton, 1962).

defense hierarchy

An interesting inference of this conceptualization is that

psychic defense structures may have a sequential and hierarchical development of their own, dependent in part on maturation, development, and external events. A simplified schematic representation is shown in Table 1. In this diagram the vertical columns indicate the interacting forces of maturation, intrapsychic development, and external environment at each stage of development. This interaction determines, in part, the kind and degree of defense activity, shown in the bottom line of each vertical column. Thus, in the age period 3 to 6 years ("early childhood") the increased awareness and curiosity, the fears associated with body injury and castration, and the presence of specific real events, such as tonsillectomy, may characteristically foster the use of phobic mechanisms. In the school age child, say 7 to 11 years of age, a more obsessional organization is seen, as will be described in the next chapter.

NOTE 10

Freud, S., 1905. *Three Essays on the Theory of Sexuality.* Standard Edition. London: The Hogarth Press, 1953, pp. 125–243.

Summary [1]

. . . . We started out from the aberrations of the sexual instinct in respect of its object and of its aim and we were faced by the question of whether these arise from an innate disposition or are acquired as a result of experiences in life. We arrived at an answer to this question from an understanding, derived from psychoanalytic investigation, of the workings of the sexual instinct in psychoneurotics, a numerous class of people and one not far removed from the healthy. We found that in them tendencies to every kind of perversion can be shown to exist as unconscious forces and betray their presence as factors leading to the formation of symptoms. It was thus possible to say that neurosis is, as it were, the negative of perversion. In view of what was now seen to be the wide dissemination of tendencies to perversion we were driven to the conclusion that a disposition to perversions is an original and universal disposition of the human sexual instinct and that normal sexual behavior is developed out of it as a result of organic changes and psychical inhibitions occurring in the course of maturation; we hoped to be able to show the presence of this original disposition in childhood. Among the forces restricting the direction taken by the sexual instinct we laid emphasis upon shame, disgust, pity and the structures of morality and authority erected by society. We were thus led to regard any established aberration from normal sexuality as an instance of de-

1. All footnotes omitted.

Table 1

DEVELOPMENT OF DEFENSE HIERARCHY

Correlations	Developmental Stages			
	Infancy	Early Childhood	School Age Child	Adolescence
Maturational Skills	biological helplessness limited awareness limited motor control	increased perceptual capacities early motor control	broad range of controlled, perceptual, motor and psychic activity	extensive quantitative and qualitative changes in physical and psychological changes associated with puberty
Psychological Development	symbiotic state need-satisfying object loss of love anxiety	object constancy recognition of whole object sexual development castration anxiety	formal logic autonomous ego development in latency guilt	intrapsychic reorganization in the face of such adolescent tasks as: identity crisis, body image changes, separation and object choice, impulse control etc.
Reinforcing Parallel External Events	loss of the object	fear of mutilation aggravated by an actual event, *e.g.* tonsillectomy	school learning patterns	career choice, move to college or military service
Simplified Defense Hierarchical Sequence	projection introjection	phobic organization	obsessional organization	intellectualization

velopmental inhibition and infantilism. Though it was necessary to place in the foreground the importance of the variations in the original disposition, a cooperative and not an opposing relation was to be assumed as existing between them and the influences of actual life. It appeared, on the other hand, that since the original disposition is necessarily a complex one, the sexual instinct itself must be something put together from various factors, and that in the perversions it falls apart, as it were, into its components. The perversions were thus seen to be on the one hand inhibitions, and on the other hand dissociations, of normal development. Both these aspects were brought together in the supposition that the sexual instinct of adults arises from a combination of a number of impulses of childhood into a unity, an impulsion with a single aim . . . .

. . . . We found it a regrettable thing that the existence of the sexual instinct in childhood has been denied and that the sexual manifestations not infrequently to be observed in children have been described as irregularities. It seemed to us on the contrary that children bring germs of sexual activity with them into the world, that they already enjoy sexual satisfaction when they begin to take nourishment and that they persistently seek to repeat the experience in the familiar activity of "thumb-sucking". The sexual activity of children, however, does not, it appeared, develop *pari passu* with their other functions, but, after a short period of efflorescence from the ages of two to five, enters upon the so-called period of latency. During that period the production of sexual excitation is not by any means stopped but continues and produces a store of energy which is employed to a great extent for purposes other than sexual—namely, on the one hand in contributing the sexual components to social feelings and on the other hand (through repression and reaction-forming) in building up the subsequently developed barriers against sexuality. On this view, the forces destined to retain the sexual instinct upon certain lines are built up in childhood chiefly at the cost of perverse sexual impulses and with the assistance of education. A certain portion of the infantile sexual impulses would seem to evade these uses and succeed in expressing itself as sexual activity. We next found that sexual excitation in children springs from a multiplicity of forces. Satisfaction arises first and foremost from the appropriate sensory excitation of what we have described as erotogenic zones. It seems probable that any part of the skin and any sense-organ—probably, indeed, *any* organ—can function as an erotogenic zone, though there are some particularly marked erotogenic zones whose excitation would seem to be secured from the very first by certain organic contrivances. It further appears that sexual excitation arises as a by-product, as it were, of a large number of processes that occur in the organism, as soon as they reach a certain degree of intensity, and most especially of any relatively powerful emotion, even though it is of a distressing nature. The excitations from all these sources are not yet combined; but each follows its own separate aim, which is merely the attainment of a certain sort of pleasure. In childhood, therefore, the sexual instinct is not unified and is at first without an object, that is, auto-erotic.

The erotogenic zone of the genitals begins to make itself noticeable, it seems, even during the years of childhood. This may heppen in two ways. Either, like any other erotogenic zone, it yields satisfaction in response to appropriate sensory stimulation; or, in a manner which is not quite understandable, when satisfaction is derived from other sources, a sexual excitation is simultaneously produced which has a special relation to the genital zone. We were reluctantly obliged to admit that we could not satisfactorily explain the relation between sexual satisfaction and sexual excitation, or that between the activity of the genital zone and the activity of the other sources of sexuality.

We found from the study of neurotic disorders that beginnings of an organization of the sexual instinctual components can be detected in the sexual life of children from its very beginning. During a first, very early phase, oral erotism occupies most of the picture. A second of these pregenital organizations is characterized by the predominance of sadism and anal erotism. It is not until a third phase has been reached that the genital zones proper contribute their share in determining sexual life, and in children this last phase is developed only so far as to a primacy of the phallus.

We were then obliged to recognize, as one of our most surprising findings, that this early efflorescence of infantile sexual life (between the ages of two and five) already gives rise to the choice of an object, with all the wealth of mental activities which such a process involved. Thus, in spite of the lack of synthesis between the different instinctual components and the uncertainty of the sexual aim, the phase of development corresponding to that period must be regarded as an important precursor of the subsequent final sexual organization.

The fact that the onset of sexual development in human beings occurs in two phases, *i.e.* that the development is interrupted by the period of latency, seemed to call for particular notice. This appears to be one of the necessary conditions of the aptitude of men for developing a higher civilization, but also of their tendency to neurosis. So far as we know, nothing analogous is to be found in man's animal relatives. It would seem that the origin of this peculiarity of man must be looked for in the prehistory of the human species.

It was not possible to say what amount of sexual activity can occur in childhood without being described as abnormal or detrimental to further development. The nature of these sexual manifestations was found to be predominantly masturbatory. Experience further showed that the external influences of seduction are capable of provoking interruptions of the latency period or even its cessation, and that in this connection the sexual instinct of children proves in fact to be polymorphously perverse; it seems, moreover, that any such premature sexual activity diminishes a child's educability. . . . .

NOTE 11

Bornstein, B., 1949. The analysis of a phobic child. *The Psychoanalytic Study of the Child*, III/IV, New York: International Universities Press, Inc., pp. 181–226.

Frankie, a $5\frac{1}{2}$-year-old boy of superior intelligence who was eager to learn, was brought into analysis because of a severe school phobia. He liked to play with other children and was friendly and amenable with them, but shy and withdrawn in the presence of any stranger. He became panic-stricken if his mother or nurse were out of sight. Even when left with his father in his own home, he was occasionally overwhelmed by attacks of anxiety. His phobic symptom had existed for more than 2 years. . . . .

When Frankie was 2, it became especially difficult to put him to bed at night. Regularly, he screamed for an hour before he fell asleep, and also whenever he awoke during the night. A third screaming period occurred at the age of $4\frac{1}{2}$ years and was stopped only after the nurse threatened to punish him. . . . .

The child's anxiety reached its first peak when he was brought to nursery school at the age of 3 years and 9 months. At that time, his sister's nurse had just left the home, and he had to share his own nurse with the baby (aged 9 months). He went to school for only 2 days. Each time, he had to be taken home because of his wild attacks of fear and screaming, and nothing could make him return to school. . . . .

The analyst suggested that treatment be postponed until after a period of preparation for analysis in which the school was to cooperate with the analyst. . . . .

Frankie started his first session by building a hospital which was separated into a "lady department", a "baby department", and a "men's department." In the lobby, a lonely boy of 4 was seated all by himself, on a chair placed in an elevated position. The child's father was upstairs visiting "a lady" who, he informed us, when questioned, "is sick or maybe she's got a baby, maybe—I don't know, never mind." He made the point that newborn babies and mothers were separated in this hospital. Casting himself in the roles of a doctor and a nurse, he attended to the babies in a loving way, fed and cleaned them. However, toward the end of the play, a fire broke out. All the babies were burnt to death and the boy in the lobby was also in danger. He wanted to run home, but remembered that nobody would be there. Subsequently he joined the fire department, but it was not quite clear as to whether the firemen had started the fire or put it out. Frankie announced: "Ladies, the babies are dead; maybe we can save you!" Actually only those lady patients who had no babies were rescued by him. The one whom he several times—by a slip of the tongue—had addressed as "Mommy", however, was killed in the fire. No particular attention was given to the men's department. Most of the men had died anyway.

This game, which was repeated in the analysis for many weeks, betrayed the intensity of the boy's fury against his mother and sister. He could not forgive his mother for her unfaithfulness. He took her going to the hospital as a desertion of him and a sign of her lack of love. She must suffer the same tortures which he had suffered when she left him. He said, as it were: "I don't love you either; I hate you, I don't need you, you may die in the hospital. If you hadn't had a baby I would love you.". . . .

Frankie, who so thoroughly punished his mother by the withdrawal of his love, naturally lived in continual fear of retaliation. He could not stay at home or go out without his mother because he needed the presence of just that person against whom his aggressive impulses were directed. The presence of the ambivalently loved person prevents the phobic from being overwhelmed by his forbidden impulses and assures him that his aggressive intentions have not come true. But while the unconscious hatred directed at the protecting person is usually difficult to uncover in the analysis of adults, it was still very close to the surface in this 5½-year-old boy. . . .

The danger which threatened the mother from relations with men would result in what was the gravest danger to him: the arrival of a new baby. He had to guard against a repetition of this traumatic experience.

It was this concern that was responsible for the insomnia which became acute at this point of his analysis. There had been previous occurrences of insomnia when he was 2½ and again when he was 4½. Now again it took him hours to fall asleep. He listened silently and anxiously to the noises at night. Whenever his parents spent an evening at home, he ran back and forth between the living room and his bedroom. He wanted to know, as he expressed it, what plans they were making. They might eat something special and he wanted to share it. Or someone might come and hurt Mommy. Ideas about the problem of procreation filled the hours of his severe insomnia. . . .

One element which was already present in his wild performances became the predominant and all-important feature: a strong inclination to gain pleasure by use of his eyes. This voyeuristic element led him to a new impersonation, that of an omniscient God.

In this new role he made the analyst a frightened, sleeping child into whose ears God whispered dreams of wild colliding horses, of violent scenes in which "Daddy throws Mommy out of the window so that she has to go to the hospital for eighteen days." The "sleeping games" revealed his suspicions of something frightful happening between his father and mother during the night—something he would have liked to observe. As God, he had the right to see and watch everything. His new role of God provided him with greater power than he had previously enjoyed as attacker, judge, or policeman—roles in which he had experienced the triumph of the conqueror, but also suffered the pain of the conquered. . . .

Later, however, when he realized that God was not only his own creation but a concept shared by others and that he could not rule "his" God to the extent necessary to be protected from anxiety, he replaced his fantasy of an omniscient God by an imaginary television apparatus which belonged exclusively to his fantasy and thus was completely at the disposal of his wishes and plans. ("God sees everything, but the television apparatus sees only if I turn it on.") The television apparatus brought the child closer to reality. When he was God, he made the analyst dream about those frightful scenes between his parents, while with the introduction of his imaginary television apparatus, he himself attempted to face those scenes. The analyst was made a co-observer of eating scenes for which Frankie provided the music (another auditory manifestation) while explaining the observed events to the analyst. He reassured the analyst many times that the observations were "make believe" and actually he never again reached the previously described state of excitement and anxiety. By means of his invention of the television apparatus, he removed himself not only from the scenes he imagines, but also from the feelings of desire and concomitant guilt which those scenes aroused. . . .

The following is one of the scenes observed through the apparatus: Father was in the restaurant and ordered the most delicious food for Mother from the restaurant owner. Then he had a secret talk with the owner. As soon as Mother had eaten, she collapsed and died; the food was poisoned. (In his thoughts, eating was linked with being impregnated, for which Frankie had not yet forgiven his mother, and for which he still punished her by death.) Father and the owner of the restaurant were unconcerned by her death; they continued their pleasant talk and play, shoving Mother under the table.[13] Some drawings of this time show God and God's wife feasting at a dinner table, disturbed by "little gnomes" who alternately attack God and his wife.

These games helped the investigation and understanding of a past period of his life: We had reason to assume that when he was $4\frac{1}{2}$, his screaming attacks had reappeared as his reaction to audible primal scene experiences. His father once wrote us that in former times, "in his prankish days", he used to pinch his wife and throw her into the air, "all in fun and for exercise. . . ., I can imagine what it must have seemed like to someone who heard it but did not see what actually happened." Frankie's running back and forth between his bedroom and the living room occurred in reaction to auditory stimuli and continued until his nurse quenched his active interest, and nightly curiosity by a threatening and punishing attitude.

With the process of internalization of his conflicts the actually threatening nurse was replaced by imaginary objects, mainly wolves, who stood guard under his bed and kept him from getting up and investigating what might be happening in the parental bedroom.

These imaginary wolves under the bed were able, like the God he had played, to see what he did and to surmise his intentions. As soon as he put out hand or foot

---

13. The scene is rich in its overdetermined factors; it permits the reconstruction of Frankie's oedipus complex. The element, "Mother is shoved under the table", refers to the child's resentment against his mother, who did not pay any attention to him when he, sitting under the table, tried to disturb his parents' meal. The next element, "Father and restaurant owner confer about the food for Mother (from which she dies)" is an indication of Frankie's wish to participate in his father's sexual activities. Frankie's position as restaurant owner was evident in many daydreams: he possessed "all the restaurants in New York". This detail makes us anticipate that Frankie's hostility toward his mother contained also some envy of her role as father's wife. Owner and father-Frankie and father do together what otherwise mother and father do. We shall see later how strong the child's desire was to take the passive role with the father.

to go into his parents' bedroom,[14] the wolves would snap at him; "but they would let me go to the bathroom." For a protection from their attacks the boy armed himself with many weapons, preferably with a long stick, in order to beat the wolves down when they raised their heads. He maintained that they observed all his movements, and he in turn countered with an equally watchful attitude. His configuration of the wolves contained as elements the punitive and protective parent figures as well as his own impulses. The wolves punish his intentions and prevent their fulfillment. Their symbolic role as superego was strikingly confirmed in a drawing which Frankie called the WOLVES' STATUE. It showed an oversized wolf (in human form) with outstretched arms, floating above Frankie in his bed, under which a number of smaller-sized wolves (also in human form) were engaged in mysterious activities, obviously of a sexual nature. In his comments on this picture, Frankie said: "It shows what the wolves hope for, what they will look like some day."

The dread of wolves which had haunted the child for weeks finally led to the analysis of his castration fear. In his stories and in his play, the mother's attackers who previously had been punished by death, now were punished by almost undisguised castration. In his pictures he endowed God with monstrously elongated arms and legs, only to cut off these limbs with scissors. Immediately after such operation he tried to undo this symbolic act of castration by drawing innumerable new arms and legs. Frankie derived reassurance from the idea that destruction is not necessarily irrevocable and consequently dared to express the thoughts of castration without any symbolic disguise. Mother's attackers were imprisoned and he, as a doctor, subjected the prisoners to operations which usually threw him into a state of exaltation. Playing the doctor, he exclaimed: "Those criminals, they have to be operated on. Off with their wee-wees. It has to come off!" In his play he guarded himself against any awareness of his fear by identifying himself with the person performing the act of castration. His fear of the anticipated retaliation found expression in his behavior toward his pediatrician. Frankie had always been a difficult patient, but during this period he absolutely refused to be examined, and assaulted the doctor by throwing blocks or potatoes which he carefully had stored under his bed for this purpose.

references

1. Bornstein, B., 1949. The analysis of a phobic child: some problems of theory and technique in child analysis. *The Psychoanalytic Study of the Child*, 3/4:181–226.

2. ——, 1953. Fragment of an analysis of an obsessional child: the first six months of analysis. *The Psychoanalytic Study of the Child*, 8:313–332.

14. The element of uncovering the hands and feet is overdetermined and it is obviously a presentation of its opposite, *i.e.*, a reverse of the original warning against touching his genital under the bedcover.

3. Brieland, D., 1965. Adoption research: an overview. In: *Perspectives on Adoption Research*, Child Welfare League of America, Inc., p. 58.

4. Brunswick, R. M., 1940. The preoedipal phase of the libido development. *Psa. Quart.*, 19:293.

5. Buhler, C., 1930. *The First Year of Life*. New York: John Day.

6. Buhler, K., 1930. *The Mental Development of the Child*. New York: Harcourt, Brace & World Inc.

7. Campbell, M., 1951. *Clinical Pediatric Urology*. Philadelphia: W. B. Saunders Co., p. 801.

8. Erikson, E. H., 1940. Studies in the interpretation of play: 1. Clinical observation of play disruption in young children. *Genetic Psychology Monographs*, 1940, p. 22. Reprinted in *Contemporary Psychopathology*, S. S. Tompkins (ed.). Cambridge: Harvard University Press, 1943, 91–122.

9. ——, 1959. Initiative versus guilt. *Identity and the Life Cycle, Psychological Issues*, 1(1):74–82.

10. Fischer, C., Gross, J., and Zuch, J., 1965. Cycle of penile erection synonymous with dreaming (R.E.M.) sleep. *Arch. Gen. Psychiat.*, 12:29–45.

11. Fisher, C., 1970. A psychophysiological study of nightmares. *J. Amer. Psa. Assoc.*, (October), 18(4):747–782.,

12. Flavell, J. H., 1963. *The Developmental Psychology of Jean Piaget*. New York: D. Van Nostrand Co., Inc., pp. 150–163.

13. Freud, S., 1900. *The Interpretation of Dreams.* Standard Edition 4, (1953), London: The Hogarth Press, 261–3.

14. ——, 1905. *Three Essays on the Theory of Sexuality.* Standard Edition, 7, (1953). London: The Hogarth Press, 125–243.

15. ——, 1905. *Fragment of an Analysis of a Case of Hysteria.* Standard Edition 7, (1953), London: The Hogarth Press, 7–124.

16. ——, 1908. *On the Sexual Theories of Children.* Standard Edition 9 (1959), London: The Hogarth Press, 205–226.

17. ——, 1909a. *Family Romances.* Standard Edition 9 (1959), London: The Hogarth Press, 235–241.

18. ——, 1909b. *Analysis of a Phobia in a Five-Year-Old Boy.* Standard Edition 10 (1955), London: The Hogarth Press, 5–152.

19. ——, 1909c. *Notes Upon a Case of Obsessional Neurosis.* Standard Edition 10 (1955), London: The Hogarth Press, 155–318.

20. ——, 1918. *From the History of an Infantile Neurosis.* Standard Edition 17 (1955), London: The Hogarth Press, 7–122.

21. ——, 1919. '*A Child is Being Beaten*': *A Contribution to the Study of the Origin of Sexual Perversions*. Standard Edition 17 (1955), London: The Hogarth Press, 179–204.

22. ——, 1924. *The Dissolution of the Oedipus Complex*. Standard Edition, 19, (1961), London: The Hogarth Press, 171–179.

23. Gastaut, H. and Broughton, R. J., 1964. Conclusions concerning the mechanisms of enuresis nocturna. *E.E.G. Clin. Neurophysiol.*, 16:625.

24. Gerard, M., 1939. Enuresis: a study in etiology. *Amer. J. Orthopsychiat.*, 9:48.

25. Green, M. and Richmond, J. B., 1954. *Pediatric Diagnosis*. Philadelphia: W. B. Saunders Co., 228.

26. Harper, P. A., 1962. *Preventive Pediatrics*. New York: Appleton-Century-Crofts, p. 32.

27. Hartshorne, H. and May, M. A., 1928–1930. *Studies in the Nature of Character. Vol. I, Studies in Deceit; Vol. II, Studies in Self-Control; Vol. III, Studies in the Organization of Character*. New York: Macmillan.

28. Hawkins, M. O., 1946. Jealousy and rivalry between brothers and sisters. *Child Study*, pp. 2–5.

29. Hawkins, D. R., Scott, J., and Thrasher, G., 1965. Sleep patterns in enuretic children. *A.P.S.S.*

30. Herzog, E. and Sudia, C. E., 1968. Fatherless homes: a review of research. *Children*, Sept.-Oct., 177–182.

31. Hoffer, W., 1949. Deceiving the deceiver. In: *Searchlights on Delinquency*, K. R. Eissler (ed.). New York: International Universities Press, Inc.

32. Johnson, A. M., 1949. Sanctions for superego lacunae of adolescents. In: *Searchlights on Delinquency*, K. R. Eissler (ed.). New York: International Universities Press, Inc., 225–245.

33. Jones, E., 1929. Fear, guilt and hate. *Int. J. Psa.*, 10(4):383–397.

34. Katan, A., 1946. Experiences with enuretics. *The Psychoanalytic Study of the Child*, 2:241.

35. Kirk, H. D., 1964. *Shared Fate*. The Free Press of Glencoe, Toronto: Collier-Macmillan.

36. Kohlberg, L., 1964. Development of moral character and moral ideology. In: *Review of Child Development Research*, M. L. Hoffman and L. W. Hoffman (eds.), Vol. 1, pp. 383–431. New York: Russell Sage Foundation.

37. ———, 1968. Early education: a cognitive developmental view. *Child Development*, 39(4):1013–1062.

38. Lemkau, P. W., 1955. *Mental Hygiene in Public Heatlh*. Second Edition. New York: McGraw-Hill.

39. Levy, D. M., 1937. Studies in sibling rivalry. *Research Monograph No. 2.* New York: Amer. Orthopsychiat. Assoc.

40. Lewis, H., 1965. The psychiatric aspects of adoption. In: *Modern Perspectives in Child Psychiatry,* J. G. Howells (ed.), Springfield: Charles C Thomas, 428–451.

41. Lipton, S. D., 1962. On the psychology of childhood tonsillectomy. *The Psychoanalytic Study of the Child,* 17:363–417.

42. Masters, W. H. and Johnson, V., 1966. *Human Sexual Response.* Boston: Little, Brown & Co., pp. 66–67.

43. Musto, D., 1969. The Youth of John Quincy Adams. *Proceedings of the Amer. Philosophical Society,* 113(4):269–282.

44. Neubauer, P. B., 1960. The one-parent child and his oedipal development. *The Psychoanalytic Study of the Child,* 15:286–309.

45. Peller, L., 1961; 1963. Comments on adoption and child development. *Bull. Phila. Assoc. Psychoanal.,* 11:1961; 13:1963.

46. Piaget, J., 1926. *The Language and Thought of the Child.* New York: Harcourt, Brace and World.

47. ———, 1951. *Play, Dreams and Imitation in Childhood.* C. Gattengo and F. M. Hodgson (trans.). New York: W. W. Norton.

48. Pierce, C. M., Whitman, R. R., Maas, J. W., and Gay, M. I., 1961. Enuresis and dreaming. *Arch. Gen. Psychiat.,* 4:166–170.

49. Rapaport, D., 1967. *The Collected Papers of David Rapaport.* M.M. Gill (ed.), New York: Basic Books, Inc. p. 589.

50. Reding, G. R., Rubright, W. C., Rechtshaffen, A., and Daniels, R. S., 1964. Sleep pattern of tooth grinding: its relationship to dreaming. *Science,* 145: 725–726.

51. Schecter, M., Carlson, P. B., Simmons, J. Q., and Work, H. H., 1964. Emotional problems in the adoptee. *Arch. Gen. Psychiat.,* 10:37.

52. Sherfey, M. J., 1966. The evolution and nature of female sexuality in relation to psychoanalytic theory. *J. Amer. Psa. Assoc.* (January), 14(1):28–128.

53. Spitz, R. A., 1962. *The First Year of Life.* New York: International Universities Press, Inc.

54. Toussieng, P. B., 1966. Thoughts regarding the etiology of psychological difficulties in adopted children. *Child Welfare,* (Feb.), p. 59.

55. Waelder, R., 1933. The psychoanalytic theory of play. *Psa. Quart.,* 2:208–224.

56. Wittenborn, J. R., 1957. *The Placement of Adoptive Children.* Springfield, Ill.: Charles C Thomas, IX, p. 189.

Chapter 5

THE ELEMENTARY SCHOOL AGE CHILD

maturation

Something clearly happens in the development of the child between 6 and 11 years of age that gives rise to the impression that something qualitative as well as quantitative has locked into place. The pieces of earlier development seem almost suddenly to fit together and function in a smoother, more integrated fashion. The child not only learns new motor skills, such as balancing on a bicycle, but at some point, perhaps around 9 years of age or so, does so with ease—the skill, so to speak, has "clicked" and become an automatic, established, unselfconscious act requiring no effort of concentration. Language skills similarly become more fluent, and the child becomes capable of more abstract thought.

personality development

Essentially this is a period of consolidation of all earlier developments. All the relatively autonomous, enduring functions that are conceptualized within the structural view of the personality show clear maturation as they become increasingly established. For example, the maturation of certain ego functions, such as defense mechanisms and reality testing, become more clearly manifest at this stage. Besides the shift from a general phobic organization to a normal obsessional organization characteristic of an elementary school age child, there is a much greater capacity for thinking, memory, speech, and conceptualizing ability. It is at this stage that certain concepts of inevitability such as death, birth, and sex differences become established. (The child's reaction to death will be discussed in Chapter 7.) Logical "secondary process" thinking is clearly dominant, and the child has a far greater capacity to delay and divert the expression of a given impulse. He is able to take care of his body quite well, and now usually thinks of food as food rather than as a symbol. The psychological defenses are greatly strengthened, with a remarkable amnesia of earlier infantile urges reinforced by such reaction formations as shame, disgust, and guilt against exhibitionistic, messing, and aggressive urges.

Concomitant with his successful management of impulses, more acceptable forms of gratification become sufficiently satisfying for the child. There is a diminution of observable sexuality, the conflicts of the oedipal period are now experienced in a less intense way, and the child is altogether more responsive to his environment. There may be occasional, temporary, regressive phenomena, but on the whole the child's ego is more robust at this stage. To the extent that he no longer has to consume his energy in dealing with his impulses, then to that extent energy is free for other activities that are not ordinarily conflict-laden, allowing the child a greater degree of autonomy (Hartmann, 1955). Thus, energy becomes available for learning, exploring, and the widening and deepening relationships with others, to be described shortly.

latency

It is this total complex of phenomena that are subsumed under the term "latency" in psychoanalysis. However, many of the behavioral manifestations that occur during this period of psychosexual and psychosocial change are modified by cultural factors. For example, in some societies overt sexual activity occurs throughout this period of development, particularly when there are no sanctions against such activity. This was seen quite clearly in the Trobriand Islanders studied by Malinowski (1927). Moreover, in present Western society, there is an atmosphere of greater freedom which permits, for example, a more open expression of sexual interests. The term latency should perhaps be confined to the intrapsychic changes that are taking place, particularly with respect to those functions that provide for an increase in internal controls, *e.g.* mechanisms of defense, increasing capacities for socialization, formation of a sense of moral values, and changes in relationships.

superego development

While initially (say, 6 to 8 years of age) the superego is strict, with signs of a heightened ambivalence and a marked conflict over masturbation, gradually this struggle abates so that in the second half of this period (say 8 to 10 years of age) the superego is less strict, sublimation is more successful, and the child begins to experience pleasure again from sexual gratification (Bornstein, 1951).

relationship with parents and peers

The child in his relationships with others at this stage begins to feel somewhat disillusioned with his parents, and may even feel they are not as great as the parents of his friends (Pearson, 1966; see Note 12). Family romance ideas are especially prominent at this time. He may turn his interests to other adults, such as teachers, scout leaders, ministers, and others whom he may overvalue. These fantasies and behavioral tendencies are part of the process of increasing separation and autonomy. Most of all, he needs peers with whom he can identify and play (Campbell, 1964).

imaginary companion

One curious form of "peer" relationship seen in childhood is the imaginary companion. In one questionnaire study of 700 adults recalling their own childhood, approximately one third of the women and one quarter of the men recalled having an imaginary companion during their childhood (Hurlock and Burnstein, 1932). McKellar (1965) described a colleague who recalled an imaginary blue fairy called "Tinkerbell" who was a friendly figure. The girl still kept Tinkerbell as a companion even though, at age 5, she knew that Tinkerbell did not really exist. Tinkerbell persisted as a kind of half-belief until about 9 or 10 years of age.

Sometimes the imaginary companion takes the special form of a conscious fantasy of having a twin, which builds up during latency "as the result of disappointment by the parents in the oedipus situation, in the child's search for a partner who will give him all the attention, love and companionship he desires and who will provide an escape from loneliness and solitude" (Burlingham, 1945). In this sense the imaginary companion is a variant of the family romance fantasies and animal fantasies that are prevalent during this period (Freud, A., 1937).

Imaginary companions appear to serve different functions at different levels of development (Nagera, 1969). They may serve as an auxiliary conscience whom the child consults; may act as a scapegoat when the child acts upon a forbidden impulse; or they may become the vehicle for some vicarious gratification. In addition, the imaginary companion may be invoked to ward off regression and to master anxiety, thus serving healthy, adaptive aims.

While all this development and consolidation is taking place, the child becomes noticeably more pleasant for adults. There is, in fact, now a pull away from earlier childhood urges, or a strong force to push them down, which is syntonic with the adult position. This is in contrast to the regressive pull of earlier childhood to which young children frequently succumb and which adults often find distinctly uncomfortable. The child now becomes in general a more social being.

social preparation

In terms of his social development, the child is also aware at this time that there is a time for play and a time for what is increasingly being called work. He seems to be aware that he must start to prepare himself more earnestly for adult roles. Erikson calls this the stage of industry versus inferiority, and notes that the child must accomplish at this stage the enjoyment of work, a sense of growing possibilities, and a feeling of capability (Erikson, 1959).

What is of further interest is that the child now begins to experience more directly the impact of the environment outside the family, especially the school and the community. Acculturation still continues to occur mostly through the family, but the family itself is also subject to the influence of society. Hence the role of society must be considered, at least in its broadest terms, at this point.

Acculturation and adaptation through this kind of cultural transmission process is, of course, much more rapid than adaptation by means of the survival of adaptive traits in the ordinary selective process of evolution. Lorenz put it well when he said: "within one or two generations a process of ecological adaptation can be achieved which, in normal phylogeny and without the interference of conceptual thought, would have taken a time of an altogether different, much greater, order of magnitude" (Lorenz, 1966). Yet, a certain period of time, perhaps a generation, perhaps more, is still necessary to effect these adaptive changes that will assist effective adjustment to a slowly evolving and changing society. But what if society evolves and changes at a more rapid rate than usual? How is the adaptive process effected, and can it keep up?

Today there is a scene of rapidly changing social and moral values. Further, the increasing rate of automation has led in some instances to obsolescence of a skill or career before it has been fully developed by the individual. Moreover, new skills and careers appear at a rate more rapid than even the most thoughtful future planning can anticipate. Instantaneous telecommunications and the rapidly increasing rate of technological development add to the fear of being overwhelmed and out of control. At the same time, the marked and probably increasing mobility of the American population has at times been associated with family isolation and generation isolation. This tendency has been aggravated by the trend toward larger impersonal cities and larger impersonal campuses. Moreover, the absolute and relative increase in the adolescent and youth population with respect to the adult population has contributed to some of the polarization of viewpoints that has occurred in recent years.

The effect of some of these trends is partly reflected in some of the unrest seen in adolescents. Some of the alienation syndromes that have been described will be mentioned later. But the effect is also now beginning to erode pre-adolescents, partly through the uncertainty and insecurity transmitted through young parents, teachers, and unsettled adults, who are affected by this scene of rapid change. This now presents our schools and our society with a most serious challenge extending far beyond any provincial concern with minor curriculum changes.

play development

Some of the previously mentioned personality characteristics and developments permeate the play of the child at this stage (Peller, 1954; see Note 13). The play is typically cooperative play, with team games and board games prominent. He enjoys special clubs, and especially enjoys making the rules. Boys at this stage, for example, in deciding to play baseball may choose the teams, mark out the field, decide on the rules, and have a great time— without ever having thrown the ball! At the same time, some of the intensity with which these games are played, with aggressive attacks and sexual excitement, seem to represent the fears, wishes and anxieties of the child in relation to his parents, brothers and sisters. Furthermore, the very fact of a number of teammates, with sharing of defense as well as attack, serves often to reassure the individual child by warding off the anxiety of being alone against adults and by a feeling of kinship with others who have the same handicaps and frustrations. As a matter of fact, the play is so gratifying at times that it absorbs some of the oedipal longings of the child.

cognitive development

The increased capacity at this time for more complex thought has been studied in detail by Piaget, who has called this the stage of concrete operations, spanning the years 7 to 11 approximately (Inhelder and Piaget, 1958). Two outstanding characteristics of this stage have been noted by Piaget. One is the now permanent possibility of returning to the starting point of a mental operation, *e.g.* the child not only can say $6+4=10$, but also $10-6=4$. This "reversible" operation is an internal action resulting from the integration of other such actions. The other characteristic is that the child is no longer dominated by a configuration he perceives at any given moment, but can now take into account two or more variables. A well-documented example is the child who can differentiate height and width as variables when an identical quantity of water is poured into a cylinder and a beaker, realizing that the amount of water is still constant (Piaget, 1928). Hitherto, he may have been bound by either the height or the width, and might have said that the cylinder, or the beaker, had more water because of either single dimension. While it is known that conservation of amount of substance appears to precede conservation of weight and various other measures, the precise mechanism by which conservation is attained by the child is unclear (Wallach, 1969). Nevertheless this step in cognitive development is an important factor in the child's capacity for learning at this stage as he enters first grade at the age of 6 years.

prerequisites to school learning

However, the process of learning has been developing long before the child enters elementary school or even nursery school. It is necessary, therefore, to review briefly at this point some of the child's earliest learning experiences. Learning is, in fact, to some extent dependent upon the earliest foundations for the process of learning itself. The earliest experiences form the basis for much of the later information-processing patterns, and it is possible that so-called "autonomous central processes" are laid down and become relatively fixed at an early age (Hebb, 1949). Many workers have demonstrated that the preschool years are of great importance for intellectual as well as social and emotional development (Stevenson, et al., 1967; Scott, 1968). However, as Elkind has pointed out, this is not to say that formal instruction is indicated in the nursery school; rather, preparation for such instruction is what seems to be appropriate. Such nursery school preparation usually includes fine and gross motor play to learn about balance, height, gravity and basic perceptuo-motor coordination necessary for later reading; role playing to learn about later social roles and adult behavior; and freedom to experiment through which the child acquires the pleasures of discovery and accomplishment. Through these and other kinds of experiences the child accumulates the necessary concepts, relationships, attitudes and motivations necessary for the learning that is now required in elementary school (Elkind, 1970). When elementary school is reached, the learning process becomes more complex, involving many factors, and each factor is affected by a specific cluster of variables, some of which will be described shortly (pages 127, et seq.).

developmental strain and developmental imbalance

The developmental process at this stage is vulnerable at a number of points. Developmental strain is almost universal until the child eventually acquires a new mastery of his impulses and the demands of reality. However, sometimes an imbalance occurs: the defenses may be too weak at first, leading to impulsive behavior caused by the child being flooded by his own instincts. At other times the defenses may be too rigid, leading to a shy, inhibited child who is mobilizing all the defenses he can (repression, reaction formations, obsessional and compulsive tendencies, sublimation, etc.) to keep his instincts under control (Fries, 1957).

The factors that lead to one or another of these polarities are multiple. Clearly the strength of the previous oedipal sexual longings and aggressive wishes, and the degree to which they had been contained by the ego, are one important balance that will influence the outcome of the oedipal struggle. Strong oedipal longings poorly contained by the ego would require an especially strong superego to prevent the direct discharge of sexual and aggressive drives. The impact of the parents here is a vital factor in determining the strength of the superego (Freud, S., 1923; see Note 14). In a sense it is the strength of the superego of the parents that is the significant factor.

Another factor that influences the direction of the balance is the degree to which conflicts are present. Conflicts about masturbation are especially prominent at this stage of development. Sometimes the discomfort produced by the urge to masturbate is so great as to overwhelm the child and leads to periodic and compulsive bouts of asocial behavior, e.g. firesetting. Here the strength of the impulse is greater than the power of the ego to modify adequately the urge for direct discharge, even under the impetus of the superego. This kind of conflict is really an example once removed of the situation in which the strength of the drive determines in part whether the child's ego will be swamped.

ego psychopathology

If the crises are not mastered, and the individual remains threatened, persisting symptoms of internal conflict appear. The symptoms themselves sometimes indicate the area of conflict. In any case, whole areas of ego functioning may be impaired. For example, in the area of social adaptation various forms of asocial behavior may occur. Conflict-free ego activity may be constricted and invaded, leading to such educational problems as learning difficulties and reading difficulties, to be discussed shortly. Particular conflicts may fail to get resolved, leading to a persistence of such specific syndromes as school phobia (see page 134), sexual deviancy (see page 135), enuresis (see page 104), encopresis (see page 70), tics, and obsessive-compulsive disorders.

learning difficulties

Perhaps the single most common manifestation of psychological difficulties found in school age children who come to child guidance clinics is some form of school learning difficulty. However, before considering the nature of some of these psychological difficulties it is important to review briefly the role of maturation, lateralization, C.N.S. integration and minimal cerebral dysfunction, intelligence, emotional environment, language, and problems of temperament in learning and reading difficulties.

learning and maturational readiness

There is considerable evidence to suggest that certain children have a developmental lag in their capacity to understand the written symbols of language, giving rise to the syndrome called developmental dyslexia (Critchley, 1964). Reading for these children is an inordinately difficult task. There may be associated speech and language problems, motor awkwardness, some spatial disorientation, mixed or delayed laterality, and a family history of slowness in reading development. Parents will sometimes recall that something seemed to click for themselves at a certain age, perhaps as late as age 12 years, when, more or less suddenly, reading became easy. Unfortunately, the delay in reading caused by delayed laterality, especially when misunderstood, sometimes results in frustration and a feeling of defeat, causing secondary psychological difficulties which further impair the capacity to learn and read.

learning and lateralization

Lateralization itself appears to follow a logical sequence, with each higher level dependent on the level preceding it. The sequence flows from motor laterality through sensory laterality to lateralization of language (Semmes, 1968). Verbal skills represent the highest level of language differentiation and lateralization (Penfield and Roberts, 1959). Working specifically with children diagnosed as having developmental dyslexia, Sparrow (1969) found that retarded readers could be differentiated from normal readers on all the currently used higher level perceptual-cognitive measures of lateralization, although no differences could be found between dyslexics and normals on less complex measures such as manual dexterity. Sparrow hypothesized that a developmental lag in the process of lateralization, defined as the representation or control of functions by one cerebral hemisphere, frequently resulted in deficits which interfere with learning to read, and in the case of reading-related behaviors it was almost always the left hemisphere.

learning and C.N.S. integration

Intactness of specific organic functions is an obvious factor in learning. Visual, auditory, and central nervous integration is a necessary condition for learning in the ordinary school setting. Impairments of any of these special functions require a special adaptation on the part of the environment to enable learning to proceed along an approximately normal course. For example, special intervention is necessary in the case of blind children if learning of the most basic kind is to occur at all (Fraiberg and Freedman, 1964; Fraiberg, et al., 1966).

minimal cerebral dysfunction and learning disabilities

The role of central nervous system integration in learning raises the question of so-called "minimal cerebral dysfunction" in children. The difficulty with the earlier clinical term "minimal brain damage" as a name for a syndrome was that it was used as an all-inclusive diagnostic label representing a group of symptoms, a dynamic concept and a presumed etiology. Unfortunately, even this usage was not consistently maintained, resulting in confusion when the term was sometimes used in the narrower sense as the single cause of a group of symptoms. Furthermore, this narrow usage sometimes engendered the unhappy connotation that any child with such a diagnosis was unable to benefit from psychotherapy and special educational techniques.

Brain damage in children may or may not manifest itself as a neurological deficit. Some of these children with presumed, or initial, or later persistent deficits may also exhibit certain common behavior traits. It is this whole complex that constitutes the clinical syndrome of "minimal cerebral dysfunction." It should be emphasized that this syndrome is not caused by the single onslaught of an injury to the brain. To begin with, our diagnostic skills are not sufficient always to detect, or at least differentiate, minimal brain damage in what is after all a complex functional problem. Then again, there is no evidence at present to prove a direct correlation between a single behavior item and a manifest neurological deficit or an earlier presumed deficit. The danger here lies in falling into the trap of supposing a simple, static and direct relationship as the only valid operational basis, a legacy from an earlier period of medicine.

Children with actual brain damage may experience difficulties in a broad range of functions, of which the process of learning may be an important one. The damaged brain of the child, however, does not remain static. While the original injury to the brain may have been of limited intensity, duration and extent, its importance lies in its subsequent effects on the child's psychological development. For example, the timing of the brain injury with respect to the stage of development of the child may well be crucial. An injury which may be trivial at, say, 6 years of age, may have a devastating effect on an infant age 6 months, at least from the point of view of subsequent development. Yet, here too, caution is necessary, since as maturation proceeds, new capacities may emerge which will enable the child to compensate for an earlier injury to the extent that the signs of the original brain damage may later disappear. In any case, the brain functions as a whole and not simply as an aggregate of separate parts, a so-called "mass action" effect (Eisenberg, 1957.) The significance of this overall dynamic-time factor lies in the different meanings the original injury and any consequent handicap had or continues to have for the child as well as his parents.

In the "minimal cerebral dysfunction" syndrome one can say that, in a significant number of cases, both an injury to the brain of varying detectable degrees and a group of behavior characteristics are present. From this observation one may suggest the hypothesis that in some cases the injury may manifest itself, under certain conditions, with a commonly occurring group of behavioral characteristics. The commonest behavioral characteristics include a short attention span, marked distractibility, hyperkinesis ("organic drivenness"), lability of mood and reduced frustration tolerance, "catastrophic" anxiety, and certain specific intellectual deficits such as a poor ability to distinguish between figure and background, perceptuo-motor difficulties and some impairment of the capacity for abstraction.

The syndrome of "minimal cerebral dysfunction" can then usefully be regarded as a result of a dynamic interaction involving numerous factors, such as the degree and timing of the original injury to the brain; the psychological state of the child and his parents before, during, and after the injury; the meaning of the injury to both child and parents; the prevailing conditions which may aggravate or relieve the symptomatic behavior; and the attitudes adopted by both child and parents in attempting to deal with the situation. The etiological factors in the syndrome of "minimal cerebral dysfunction" are seen to be both physical and psychological, influenced by both endowment and environment, changing with maturation and development. It is this continuing state of flux that is important to bear in mind as the child is confronted with successive stages in his development and encounters the school learning situation.

learning and intelligence

General intelligence constitutes another factor in learning.

However, over and above native endowment, functional intelligence is in part determined by the degree of motivation, stimulation, model adequacy, and opportunity. For example, Zigler and Butterfield (1968) have noted that deprived nursery school children suffer from an emotional and motivational deficit which decreases their usual intellectual performance to a lower level than would be expected from their intellectual potential as measured in an optimizing test situation. The importance of this kind of observation of children in nursery school and kindergarten lies in the possibilities for predication, since most studies of children who appear to develop learning difficulties in elementary school reveal a much earlier onset (Cohen, 1963).

emotional freedom to learn

This leads to a further general factor, namely, that learning takes place in an environmental climate that may facilitate or hamper the process of learning. A climate of emotional freedom to learn includes the concept that the child must have such areas of functioning as attention, memory, speech, etc., sufficiently conflict-free that he can devote himself to learning. Clearly a large number of factors that cause anxiety may reduce the level of functioning in these areas because of the anxiety aroused. Some of these factors will be described shortly. (See page 132.)

language problems and learning difficulties

The specificity of a particular language is a special kind of contributing factor to certain reading disabilities. The prevalence of reading disability, for example, varies with the language used, being highest in English-speaking countries, lower in German-speaking countries, lower still in Latin-speaking countries such as Italy or Spain, and only 0.98% among Japanese children (Makita, 1968). Makita postulates that this rarity is based upon the fact that in Japanese KANA script there is "almost a key to keyhole" situation in the script-phonetic relationship, and that the reading disability of many children in English-speaking countries might be "more of a philological than a neuro-psychiatric problem."

temperament and learning disabilities

Chess (1968) has drawn attention to the temperament of the child in learning, and has suggested that even in cases where the cognitive or motivational element is the primary issue in a learning difficulty, the implementation of an appropriate remedial or therapeutic plan may depend upon what she terms the child's "temperamental individuality." Chess identified and described 9 categories that constitute the temperament: activity level; rhythmicity of such functions as hunger, elimination and sleep-wake cycle; approach or withdrawal in response to, say, a person; adaptability to an altered environment; intensity of any given reaction; threshold of responsiveness; quantity and quality of moods; degree of distractibility; attention span and persistence in the face of obstacles. The therapeutic plan was devised appropriate to the temperament as defined by these nine characteristics.

school underachievement

With this general background it is now profitable to describe some of the more specific psychological conflicts involved in school learning difficulties. Underachievement in school is found far more commonly in boys, and also tends to manifest itself earlier in boys than in girls. For example, in one study boys tended to become chronic underachievers even during the first few grades of elementary school, while girls tended to show signs of underachievement in the grades just prior to and at junior high school (Shaw and McCuen, 1960). Among all the different causes of learning difficulties, anxiety from a number of sources is perhaps the most common interfering factor (Pearson, 1952). Anxiety may be derived from sexual conflicts, illness, sibling problems, or tension between the parents. The anxiety may interfere with the capacity to assimilate or utilize new information. Sometimes these conflicts give rise to negativism, delinquency, truancy, or school phobia, with subsequent secondary impairments of learning.

anxiety and aggression

One common cause of anxiety arises from a difficulty in controlling aggressive impulses, giving rise to a learning block

(Blanchard, 1946). The child may shut himself off from all possibility of having his aggressive fantasies stimulated, or he may experience the act of learning itself as an aggressive act, making non-learning a counter-aggressive move. Learning difficulties are, of course, most often multidetermined; however, one component may be the hostility the child feels toward parents, and his unconscious refusal to please them. In failing to perform, the child simultaneously punishes himself, thus warding off guilt.

anxiety and depression

Sometimes the anxiety may be part of a more pervasive depressive disorder with self-denial, self-punishment, and an appearance of stupidity as outstanding features. Depression in children may also present as school failure, or with somatic complaints accompanied by feelings of inadequacy, worthlessness, low self-esteem, helplessness and hopelessness. Temper tantrums, disobedience, running away, truancy and, in adolescents, delinquency, may also be signs of depression in childhood (Glaser, 1967).

anxiety and the appearance of stupidity

A child may also present himself as "stupid" when he is trying to maintain a secret; is reacting to his frustrated sense of curiosity; wishes to avoid competition; or is caught in a conflict between obedience and rebellion and elects to do neither and both at the same time. Secretiveness and lying on the mother's part, especially when there is a close bond between mother and child, often forces the child to appear ignorant and not curious, not only about the forbidden topic but in a more generalized way too (Hellman, 1954). The secret of the mother is frequently about an extramarital love affair.

anxiety and symbolic association

Very rarely an unconscious and symbolic association between certain conflicts and particular words, or even letters, leading to a reading inhibition, is discovered during intensive psychotherapy or psychoanalysis of a child (O'Sullivan and Pryles, 1962).

anxiety and truancy

Truancy may be a further manifestation of anxiety. The act of truancy may represent a wish to get away from an untenable home situation. Sometimes the truancy represents a flight from reality and a retreat into fantasy. The family ties may be so insufficient that truancy is facilitated. At other times the truant child may be seeking a lost love object, or may be attempting to create a sense of guilt in the parents. Occasionally, the truant child wishes to avoid school because of a primary learning difficulty, or a fear of criticism or punishment from classmates or teachers.

anxiety and school phobia

Reference was made earlier to specific syndromes arising from internal conflict that may interfere with learning. So-called "school phobia" is one such syndrome. Separation anxiety may become exacerbated, or make its first appearance, during the elementary school stage; this anxiety may give rise to the symptom of school avoidance. There is often a history of a poorly resolved dependency relationship between mother and child (Waldfogel, *et al.*, 1957). Often some acute anxiety is precipitated just prior to the onset of the symptom. This anxiety may be produced by an illness, or an operation such as tonsillectomy, or an external event so similar to an internal fantasy that it intensifies the fantasy to the point where the child may fear its being realized. Sometimes hysterical or compulsive reactions may be mobilized to deal with the anxiety. In the face of this anxiety the child may regress and experience an increased urge of his dependency wishes. At the same time, the mother herself may be experiencing anxiety, most often brought about by some threat to her security. Such threats might arise from marital unhappiness, economic deprivation, or simply overwhelming demands that she resents. She then exploits the child's wish for dependence as a means of gratifying her own frustration, loss, and anxiety. Mother and child then become locked together in a mutual act of regression and dependency, usually combining hostile fantasies which each must hold in check by each keeping close to the other. Often the mother encourages her child to stay home because of fears for his safety based on her own angry wishes toward him. The child, in turn, is afraid to leave mother for fear something will happen to her in his absence. The absence from school and the anxiety aroused may interfere considerably with the child's learning.

ego and superego deviations

Almost any deviation from normal development may present itself in part as a learning difficulty. However, the deviations described below more commonly present as difficulties in their own right. The deviations may be conceptualized as falling into two broad categories, ego problems and superego problems. Among the ego problems certain types of sexual difficulties will be discussed. Among the superego problems, stealing and lying will be discussed.

sexual difficulties

Expressions of normal sexuality may take a variety of forms during childhood (Freud, S., 1905). At the same time, signs of sexual problems may emerge during this period of development. However, deviant-appearing behavior does not necessarily have the same significance as similar behavior exhibited during adult years when the individual should have reached maturity. For example, manifest homosexual and heterosexual preferences have different cycles and different meanings during early development. An infant may show affection for an adult, regardless of sex, provided the adult meets the caring and protecting needs of the infant. A pre-school child begins to show strong feelings, both positive and negative, toward both parents, based on the sexual attributes and roles of those parents. In this sense, a pre-school child may show homosexual and heterosexual preferences. During the elementary school years a boy may "love" a particular adult who has shown him empathy and understanding. If the adult is male, the relationship appears homosexual; if the adult is female, it appears heterosexual. But in neither case is it necessarily based on the sex of the person, but rather again on the function performed by that person. At the same time, the child's relationship with his peers may appear singularly homosexual in terms of preferred sex of the playmate, yet not represent homosexuality at all. For example, some school-age boys may show a disdain for girls, wishing only to play with other boys. Such boys are not at all destined to become homosexuals; as a matter of fact, a boy who at this age prefers to play with girls is more likely to be vulnerable to later homosexual influences. The key to understanding this paradox lies in the realization that the choice of playmates at this stage is often made largely on the basis of identification and not of actual sexual love for the selected playmate.

homosexuality

Nevertheless, there are certain influences that may mold a child in the direction of homosexuality. Besides any innate bisexual or homosexual tendency that cannot as yet be documented, some children persist in forming narcissistic relationships in which they identify with persons of the same sex. Further, continuing attachments to adults on the basis of persistent attempts to gratify early needs may also lead to persisting homosexual relationships. Sometimes disguised sexual assaults upon children, with erotic components, *e.g.* enemas, rectal temperature taking, vaginal douches, etc., may lead to a persisting passive homosexual longing. Also, if the oedipal feelings are not adequately resolved, the child may remain fixated at the level of an intense homosexual tie. Lastly, if the child is unable to mobilize effective defense reactions against homosexuality, or has no satisfactory parent models with whom to identify, there is a further likelihood of homosexual tendencies outweighing heterosexual strivings (Freud, A., 1965).

Yet, still, the balance of factors to be weighed makes prediction of the ultimate sexual outcome precarious. For example, besides the qualities in the parents and their conflicts, there are numerous conflicts and anxieties that may arise in the child, which may be aggravated by such external factors as illness, divorce, seduction, incest, rape, etc., (Lewis and Sarrel, 1969), not to mention the myriad of opportunities and lost opportunities for satisfactions or frustrations. (Homosexuality will be discussed further when adolescence is considered; see page 166.)

transvestite behavior

A specific variety of homosexuality seen in children consists of transvestite behavior. Boys who dress up as girls are regarded with greater concern in our society than girls who dress as boys. As a matter of fact, girls are sometimes encouraged to dress as boys, wearing pants, shirts, etc. Perhaps part of the reason for this is that it represents a more "normal" solution to the girl's rivalry and envy of boys, and is also an acceptable escape from the feeling of guilt she may have as a result of her belief that she has done herself harm while masturbating.

Boys who dress as girls on the other hand seem to be coping less adequately with their intrapsychic difficulties. They may be trying to win their mother's love, especially when they also sense that their mother does not really like them. They may also be attempting to deal with a loss through the normal process of identification. That is to say, if they more or less suddenly lose the mother they love (either in actuality or at least in psychic reality), they may attempt to make up for this loss by identifying with, and holding onto, the internalized image of the mother. In still other cases the boy may be acting out hostile, aggressive impulses against the mother by caricaturing how a woman behaves or dresses.

The mothers of such children often have a disturbance in their own sexual identity and their object relations (Stoller, 1967). They may dislike men for a variety of reasons and then start the boy off on cross-dressing as soon as he shows any signs of developing a masculine identity. She nips it in the bud, so to speak. Other mothers may regard their son as an extension of themselves, and then find themselves unable to tolerate any separation. Such mothers will then so gratify their son that the boy's gratitude becomes profound enough to lead to a strong identification with the mother.

Unfortunately, the fathers of such children are usually inadequate models of masculinity and, furthermore, they fail to protect their sons from the influences of the mother.

One important clinical point is the degree to which the child becomes sexually excited during the act of dressing up in the clothes of the opposite sex. Children who get sexually excited usually find it hard to give up the gratification, and almost become addicted to the behavior. They may resent any interference, and even fly into a rage.

sexual promiscuity in girls

Homosexuality is not the only risk of such influences. Exaggerated heterosexual activity may also be an outcome. In some instances a girl may repeatedly act seductively, engage in intercourse and become pregnant. Some of this compulsion to repeat may represent an attempt to work through an earlier traumatic incestuous relationship, as illustrated in this very brief case summary.

When Cathy was a young girl, she lived in a home in which her father was given to violence. When she was about 6 or 7 years of age, her father committed incest with her. In later years, when Cathy became an adolescent, she found herself involved again with a boy who was many years older than herself, and who was given to violence. Her particular boy friend at the time had a criminal record involving robbery with illegal possession of a gun. Eventually, at age 15 years, Cathy became pregnant with her 24-year-old boy friend. (This case will be discussed again on page 155.)

The repetitive behavior may also be part of a larger problem of poor impulse control, resulting from such factors as inadequate models for controls in the parents, over-stimulation, or unresolved highly ambivalent child-parent relationships. Moreover, in some cases the girl may be acting out an unconscious wish of her mother to have an affair or care for a baby again.

superego problems

Another group of problems that occur at this stage appear to have in common an antisocial aspect. Such problems include stealing, lying, and truancy (see page 134). From a psychoanalytic viewpoint these symptoms often represent a deviation in superego development.

stealing

Stealing is a particularly common symptom. The significance of stealing depends upon whether it is a developmental phenomenon or a neurotic symptom. In the infant, the child simply lacks the distinction between self and object, between "what's mine" and "what's not mine." The pre-school child also has a tendency to hoard, and may "acquire" the objects that belong to another child to add to his collection. In the nursery school period, object relations usually advance to the point of learning what belongs to others, so that taking something that belongs to someone else begins to be called stealing. If the child is delayed in his development, and continues to be relatively more immature and have poor impulse control, the impulse to take things that belong to others will continue, especially if there is added stress from any kind of deprivation.

Once the child has gone beyond this stage of development, the act of taking something that belongs to someone else is more properly called stealing. Many motivations may now lie behind this act. Sometimes it is an expression of a wish to obtain love, or to bribe a person into friendship. At other times it is an expression of hostility toward the parents who are chagrined at the act. Yet, some parents are not chagrined and some may even seem to condone the act. For example, a boy confessed to stealing some table tennis balls from a large department store. His father responded by saying he was not concerned because "the store could stand the loss." The distortion of reality values and the implied condoning of the act were clear. In this case the boy had no more sense of guilt about what he had done than had the father. Such a child may have quite adequate superego injunctions in other areas, but because the parents themselves are delinquent and provide no taboos against stealing, this aspect, too, of the parents is taken in whole by the child, resulting in a superego or conscience that has noticeable deficits.

Occasionally, the act of stealing is a poor sublimation for an intense desire to damage, mutilate, and castrate another person. Instead of hurting a part of the other person's body, his "treasured possession" is taken away. Sometimes such an unacceptable impulse gives rise to a feeling of guilt, which is then vitiated by the punishment which is incurred when another "crime" is committed. The act of stealing serves this function when it is performed in such a way that it demonstrates a clear wish to be caught. (Sometimes the item stolen provides a clue to the initial unacceptable impulse.)

Stealing may also be part of a more general behavior trait.

For example, a child may have a tendency to behave in a counter-phobic way. That is to say, he will try to deal with a fear by repeatedly and increasingly risking the danger he most fears. Stealing may be just such a "daring act," defying authority and experiencing the thrill of near misses. Sometimes it is an act performed in the service of identification with a group, or a particular leader, or as a reluctant follower of the commands of such a person.

lying

What has been said about stealing could also be said about lying. In infancy, fantasy and reality are not well distinguished. There is throughout childhood a tendency, especially under stress, to revert to the pleasure of fantasy and primary process thinking, so that the verbal distortion of reality more likely represents the lack of distinction between fantasy and reality, or the regression to fantasy, rather than a conscious effort to distort reality. Later, when the distortion of the truth can be more properly called lying, motivations similar to those found in stealing may give rise to lying.

Note 12

Pearson, G. H. J., 1966. The importance of peer relationship in the latency period. *Bulletin of the Philadelphia Association for Psychoanalysis,* 16:109–121.

As we observe children we note that around the age of five and six, the child begins to remove himself from his family and seeks friends of his own age outside the home. . . . Real playing together becomes more definite from five or six on. By the time he is about six or seven, he gradually spends more and more time with his friends than with his family. He begins to share his interests and ideas more with his friends and less with his parents, and he definitely begins to keep his secrets for his friends and no longer tells them to his parents.

By the time he is eight or nine, this behavior has become quite marked and of course continues into and through adolescence. At the same time he begins to question, both by himself and with his friends, his former concept of his parents as deities who can do no wrong. He begins gradually to recognize that they, like all other adult human beings, are mortal and comes to believe that adults, as a general rule, are not to be trusted. As he finds himself being aware of his parents' and other adults' shortcomings, he relies more and more on the support and cooperation of his peer companions. Somewhere between eight and ten these form a group, tend to gang together against the adults and the adults' authority, and find pleasure in thwarting the adult as much as possible. This turning away from the former worshipful admiration of the parents and other adults and the consequent deprecating of their importance is regarded by the parents, and other adults, with distinct displeasure. . . .

Withdrawal from parents and adults and relating more closely to peers reinforces repression of the oedipal conflict and thus becomes an important factor in personality development. Relationship with peers in itself develops skills in socialization. . . . this is as necessary an individual step in the total development of the human being as is the relationships with the mother. When there is interference with it or if it does not occur, the later life adjustment of the human being is crippled. . . . This developmental process can be interfered with in two ways: as the result of environmental and adult restrictions; and as the result of inner restrictions which have been produced by frustrations during the pre-oedipal and early oedipal years.

Parents who dislike the incessant activity and use of small and large muscles in the five-, six-, or seven-year-old may insist on less active behavior. As a consequence the child is forced back into the intrapsychic life of daydreaming and fantasy and is prevented from repressing and redirecting the oedipal fantasies. . . . Similarly parents who for whatever reason restrict unreasonably their child's contact with other children or resent bitterly the child's loyalty to his peer group, and the concomitant "disloyalty" to themselves, may interfere with the child's socialization and prevent the (necessary) repression. . . .

External circumstances . . . . may restrict the possibility of a child making adequate contact with his peers. . . . Sometimes an only child will be sent to a private school from the time he enters school. This school usually is a long distance from his home and no other child from his neighborhood may attend it. His peers may look with contempt on this particular child because he attends a different school. He finds that they don't accept him readily, so he comes more and more to stay by himself on his own property and often within his home. This again forces a difficulty in the solution of his oedipal problems, or at best a delay in their solution. Of course, the opportunity he has for free play with his peers during school hours will help him to some extent.

Very frequent moves from one neighborhood to another during this period also may interrupt old relationships and create difficulties in adjusting to new groups of peers so that the child eventually gives up making further attempts. Long continued illnesses during this period or marked chronic physical disabilities which actively prevent peer contact are a cause in some cases but these are special instances.

Occasionally one sees a child who restricts himself from peer contact because of former painful experiences. . . .

There are a number of cases in which the child during the late prelatent and latency periods restricts himself from peer contact for unconscious reasons, usually the result of traumatic experiences during his pre-oedipal and early oedipal periods. . . .

. . . . a child who himself avoids contact with his peers during the late prelatent and latent periods or who is much, much too loyal to his parents in his thinking,

NOTE   13

Peller, L. E., 1954. Libidinal phases, ego development, and play. *The Psychoanalytic Study of the Child*, 9:178–198.

SURVEY OF PLAY ACTIVITIES

CENTRAL THEME OF PLAY; OBJECT-RELATIONS:	DEFICIENCIES ANXIETY (denied):	COM-PENSATING FANTASY:	FORMAL ELEMENTS, STYLE:	SOCIAL ASPECT:	PLAY MATERIAL:	SECONDARY PLAY GAINS:
Group I Relation to *Body* ——— Anxieties concerning body	My body is no good I am often helpless	My body (its extensions, replicas, variations) is a perfect instrument for my wishes. Imagery grandeur, of ceperfectease	Hallucinations (pos. & neg.) rather than fantasies. Imagery increases pleasure, of persisten	Solitary	Extensions & Variations of Body functions & Body parts.	Increased body skills & mastery. Initiation into active search for gratification.
Group II Relation to *Preoedipal Mother* ——— Fear to lose love object	My Mother can— desert me; do as she pleases;	I can do to *others* what she did to *me.* I can go on (or quit)	Short fantasies. Endless, monotonous repetitions. Few variations. No risk, no climax, no real plot. Tit-for-tat	Solitary or with mother. Other children rank with pets, children, and or things—not as co-players. Sporadic mirroring play	Maternal play with dolls, stuffed animals, with other mother herself. Peek-a-boo. Earliest tools.	Rage, anxiety mitigated. Ability to bear delay, frustration. Initiation into lasting object relation.
Group III starts about 3 years *Oedipal* Relations & Defenses against them. ——— Fear to lose love of love object	I cannot enjoy what grownups enjoy.	I am big; I can do as big people are doing. Family Romance	Spontaneity, Infinite variety of emotions, roles, plots, settings. Time is telescoped In later times; Drama, risk	Early co-play Attempts to share fantasy. Fantasy alway social Activity may be solitary or social	Dollplay; wide variety of events, of father, mother images; (pilot, nurse, magician etc.) Creative play, Imaginative play. Use of emblems, props, insignia	Preparation for adult roles, adult skills. Co-play prepares co-work. Initiation into adventure, accomplishment.
Group IV starts about 6 years *Sibling* Relations ——— Fear of super-ego and super-ego figures	I am all alone against threat-ening authority I canont start all over again	Many of us are united. We observed rules conscienti-ously. I can live many lives.	Codified plot & roles. Importance of rules, program, rituals, *formal* elements. Reciprocity (Piaget)	Organized co-play Fantasy tacitly shared.	Team games Board games Organized games Games with token armies	Dissolving oedipal ties. Co-operation with brothers, with followers & leaders ex-perienced as gratifying.

must show disturbances in his development.

. . . . In short, it is important to remember that the child utilizes a number of methods such as: motor activity, curiosity and interest in the external world, alliance with his peers against adults, increased loyalty to his peers with its accompanying increase in a more realistic appraisal of his parents and other adults, as mechanisms to aid his repressions, to promote separation from parents and to facilitate his own maturing.

NOTE   14

Freud, S., 1923. *The Ego and the Id.*, Standard Edition (1961), 19:34. London: The Hogarth Press.

The child's parents, and especially his father, were perceived as the obstacle to a realization of his Oedipus wishes; so his infantile ego fortified itself for the carrying out of the repression by erecting this same obstacle within itself. It borrowed strength to do this, so to speak, from the father, and this loan was an extraordinarily momentous act. The superego retains the character of the father, while the more powerful the Oedipus complex was and the more rapidly it succumbed to repression (under the influence of authority, religious teaching, schooling and reading), the stricter will be the domination of the super-ego over the ego later on—in the form of conscience or perhaps of an unconscious sense of guilt.

references

1. Blanchard, P., 1946. Psychoanalytic contributions to the problems of reading disabilities. *The Psychoanalytic Study of the Child*, 2:163–187.

2. Bornstein, B., 1951. On latency. *The Psychoanalytic Study of the Child*, 6:279–285.

3. Burlingham, D., 1945. The fantasy of having a twin. *The Psychoanalytic Study of the Child*, 1:205–210.

4. Campbell, J. D., 1964. Peer relations in childhood. In: *Review of Child Development Research, Vol I.*, M. L. Hoffman and L. W. Hoffman (eds.). Russell Sage Foundation, 289–322.

5. Chess, S., 1968. Temperament and learning disability of school children. *Amer. J. Public Health*, 58(12):2231–2239.

6. Cohen, T., 1963. Prediction of underachievement in kindergarten children. *Arch. Gen. Psychiat.* 9:444–450.

7. Critchley, MacD., 1964. *Developmental Dyslexia*. London: Heinemann, p. 104.

8. Eisenberg, L., 1957. Psychiatric implications of brain damage in children. *Psychiat. Quart.*, 31:72–92.

9. Elkind, D., 1970. The case for the academic preschool: fact or fiction? *Young Children*, Vol. 25, No. 3, 132–140.

10. Erikson, E. H., 1959. Industry vs. inferiority. In: *Identity and the Life Cycle, Pyschological Issues*, 1(1):65–74.

11. Fraiberg, S. and Freedman, D. A., 1964. Studies in the ego development of the congenitally blind child. *The Psychoanalytic Study of the Child*, 19:113–169.

12. Fraiberg, S., Siegel, B. L., and Gibson, R., 1966. The role of sound in the search behavior of a blind infant. *The Psychoanalytic Study of the Child*, 21:327–357.

13. Freud, A., 1937. *The Ego and the Mechanisms of Defense*. London: The Hogarth Press, pp. 73–88.

14. ——, 1965. *Normality and Pathology of Childhood Assessments of Development*. New York: International Universities Press, Inc.

15. Freud, S., 1905. *Three Essays on the Theory of Sexuality*. Standard Edition (1953). London: The Hograth Press. Inc.

16. ——, 1923. *The Ego and the Id*. Standard Edition (1961), 19:34. London: The Hogarth Press.

17. Fries, M. E., 1957. Review of the literature on the latency period. *J. Amer. Pyschoanalytic. Assoc.*, 5(3):525.

18. Glaser, K., 1967. Masked depression in children and adolescents. *Amer. J. Psychotherapy*, 21(3):565–574.

19. Hartmann, H., 1955. Notes on the theory of sublimation. *The Psychoanalytic Study of the Child*, 10:9–29. New York: International Universities Press, Inc.

20. Hebb, D. O., 1949. *The Organization of Behavior: A Neuropsychological Theory*. New York: Wiley.

21. Hellman, I., 1954. Some observations on mothers of children with intellectual inhibitions. *The Psychoanalytic Study of the Child*, 9:259–273.

22. Hurlock, R. and Burnstein, A., 1932. The imaginary playmate: a questionnaire study. *J. Genet. Psychol.*, 41:380–391.

23. Inhelder, B. and Piaget, J., 1958. *The Growth of Logical Thinking from Childhood to Adolescence*. New York: Basic Books.

24. Lewis, M. and Sarrel, P., 1969. Some psychological aspects of seduction, incest, and rape in childhood. *J. Amer. Acad. of Child Psychiat.*, 8:4, pp. 609–619.

25. Lorenz, K., 1966. *On Aggression*. M. K. Wilson (tr.), New York: Harcourt, Brace & World, Inc, p. 239.

26. McKellar, P., 1965. Thinking, remembering, and imagining. In: *Modern Perspectives in Child Psychiatry*. J. G. Howells (ed.), Springfield, Ill.: Charles C Thomas, 170–191.

27. Makita, K., 1968. The rarity of reading disability in Japanese children. *Amer. J. Orthopsychiat.*, 38(4):599–614.

28. Malinowski, B., 1927. Prenuptial intercourse between the sexes in the Trobriand Islands, N. W. Melanesia. *Psychoanal. Rev.*, 14:26–36.

29. Nagera, H., 1969. The imaginary companion. *The Psychoanalytic Study of the Child*, 24:165–196. New York: International Universities Press, Inc.

30. O'Sullivan and Pryles, C. V., 1962. Reading disability in children. *J. Pediat.*, 60(3):369.

31. Pearson, G. H. J., 1952. A survey of learning difficulties in children. *The Psychoanalytic Study of the Child*, 7:322–386.

32. ——, 1966. The importance of peer relationship in the latency period. *Bulletin of the Philadelphia Association for Psychoanalysis*, 16:109–121.

33. Peller, L. E., 1954. Libidinal phases, ego development, and play. *The Psychoanalytic Study of the Child*, 9:178–198.

34. Penfield, W. and Roberts, L., 1959. *Speech and Brain Mechanisms*. Princeton University Press, Princeton, New Jersey.

35. Piaget, J., 1928. *Judgement and Reasoning in the Child*. New York: Harcourt, Brace & World Inc., pp. 181–182.

36. Scott, J. P., 1968. *Early Experience and the Organization of Behavior*. Belmont, California: Wadsworth.

37. Semmes, J., 1968. Hemispheric specialization: a possible clue to mechanism. *Neuropsychologia*, 6:11–26.

38. Shaw, M. C. and McCuen, J., 1960. The onset of academic underachievement in bright children. *J. Educ. Psychol.*, 51:103–108.

39. Sparrow, S. S., 1969. Dyslexia and laterality: evidence for a developmental theory. *Seminars in Psychiatry*, 1(3):270–277.

40. Stevenson, H. W., Hess, E. H., Rheingold, H. L., 1967. *Early Behavior*. New York: Wiley.

41. Stoller, R. J., 1967. Transvestites' women. *Amer. J. Psychiat.*, 124(3):333–339.

42. Waldfogel, S., Coolidge, J. C., and Hahn, P. B., 1957. The development, meaning and management of school phobia. *Amer. J. Orthopsychiat.*, 27:754–780.

43. Wallach, L., 1969. On the Bases of Conservation. In: *Studies in Cognitive Development. Essays in Honor of Jean Piaget*, D. Elkind and J. H. Flavell (eds.). New York: Oxford University Press, 191–219.

44. Zigler, E. and Butterfield, E. C., 1968. Motivational aspects of changes in I.Q. test performance of culturally deprived nursery school children. *Child Development*, 38(1):1–14.

Chapter 6

EARLY ADOLESCENCE

maturation

Adolescence usually has its onset some time around the age of 10 years in girls and 12 years in boys. However, there is evidence to suggest that the menarche has been occurring earlier by approximately 4 months every 10 years in Western Europe over the period 1830–1960, and there is no evidence that this trend has stopped (Tanner, 1962). There is also evidence to suggest that in our society there are forces at work that have the effect of prolonging adolescence beyond the age of 18 years or so for girls and 20 years for boys. These were formerly regarded as the ages at which adolescence ended and adulthood began (Berger, 1969). In fact, several phases of adolescence have been described, including pre-adolescence, early adolescence, adolescence proper, late adolescence, and post-adolescence (Blos, 1962). However, this prolongation may not simply be an extension of the time period. Dynamic changes occur which seem to meet the criteria for a developmental stage. Keniston (1970a;1970b) has therefore conceptualized a developmental phase between late adolescence and early adulthood which at present has no name, although the term "youth"is often applied to this stage. The account that follows is concerned mostly with the earlier stages of adolescence.

Physical maturation occurs in almost every system of the body in both the boy and the girl (G.A.P. Report #68, 1968; Schonfeld, 1969). In addition to the changes in voice and the growth of a beard in the boy, and the breast development in the girl, such functional changes as ejaculation in the boy and the onset of menstruation in the girl serve as organizers for the gender identification of the adolescent. For example, menstruation is a pivotal biological event around which a girl organizes her sense of femininity (Kestenberg, 1961).

Delay or failure of maturation, as well as precocious or uneven maturation, are often causes for concern to an individual boy or girl. In one study based on fantasy themes, late maturing boys were found to be more likely to have feelings of personal inadequacy, feelings of rejection and domination by others, prolonged dependency needs and rebellious attitudes toward their parents (Mussen and Jones, 1957). Early maturing boys, on the other hand, were more likely to feel self-confident, independent, and seemed more capable of playing a mature role in their social relationships. They also seemed to produce more student body presidents and more athletes (Jones ,1957).

cognitive development

At the same time, psychological maturation is also taking place. An outstanding characteristic of this stage of cognitive development is a widening scope of intellectual activity, increased awareness, and a capacity for insight. Piaget has called this a stage of abstract operations (Inhelder and Piaget, 1958; Piaget, 1969, see Note 15). The essential change here is the child's beginning capacity to grasp abstract concepts such as infinity, and his ability now to reason from hypotheses. He will now use such propositional phrases as, "if so and so, then such and such," or "either/or."

"Egocentrism," which essentially refers to a lack of differentiation in some area of human interaction (Piaget, 1962), takes a unique form in adolescence. The extent to which the adolescent believes, say, that other people are as obsessed with his behavior and appearance as he is himself is, for example, a measure of the "egocentrism" of the adolescent (Elkind, 1967). Based on the (false) premise that others are as admiring or as critical of him as he is of himself, the adolescent constructs what Elkind calls an "imaginary audience," whose reaction the adolescent can of course anticipate. But by the same token, the adolescent constantly feels under scrutiny and often feels shame, self-criticism—and self-admiration. However, in his egocentrism he fails, of course, to differentiate between what he believes to be attractive and what others actually admire.

Yet, at the same time, he also regards his own feelings as quite unique, and develops what Elkind calls a "personal fable." These fables consist of stories about himself which he believes, such as a belief in his own immortality or, say, the adolescent girl's belief that she will not become pregnant and therefore has no need to take precautions, or that only he or she alone can feel with extraordinary intensity.

Gradually, by age 15 or 16 years, the "imaginary audience" gives way to a perception of the real audience through a process of repeated testing against reality. The "personal fable" also diminishes as the adolescent discovers in the intimacy of a relationship of mutuality that others have feelings similar to his or her own.

Some of these cognitive characteristics have been described from a psychoanalytic view. For example, Fountain (1961) described five qualities that distinguished adolescents from adults. First, adolescents tend to show a special intensity and volatility of feeling, with a rapid fluctuation of object choice. He seeks emotional experiences, and it is as if he must go out of his way to find emotion. Second, adolescents have a need for frequent and immediate gratification, accounting, in part, perhaps for his preference for rock music rather than Mozart or Bach. He cannot tolerate much anxiety and has a need to be kept constantly interested. Third, the adolescent is particularly likely to be unaware of the probable consequences of his actions and to misunderstand the feelings and behavior of others. Fourth, there is in adolescence a failure of self-criticism; a failure, that is, to perceive contradiction, incongruity, and absurdity in oneself. Fifth, the adolescent has an awareness of the world about him different from that of the adult; adolescents, according to Fountain, are less capable of concerning themselves with persons and events that do not impinge upon them personally. In summary, Fountain observed that "as the adolescent matures, the world about him begins to exist in its own right; he sees people as having needs of their own, independently, and he no longer perceives them only as they relate to him. He becomes to some degree 'responsible' for his fellow men." A further account of the adolescent's cognitive and emotional development in relation to society will be discussed shortly when the syndrome of alienation is considered (page 151).

personality development: universal ego tasks

Associated with the cognitive changes just mentioned, there are clear manifestations of personality development. In fact, adolescence has been conceptualized as the second stage of individuation culminating in stable, clearly defined self and object representation (Blos, 1967). At any rate, as the child enters early adolescence he undergoes a period of upheaval and turmoil. The amount of upheaval is to some extent determined by the degree to which the child has been successful in resolving the developmental crises of his life experiences so far (Freud, A., 1946). At the same time, the recurring, universal developmental crises now re-emerge in the context of the early adolescent stage in development. Besides the previously mentioned major cognitive task of conquering thought, at least four major groupings of universal ego tasks may be defined: (a) defining one's own individual self; (b) separation and coming to terms with specific feelings in relationship to one's family; (c) the development of love relationships; and (d) achieving mastery over one's impulses and one's body functions and capacities.

identity

One major task of adolescence, then, is the consolidation of ego identity (Erikson, 1956; 1963; see Note 16). Besides the obvious conscious sense of individual identity and self-conscious introspective feeling, there is also an unconscious striving for a continuity of personal character. Further, the extent to which the ego has succeeded in integrating its own functions with the forces of the drives and the demands of reality is a measure of the degree of identity formation and solidarity achieved.

reactions to identity tasks

One often sees a young adolescent trying on different roles as he struggles with the task of identity—as if to see which one fits him best. He may also keep his identity, particularly his sexual identity, fluid and ambiguous. Or again, the choice may be delayed and a psychosocial moratorium is declared. The various roles played may also serve to counterbalance feelings of inadequacy. For example, a boy who feels weak inside may parade as a bully, or a girl who is concerned about her femininity may try to play the role of a "femme fatale" (Galdston, 1967).

Occasionally, the role adopted is more like a suit of armor. And, if the role is too rigid and fixed, it may occasionally fall apart under pressure.

Daniel, a 15-year-old boy, had been conscientious and shy in his earlier years. He had grown up in a family disturbed by marital discord. In the year and a half before he came to our attention he had a spurt of growth. He forced himself to socialize more and to go out for school teams. He wanted to be the perfect all-round boy, and as far as his parents were concerned he appeared to be doing well. However, his work at school began to slip and he had repeated angry outbursts against his mother and older sister. He also began talking with his peers of the hopelessness of the world situation, how rotten people were, and that he might as well die. He would strive harder in an attempt to prove himself by engaging in strenuous physical and academic work, but these periods alternated with other periods filled with moods of sadness and desperation. His work did improve, and he decided to run for an important school office, although in retrospect it was noted that he appeared harassed and filled with remorse and hopelessness about his shortcomings. One day, following an important social event at school which he had attended just before the school election, he finally took a large dose of rat poison. He felt he could not go on. He was brought to the hospital several hours after he had ingested the poison.

This boy simply could not live up to the rigid ideals he had set for himself and was encouraged to expect by the attitudes of his parents.

alienation

Sometimes the so-called syndrome of alienation occurs (Halleck, 1967). Halleck originally described several characteristics of the alienated adolescents:

1. A tendency to live in the present and to avoid commitment to people, causes, or ideas.
2. An almost total lack of communication with parents or other adults.
3. An ill-defined self-concept.
4. A tendency toward sudden severe depression often accompanied by attempts at suicide.
5. An inability to concentrate or study.
6. Promiscuous but ungratifying sexual behavior.
7. Use of marijuana or L.S.D.

Halleck postulated that the internal mechanisms that led to this syndrome included a passive-aggressive rebellion against authority; fears of success or failure; and a feeling of being unloved. Also, several external forces contributed to this picture. The parents often gave ambivalent messages to the child, and forces and characteristics of society had a specific impact. For example, the increasing rate of social change and social values, the increasing development of automation, and the isolation of the generations were considered by Halleck to be important factors. The alienated adolescent also appeared to have a pervasive distrust of the use of words, the use of power, and of the real motivation of those in power.

It is important to note, however, that not all of these characteristics are always present. Indeed, sometimes contradictory characteristics may be seen (Noshpitz, 1970; Wise, 1970). For example, far from having a tendency to avoid commitment to people, causes, or ideas, some adolescents who manifest other features of the syndrome may also reveal a passionate commitment to causes and ideas. Berman (1970), in fact, regards alienation as an essential process in achieving a necessary physical and psychological distance from parents and society. Sometimes the alienation takes specific forms, *e.g.* the Hippie movement (Williams, 1970), while serving the same functions.

The view of adolescent alienation as a normal phenomenon has been well expressed by Settlage (1970b): "Adolescent alienation, while it can and does take pathological forms, is basically a normal and necessary developmental phenomenon; that while we should be alert to those adolescents who are individually or collectively disturbed and need our help, we should at the same time view adolescent behavior as a possible symptomatic expression of the state of our society and culture." There is now overwhelming evidence that contemporary adolescents and youth in the United States are far more aware of and concerned with the irrational aspects of the adult world than were previous generations. Further, there is increasing evidence of appropriate efforts on the part of adolescents and youth to change these irrational aspects of life. To be sure, in some cases this concern represents an externalization, a turning away from, inner irrational forces. Sometimes, too, the form of the dissent is itself unrealistic or unproductive. Yet, more often there is an appropriate rejection of corrupt values and a proper sense of urgency of the need to change society and control some of its more dangerous aspects (Settlage, 1970a; see Note 17). Keniston (1970c) has made a special plea for more attention to the positive, adaptive attempts of the adolescent who is trying "to make the world a more livable place, to create new life styles, to change others."

separation and feelings toward parents

Separation from the family and coming to terms with specific feelings toward one's family and others outside the family is another major task of early adolescence. Sometimes while seeming to be tearing himself away from the family abruptly and suddenly, the young adolescent simultaneously displaces his longing onto other people who either represent the parents or, as sometimes happens, represent their very opposite. At the moment of transfer the adolescent temporarily feels "free." However, his attachment to a leader of a group, or of a gang, may soon undergo the same vicissitudes as his relationships with his parents. It should be said here that parents feel quite keenly the sudden loss of the adolescent who attempts to separate in this way.

further reactions to the task of separation

Other adolescents may reverse the tender feelings they have

for their family members, and instead feel contempt, or hate. Such adolescents present the picture of a very uncooperative and hostile person. Sometimes the adolescent becomes excessively suspicious of others, or at other times he feels a sense of depression, depending on whether his hostile feelings are turned outward (*i.e.* projected) or inward (*i.e.* turned against the self). Depression in adolescents is often manifested by repetitive or frantic activity to ward off boredom; drug taking (see page 170); and acts of violence or promiscuous sexual behavior (Toolan, 1962). Sometimes the adolescent succeeds in detaching himself from his family, but for one reason or another is unable to find a person to love or be loved by. Such an adolescent may then turn his love interests inward and become intensely narcissistic. He may feel either enormously important, or, should his interests focus on his body, become inordinately concerned with his physical state.

love relationships

The love relationships of adolescents also seem to follow a developmental sequence (Pearson, 1958), and can be regarded as a separate developmental task. At the onset of adolescence a furtive sexual interest in the opposite sex begins to occur in both boys and girls. This is soon followed by an at first unconscious desire to attract a person of the opposite sex, manifest in feats of prowess in the boy, or giggling among girls. Very shortly this desire becomes conscious, and concerns about appearances become manifest. Boys and girls subsequently fall in love with persons of the opposite sex who are usually older—and ineligible. The girl tends to be more romantic in her fantasies, the boy more erotic. Parents may resent these new attachments, and in so doing may contribute to the adolescent's conflicts. Gradually both boys and girls become more comfortable with a variety of persons of the opposite sex who are now their peers, and tentative sexual explorations occur, usually of a somewhat aggressive kind at first, such as teasing, hair pulling, etc., suggesting regressive phenomena. Eventually the boy or girl becomes attached to one specific peer of the opposite sex, and experiences a sense of physical excitement when in the presence of the partner.

Often the partner is overvalued and exalted as a feeling of love replaces the urge for direct sexual gratification. In an almost reciprocal manner the boy or girl may feel unworthy of the object of his or her love. At first these love relationships seem to be of limited duration, and consist mostly of talking, with some petting. As the older adolescent gains experience, the narcissism of the adolescent boy or girl becomes less over-riding and a genuine concern for the real feelings of the person of the opposite sex emerges, together with an urge for genital sexual experiences. In a recent 7-year follow-up study of 45 normal adolescent boys representing a significant segment of the adolescent population, 10% had had sexual intercourse at the end of the third year in high school, rising to 50% by the middle of the third post-high-school year (Offer, *et al.,* 1970).

unresolved love relationship behavior

Displaced feelings, infatuations, and disappointments are common enough in normal adolescents (Freud, A., 1958). Sometimes an infatuation seems in some ways to re-evoke the feelings of an earlier love affair, so to speak, namely the oedipal attachment of the younger child to the parent of the opposite sex. If the oedipal struggle had been particularly difficult, the young adolescent experiences a great deal of turmoil. The case of Cathy, mentioned earlier (page 138), is relevant here.

Cathy, age 15 years, became involved with a 24-year-old man. He was a person given to violence, with a criminal record involving holdup. She became pregnant, and had a miscarriage at three months. One month later, after an argument with her mother in which Cathy was told to get out of the home and leave with her boy friend, Cathy attempted suicide by swallowing an overdose of aspirin.

In the course of her treatment it was discovered that Cathy's father was an alcoholic. He was violent at times and frequently threatened Cathy's mother. Moreover, incest took place when Cathy was 6 or 7 years old.

This adolescent girl was, in part, clearly unconsciously repeating in her relationship with her 24-year-old boy friend the earlier incestuous relationship with her father.

mastery of impulses and body

The tasks of comprehending and controlling the upsurge of impulses and the new powers of his changing body and mind are formidable for the adolescent. Early in development the child struggles to cope with his impulses. In early childhood there is the tendency to act on each wish more or less as it arises. This can be seen in the alternating loving, hating, caressing, and kicking behavior in some young children. Later, as more skills become available—for example, language development—the child learns often to think about his wishes rather than always to act on them. The child also develops the capacity for play, in which he can actively work by means of repetition and trial solutions to master a problem which is beyond his capacity in his day-to-day life. And, of course, he is usually reassured by the continuing actual presence of his parents, and by their understanding support and encouragement on the one hand, and avoidance of excessive stimulation on the other hand. He identifies with his parents and takes over their thoughts and ideals. Their modes of behavior become models for him. In all these ways—that is, by initial impulsive discharge, by thinking and fantasying, by trial solutions through play, and by identification—he learns to cope with his strong instinctual urges. If he is successful, energy becomes available to him to learn at school, and he is prepared more or less for the onset of adolescence.

drive regression

Many of these ways of coping are used again by the adolescent, although perhaps in a more complex manner. Some adolescents become almost overwhelmed by the upsurge of their impulses and allow themselves to be indiscriminately messy, or sloppy, or careless. Such adolescents may still feel like a young child inside a changing and relatively unfamiliar body, threatened by urges whose strength is also unfamiliar. In fact, many adults continue to retain a part of their life where they can be messy—the garage, the attic, their study, their bureau drawers. Occasionally, the adolescent will feel overwhelmed and will act in a sexually impulsive manner. In still others, a regression in sexual drive development occurs, leading to behavior in which the adolescent gratifies earlier components of the sexual instinct, including the voyeuristic urge, the urge to explore with the mouth, and the exhibitionistic urge.

intellectualization as a defense

Occasionally, the upsurging impulses are dealt with by repression. A common mechanism of defense employed by the adolescent to maintain that repression is intellectualization. In intellectualization, the body and its needs are almost totally disregarded and the intellect is exalted in its place. Here the adolescent puts into the service of defense his newly acquired cognitive skills. Until recently, intellectualization was regarded as the characteristic defense of adolescence. Nowadays this does not appear to be so true. On the contrary, a more common tendency is toward activity, or what Hartmann (1969) refers to as the "fashion" of acting out in groups. At the same time, much of the activity of the adolescent is adaptive and devoted to change (Keniston, 1970c).

adolescent turmoil

Adolescence in Western culture was conceptualized by Anna Freud (1969) as a developmental disturbance. When the adolescent is living in an adverse environment, the degree of disturbance may be great, yet at the same time it may be partially adaptive. In some cases it may be difficult to distinguish between adolescent turmoil and schizophrenia.

A case in point is Evelyn, the 15-year-old daughter of a severely disturbed schizophrenic mother. Evelyn complained of various physical sensations, including one in which she once felt that the veins in her arms were too large and were growing larger every moment. She was filled with alarm on that occasion, and her physician was called to reassure her. She seemed to develop a state of panic over any minor physical injury, and was fearful each time she menstruated. In addition to these symptoms, her school work was suffering. She feared she was going to die, and could not sleep at night. She had abdominal pains and insisted she had appendicitis.

Evelyn's mother, a severely disturbed woman, also suffered from a leg deformity, resulting from a chronic osteomyelitis for which several operations had been performed. She used to pick at the wound and perpetuate an infection. The mother had involved Evelyn in a complex suffocating relationship in which she was hardly permitted any separate existence at all, but in which Evelyn herself somehow found it necessary to participate, sometimes to the extent of an identification with her mother in order perhaps to satisfy some of her own longings for her mother.

Evelyn's father tried to avoid getting involved in this situation by working very long hours in a delicatessen store, and was clearly not able to withstand the onslaught of the mother's demands. He was clearly of little help to Evelyn in dealing with her mother.

In the interviews with Evelyn, it became abundantly clear that she was very anxious. Her concern about being crazy was expressed directly, and her highly ambivalent relationship with her mother was both described by her and vividly re-enacted by her with the therapist. She was depressed, and felt guilty that she could somehow never satisfy her mother. She loved her mother and consciously wanted to love her, but it was often very difficult to sustain these positive feelings.

Evelyn wanted to have a separate life, yet at the same time found it almost impossible to tear herself away from the pathological interaction between herself and her mother that always developed. This separation problem between the mother and daughter also presented a difficulty in the management of the treatment situation. One might call this a family transference phenomenon. The mother was forever intruding into the therapist's office, and would sometimes contrive to come herself instead of Evelyn.

Evelyn's manifest symptoms and anxiety gradually began to subside, and the picture that ultimately emerged was that of an essentially intact adolescent who was struggling with a sick, schizophrenic mother with whom she at times identified, albeit ambivalently.

Evelyn was able to continue at school and found outside friends. The support Evelyn derived from the treatment enabled her to extricate herself, to some extent, from a morbid relationship with her mother, and to effect some distance and gain some encouragement in her attempts to see the reality of the situation. It was not possible to go any further with her at that time.

This case illustrates how certain kinds of florid presenting symptoms might lead one to think of schizophrenia, when in fact the symptoms might more accurately represent an acute anxiety crisis, sometimes called acute adolescent turmoil. One might, for example, have considered Evelyn's symptom of body distortion (the veins in her arms seeming to be too big for her arms and growing larger all the time) as a somatic delusion, and have come to the conclusion that Evelyn was therefore schizophrenic. But it seems more profitable, and probably more correct, to regard the symptom as an expression of her intense conflict around her sense of self, her concerns about her changing body, and her quest for her own separate identity—an identity crisis, perhaps, in the form of a body image distortion. (One often finds that the concerns about body changes in general that occur during adolescence become the vehicle for the expression of deeper problems.). The rapid abatement of Evelyn's symptoms when a stable relationship was offered to her would appear to support this view of her condition. What is equally striking in this case is the strong identification with the mother.

Adolescent turmoil and more severe psychiatric disorder are sometimes difficult to distinguish. Masterson (1968), in a 5-year controlled study of 101 adolescents, attempted to distinguish between adolescent turmoil and psychiatric disorder, and regarded the psychiatric effects of adolescent turmoil as the product of the interaction between the turmoil and the personality structure of the adolescent. In the healthy personality, adolescent turmoil produced, at most, subclinical anxiety and depression. Adolescents with a character neurosis suffered psychoneurotic symptoms during the period of adolescent turmoil but retained a residue of pathological character parts after the turmoil and accompanying psychoneurotic symptoms subsided. Adolescents with pre-existing schizophrenia and personality disorder suffered a worsening of their condition during adolescent turmoil that also persisted into adulthood. Masterson was concerned that a psychiatrist who saw an adolescent with a personality disorder might attribute the difficulties in diagnosis to the fact that the patient was an adolescent rather than that the patient indeed had a personality disorder. More often the danger would seem to be over-diagnosing a transitory developmental stage.

reactions of parents

The adolescent, of course, is not behaving in a void; he behaves in the context of his family and society, who in turn react to him. Parents cannot help but react to the adolescent for at least three reasons.

1. The parent is in a sense faced from the other side with the very same problems that face the adolescent. For example, in regard to identity choice, the parent may want the adolescent to follow a certain career, while the adolescent may have quite different ideas, and sometimes several at a time, for himself. Involved in this, too, is the narcissistic wound that the parent feels, often expressed in a competitive relationship with their daughter or son.

A mother may unconsciously try to attract her daughter's date or a father may do likewise with his son's date. Some parents may be particularly sensitive to the impending separation of their teenager and, instead of giving assistance in the transition, may actually try to increase the tie to family by making the home too comfortable, *e.g.* making the bed, getting the breakfast, etc. Then again, some parents unknowingly may find themselves uncomfortably aroused by the sight, smell, or touch of their adolescent son or daughter.

A mother once expressed concern, even alarm, that her 15-year-old son, with whom she lived alone, was having violent temper tantrums. When an inquiry was made as to what the temper tantrums were like, it turned out that when he watched television and saw his team lose at football, he would throw a pencil down on the floor (gently!) and say "damn!" (quietly!). Subsequently, it was found that the mother was concerned about her own sexual and aggressive fantasies related, in part, to her husband who had abandoned her many years earlier. These fantasies were now being displaced and projected onto her 15-year-old son, who was in fact a very subdued adolescent.

Thus, parents may unwittingly use the adolescent daughter or son to act out unconscious wishes of their own.

2. Parents react to adolescents because the defensive pattern of behavior of the adolescent arouses discomfort and concern. For example, if an adolescent is careless, messy, unreasonable, sarcastic, unpredictable, alternately affectionate or hostile, sometimes erupting into violent anger in response to an innocuous question, it is not surprising that a parent might react to such behavior on the part of the adolescent with feelings of anger, or guilt, or both. Sometimes the parent so reacts because the behavior of the adolescent is an uncomfortable invitation to act likewise, stirring up in the parent a tendency to regress. Sometimes the parent so reacts because the parent's own adolescent struggle was incompletely mastered, and the immediacy of the adolescent boy or girl arouses past conflicts that the parent does not wish to relive. The adolescent often senses this and turns to a more neutral person, a less highly charged person, such as an uncle or an aunt. However, it should also be said that some parents may also find that the presence of an adolescent offers them an opportunity for further working through of some of their own earlier conflicts.

3. This has to do with the developmental stage of the parents. Parents of an adolescent may be in their forties, a period of life which has its own developmental aspects and corresponding anxieties. For these parents, the troublesome adolescent may be a further source of anxiety. This anxiety is perceived by the adolescent, who in turn feels more insecure, thus creating a vicious cycle.

Sometimes a family in crisis may characteristically select the adolescent as a scapegoat, perhaps because the adolescent is at that time, for a variety of reasons, the source of great discomfort to the parents. The adolescent himself may contribute to this selection, and aggravate the situation by his own provocative behavior. When this interaction occurs, the adolescent is prone to act impulsively, in part because his defenses are impaired and implicit sanction is given for the breakthrough of previously forbidden impulses (Courts, 1967).

society and adolescents

Society[1] in general is also part of the environment with which the adolescent interacts. Society may play a structuring role. Evolving as it does through generation after generation of adults, society has over the years erected structures to channel the problems of adolescence, with varying success. Such structures range from primitive rites and rituals to highly organized systems of apprenticeships and examinations.

But, by the same token, when society itself is in a state of turmoil, unrest, and danger, the adolescent will feel less secure and more upset. He may then feel impelled toward acts of violence against others or against himself. For example, at the time of the

---

1. "The term *society* denotes a continuing group of people who have developed certain relatively fixed ways of doing things which express their particular ways of viewing reality, and which employ specific symbols embodying these views. The society creates a whole universe of rules, laws, customs, mores, and practices to perpetuate the commonly accepted values and to cope with the various issues (birth, death, marriage, puberty, etc.) experienced by all members. All of these socially patterned ways of behaving constitute the society's culture."(G.A.P., 1968, page 763.)

assassination of President Kennedy, an increased number of adolescents attempted suicide. The whole matter of the impact of the conditions of our times on the individual human condition during adolescence is now in the forefront of many studies (Noshpitz, 1970; Settlage, 1970a). For example, Settlage has noted that the adolescent has to learn how to live with the constant and rapid social change that is the scene today, along with uncertainty, ambiguity, and relativity. Adequate models for identification as civilization becomes increasingly complex become less available. Many middle-aged parents today are utterly baffled at the social changes they are witnessing. The current information explosion in the midst of social misery has led some adolescents to demur and seek "relevance" in social action, while others have tried to create a simpler society of their own. Previously held notions of child rearing and education may not be appropriate for the special adaptation to change that is now required. At this point the question goes beyond the interaction between the adolescent and society, and becomes one of priorities in living for the future of mankind.

adolescent conflicts and physical illness

Psychopathology in adolescents may occur around any of the developmental tasks just described and manifest itself in a variety of forms, some of which will be described shortly. Often the psychological conflict may seek expression through an intercurrent event, such as a physical illness. Children with chronic illnesses often unconsciously make use of their condition to express anxiety around problems involving control of the body and its impulses, and independence from parental restraints. This is illustrated in the following case.

Johnny first came to the attention of the pediatrician at the age of 10 years with symptoms suggesting diabetes. Initially, the pediatric management of the diabetes presented no outstanding problem. Then, as Johnny entered adolescence, around the age of 13 or 14, the pediatrician noticed that the diabetes was becoming more difficult to control. Johnny began having attacks of severe acidosis with coma. He also seemed uncooperative at this time, and unhappy, with considerable lassitude. Further, Johnny consistently aroused the antagonism of the medical staff through each of his many admissions to the hospital. He seemed also to have an extreme fear that his mother would leave him each time she went out.

It soon became evident that there was more to this problem of control of the diabetes than the managment of a refractory pancreas, difficult as that was. Interest was therefore focussed more specifically on other aspects of Johnny's life, with the result that many significant findings came to light.

Johnny's father had died when Johnny was age 13 years, just before the diabetes began to become difficult to control. His father had been a diabetic who had died tragically from a staphylococcal infection. Johnny could not believe his father had died when he first heard about it, and was for a short while afterward angry at almost everyone.

Johnny's mother was hypertensive and obese. She seemed to have conflicts around the issue of dependency, but had maintained a marriage to her husband whom she knew to be a diabetic before she married him. The marriage seemed in some ways to fulfill some of her needs to grapple with a situation that would be bristling with difficulties.

After the father's death the mother seemed to take an intense interest in Johnny's diabetic problem to the extent of deciding herself what medication Johnny should have. At times she confused the many doctors she involved in Johnny's care. It appeared that the mother's anxiety about Johnny's future life expectancy prevented her from being able to trust doctors. Also, the anxiety seemed related to her own fears and wishes about death, in which one might say that brinkmanship was constantly being reenacted.

As far as Johnny was concerned, it became clear that the whole matter of "control" of the diabetes was related in part to his ability to "control" his body and his impulses. The illness itself seemed to be experienced as a threat to the sense of integrity toward which he had been striving. The attacks of coma also bore a close affinity to an attempt to test out a self-destructive fantasy; that is, they appeared to be suicidal equivalents. It was as though Johnny was seeking to rejoin his dead father and identify with him. In addition, Johnny was violently struggling to free himself from his mother's control, as well as at the same time acting out what seemed to be an unconscious wish of his mother, namely, to have Johnny replace her husband. It should be emphasized that these aspects of Johnny's illness were clarified through intensive psychotherapy and are not immediately obvious from the skeleton of the case presented here.

It was only when this total view of a rather complex state of affairs was clarified that the physical illness could be seen in perspective as part of a life crisis.

attempted suicide

Attempted suicide as a solution to life's problems has a peak during adolescence. Suicide is the fourth commonest cause of death during the age group 15 to 20 years. Most of the common dynamic factors involved in attempted suicide in adolescents are clearly related to the developmental tasks of adolescents just mentioned (Lewis and Solnit, 1963). For example:

1. The adolescent may find himself overwhelmed by the task of dealing with his sexual and aggressive feelings toward his parents, or the persons on whom these feelings have been displaced, and act impulsively. Sometimes catastrophic social events, *e.g.* plane crashes, civil disturbances, violent warfare, intensify the adolescent's problems and lead to attempted suicide.

2. Occasionally, the adolescent is motivated by an unconscious wish to join a dead relative, *e.g.* a father who was lost early in childhood.

3. When faced with the identity struggle, the adolescent may fear his identity dissolution, and paradoxically attempt suicide to avoid that fate.

4. Some adolescents are simply desperate and can think of no other solution for dealing with their depression, guilt, and anxiety, or their intolerable home situation. Fortunately, in some of these cases there is also a strong wish to be rescued.

5. Occasionally, the adolescent attempts suicide as an act of revenge, or as an attempt to manipulate his family into change.

6. Sometimes the adolescent concerned is schizophrenic; or his reality testing may be impaired by brain injury or acute toxic states, caused by infection or drug-induced.

illegitimate pregnancy

A further significant manifestation of adolescent upset related to adolescent developmental tasks is the occurrence of illegitimate pregnancy. Adolescent girls who become unwed mothers are not rare in our society and come from every social class. In 1960, adolescent girls gave birth to 91,700 out-of-wedlock babies. In one study, 18% of 2,000 single females who had premarital coitus became pregnant (Kinsey, 1953). For the adolescent the event of pregnancy may be related to an attempt to cope with any of the developmental tasks described earlier. In many instances there is an unconscious, or even conscious, wish to become pregnant. The wish may be derived from a number of sources. Some girls believe that by producing a baby they will be able to rid themselves of the feeling that they are defective (Bonan, 1963). In others, there is a depression and fear of loss of the tie to the mother, which is dealt with in part by an attempt to identify strongly with the mother, and produce a child whom the adolescent can mother as she herself wished to be mothered. Occasionally, the wish to have a baby is an attempt to satisfy an urge to give a baby to someone, often the mother. Indeed, the adolescent may be acting out the unconscious wish of her mother to have another baby. Often, pregnancy is the accidental result of a wish for closeness with a boy. Rarely is the unwed pregnant teenager "promiscuous" in the common sense of the word.

The wish of the mother may arise because she is menopausal at the time and feels particularly in need. The message may be conveyed, for example, by turning a blind eye to late nights, by stimulating sexual conversation, by misplaced "permissiveness," or by too early provision of contraceptives. Sometimes a pregnancy results through a prophecy-fulfillment mechanism: the parents "expect the worse" for their child, and the child obligingly lives up to this expectation (Bowman, 1958). This is sometimes seen in adopted girls who have assumed, as have their parents, that they are illegitimate.

Rarely, an adolescent will impulsively become pregnant in an attempt to rid herself of what she feels to be an intolerably bad wish, somewhat along the lines of Oscar Wilde's dictum: "the only way to get rid of a temptation is to yield to it." The conflict is then externalized as the parents and social agencies struggle to help the adolescent decide what to do about her pregnancy: whether the outcome will be abortion, adoption, marriage, or keeping the baby. For some deprived, adolescent, unwed mothers the baby is a source of gratification (Khlentzos and Pagliaro, 1965).

During an illegitimate pregnancy the adolescent girl may experience feelings of shame, guilt, or helplessness and may not take adequate care of herself (perhaps in the hope of inducing an abortion). There usually are considerable fears about the parents' reactions. Parents in most cases find it hard to accept the pregnancy, no matter what their social class (Malinowski, 1966). There may also be much conflict about making suitable plans. Rarely does the unwed pregnant minor see her pregnancy as a symptom of emotional conflict.

Again, a striking aspect of such pregnancies is its relation to the struggles with impulse control, the concerns about the body, the striving for a sense of integrity and identity, and the power of the regressive pull in the face of the demands of reality, all of which characterize the normal disturbance during adolescence.

homosexuality

Mention has been made of the fact that achievement of an appropriate sexual identity and heterosexual relationship is a primary concern of the adolescent. Sometimes a deviation in the direction of homosexuality receives a particular impetus during adolescence. However, it is important to realize that a wide variety of homosexual experiences are normal during childhood and adolescence (Fraiberg, 1961; see also page 136). The following experiences may occur during normal adolescence:

1. Visual comparison of the size of one's penis, compared with the penis of other boys.

2. Simliar comparison of the size of the breasts in girls.

3. Group exhibitionism and grabbing of the penis of other boys.

4. Mutual masturbation.

5. Transient fellatio.

6. Hand holding, kissing, breast fondling, and genital petting in girls.

These kinds of behavior are almost age appropriate among adolescents, provided they are sporadic, not persistent, and not pervasive. Usually the behavior represents a temporary defense against the anxieties associated with heterosexual relationships.

On the other hand, an entrenchment in a homosexual identity may occur under certain conditions. For example, persistent homosexual behavior, particularly in late adolescence, with the beginnings of an exclusive preference in that direction, is a danger sign. Prolonged halting of heterosexual explorations because of anxiety may help turn the adolescent toward homosexuality. When less common homosexual activities are engaged in, *e.g.* anal intercourse, normal heterosexual relationships are less likely to occur. If the adolescent forms a love relationship, an attachment, to an adult of the same sex, it becomes more difficult for the adolescent to relinquish that relationship.

anorexia nervosa

Occasionally, the challenge of adolescence reveals the immaturity of the child, who in actuality is still dealing with conflicts from a much earlier period. The conflicts may represent, for example, fixation at earlier points in the sexual development of the child. Further, the level of object relations may still lean heavily on the need to be cared for, and unresolved earlier separation difficulties may persist. Sometimes these conflicts express themselves directly as a somatic illness. For example, among many girls exhibiting some form of the anorexia nervosa syndrome, there seems to be a regression as puberty approaches, with a recrudescence of oedipal and pre-oedipal conflicts.

Descriptively, the anorexia nervosa syndrome consists essentially of disturbances in the body image and the perception of the bodily state, along with a paralyzing sense of ineffectiveness (Bruch, 1962). An eating disturbance is prominent, and may include such symptoms as aversion to all food, strange diets, or eating at times to relieve anxiety. The child may deny she is thin, and seems unaware of fatigue. There may be feelings of shame and guilt, and the sexual function of the mouth, *i.e.* kissing, is avoided. Most of the adolescents are perfectionistic, even obsessive-compulsive in their personality traits, with food as an obsessive thought and avoidance of food a compulsive act. At the same time, they are usually somewhat infantile, dependent adolescents who are tense, and easily feel unwanted. In their object relations they are usually shallow, lacking in warmth, and have an ambivalent relationship with the mother. Their self-concept is often unrealistic, in that while they wish to be independent they are, in fact, quite incapable of taking adequate care of themselves. Lastly, in their sexual adjustment there are marked conflicts, with disgust as a prominent reaction formation.

The symptoms seem to represent in part the child's attempt to escape from adult sexual roles, and may further be in the service of regaining control of the body, the self, and the parents (Sours, 1969). More commonly, one sees pubescent girls who attempt to reject their sexual role through milder food fads and diets that alter the body.

☈ conversion reaction

Another example of the confluence of earlier unresolved difficulties and the onset of adolescence resulting in a clinical syndrome is the emergence of a conversion reaction, again particularly in girls. Descriptively, the syndrome in childhood consists essentially of using quite massive loss of functions without organic cause (Proctor, 1958). The commonest symptoms are blindness, deafness, inability to walk (astasia), inability to stand (abasia), great pain or no pain, inhibition of movement or grossly excessive movements, often resembling seizures.

These symptoms may be part of a general hysterical personality, which usually consists of marked immaturity and labile emotions. Emotional ties usually appear to be shallow, and the child is often seductive and loves to be the center of attention. Often the child imitates others. There may be an apparent lack of concern for the conversion symptom itself. Most of the children have a need to maintain a fiction of excellence and to control others, often with a demanding, dependent quality. It should be emphasized that these needs or wishes are unconscious and that the child does subjectively feel pain, or does believe he cannot walk.

What is again of interest here is that the syndrome occurs most commonly at puberty. Earlier problems and anxieties in these children often arise from what are experienced as seductions and repressed sexual conflicts. Excessive sexual stimulation of the child by immature parents, who at the same time impose excessive taboos, may have contributed to the conflicts. All remains more or less quiescent until adolescence is encountered. At that point a rekindling of the earlier conflicts occurs, with resulting florid symptom formation. The syndrome persists until the anxiety can be successfully resolved or repressed again. It would appear that it is precisely the similarity of the developmental problems of adolescence to the developmental problems of earlier childhood that stimulates the earlier conflicts and leads to anxiety and symptom formation.

delinquency

Perhaps because of the increased strength of the drives, and the corresponding vulnerability of the ego, delinquent behavior also reaches a peak during adolescence. The term "juvenile delinquency" has two definitions—one psychological, the other legal. Eissler (1955), for example, defined delinquent behavior purely on the basis of the motivation of the individual—". . . . behavior patterns which may not fall into the arbitrary delineations of juristic definition might show all the earmarks of delinquent behavior in respect to their origin, motivation, clinical appearance, and also very often their social effect." The legal definition, on the other hand, is purely on the basis of age, *i.e.* any person under the statutory age limit who has committed a legal offense. In most states the age limit varies from 16 to 20 years. The literature on delinquency is monumental, and has been well reviewed by Scott (1965). The purpose of mentioning delinquency here is to emphasize that it is a phenomenon that characteristically occurs during adolescence, and that in many instances the problems of adolescence are part of the motivation for the delinquent behavior, though the delinquent behavior may have many roots and manifest itself in many forms.

Wardrop (1967), for example, has identified five broad groupings, each with a characteristic etiology.

1. Adolescents may have poor impulse control due to some degree of organic brain damage. Family disturbance in this group may be the precipitating factor that tips the balance in the direction of delinquency.

2. Severe deprivation, due, say, to illegitimacy, or frequent foster home changes, leads to a tendency toward immediate impulse gratification. Sexual promiscuity and drug use may be a symptom in this group.

3. Neurotic conflict, due to unresolved earlier problems, may result in inadequate sexual identification, or strong feelings of guilt.

Aggressive behavior that represents bravado, or promiscuity that represents an attempt to bolster self-esteem and a feeling of inadequacy, as well as self-punishing behavior, may be seen here.

4. The adolescent may be responding to a family upset or family encouragement.

5. The cultural environment may influence the adolescent in the direction of identifying with a gang in which violent behavior is the norm.

Many other classifications are in use (Scott, 1965). The virtue of this classification is that it tries to group in a broad way some of the psychological causes of delinquency in the context of the social setting, taking into account the impact of family disturbance on personality development, the organic factor, and the degree of neurotic conflict. Each classification usually implies a theory, many of which are sociological. For example, one theory suggests that delinquency is an attempt to deal actively with the misery, frustration, rage, and envy brought about by deprivation. Thus, Cohen has suggested that "the hallmark of the delinquent sub-culture is the explicit and wholesale repudiation of middle class standards and the adoption of their very antithesis." (Cohen, 1955.) Other theories stem from other vantage points. For example, the observation that early deprivation and separation, particularly during the second year, is associated with delinquency during adolescence (Bennett, 1960) has given rise to a psychodynamic theory of delinquency involving the concepts of deformed ego and superego formation.

What remains to be emphasized is that delinquent acts reach a peak in adolescence, in part because of the adolescent characteristic of psychological imbalance caused by the increase in drive strength on the one hand, and the upset capacity for ego and superego controls on the other hand. At the same time, the etiology of a particular delinquent act of a particular child is always multideterminined.

drugs

Drug usage as a phenomenon of adolescents is currently increasing steadily. Approximately half the students enrolled in large universities or colleges near urban centers have tried marijuana and many high school students have also tried the drug (Cohen, 1969). Blum and his associates (1969), in a survey of four high schools in the San Francisco Bay area, emphasize the apparent rapidity of the spread of drug use, especially marijuana, but also including L.S.D. and the amphetamines, and made a prediction for the opiates. That prediction has now been confirmed (Kleber, 1970).

In another survey of 26,000 college students, 26% had used marijuana, 14% had used amphetamines, and 5% had used L.S.D. (Mizner, *et al.*, 1970). Almost all L.S.D. users had also tried marijuana, and most had used amphetamines. There is no evidence at present that all or most users of marijuana inevitably progress to heroin, and nothing to suggest that dependence on the one creates any kind of physiological need for the other (Stafford-Clark, 1969).

glue sniffing

In the young adolescent, a curious form of inhalation drug taking occurs, particularly among 11- to 15-year-old boys of normal intelligence. The striking feature here is that almost any substance that can be vaporized is used, *e.g.* model airplane glue, lighter fluid, paint, gasoline, etc., and the substance is inhaled through all kinds of ingenious methods (Glaser, 1966). The inhaled substance is used concurrently with tobacco and alcohol, but not usually with other narcotics. In some of these young adolescents the home has been broken by death, abandonment, or divorce. For some, the inhalation facilitates wish-fulfilling fantasies (Fawcett and Jensen, 1952), while in others it appears to be related to an erotic sensation derived during the act of sniffing, which itself may sometimes be a compulsive symptom. This symptom is often part of a regressive tendency during early adolescence.

narcotic usage

The increasing use of narcotics among early adolescents is partly due to the increase in the ready availability in high schools of drugs such as heroin at a time when the adolescent is curious and wishes to experiment (Kleber, 1970). Chein found that 16 seemed to be the age at which most experimentation starts. Many observers now find that 14-year-olds are experimenting. Ordinarily, if the drug were not so readily available, it might end there. With ready availability of narcotics, the user may go on to occasional use, followed by regular or habitual use, and then make efforts to break the habit. A user may go through all these stages, but he may also stop at any stage (Chein, *et al.*, 1964). Heroin is usually started by inhaling ("snorting") a mixture of heroin and quinine water. Subcutaneous injection ("skin popping") is then tried. Later, the adolescent may give himself intravenous injections ("main lining"). The adolescent reaches a "high" very quickly, perhaps in less than a minute, and then experiences a reversible drowsiness and sensual itching that may last from 2 to 4 hours. During the next 4 to 12 hours he may experience no particular sensations, but neither does he yet feel a need to take a further dose. Some time between 12 and 15 hours after taking a dose, withdrawal signs appear. The adolescent begins to feel anxious, his eyes and nose start running, he gets goose-flesh, and he experiences muscular twitching. During the next day or two the symptoms of withdrawal get worse, with abdominal cramps and chills. The adolescent will then often huddle in a blanket to keep warm. Usually the withdrawal symptoms subside after 4 or 5 days, leaving the adolescent feeling tired, exhausted, and aching.

Some adolescents try many different drugs. Amphetamine ("speed") is popular, although it is usually only taken for a short period of time. If an overdose is taken, the adolescent will have hallucinations, become suspicious of others, and may become wildly violent. Following a "high" with amphetamine, there is often a prolonged period of fatigue and depression, sometimes lasting for a week or two. Adolescents soon discover that heroin counteracts this after effect, and it is often this experience that is the first step to heroin addiction. Psychedelic drugs such as L.S.D., mescaline, and S.T.P. may also be taken by the adolescent. The complex etiology of adverse reactions ("bad trips") to L.S.D. have been described elsewhere (Ungerleider, *et al.*, 1968).

motivation for drug use

The motivations for drug use are multiple; some appear to be relatively superficial reasons, other have more complex roots. Mizner and his colleagues in the study mentioned earlier found that 38% of those who used marijuana for the first time said they did so out of curiosity; 60% of those who used amphetamines said they took the drug to help study or get through exams; and 45% of first-time users of L.S.D. felt it would be a worthwhile experience. At the same time, psychiatric problems are often associated with drug use. However, these psychiatric problems are comparable to the kinds of problems that plague students who avoid drugs. Paulsen (1969) has distinguished three prevailing elements in these problems: (1) disturbances of intellectual functioning (thinking); (2) anxiety, phobic, panic or depressive episodes (feelings); and (3) behavioral disturbances (action). Others have observed social factors in the motivation for drug use. Thus, adolescents in the lower social classes tend to take drugs to suppress their awareness of the squalor in which they live, while adolescents from the upper social classes tend to take drugs for the sensual experience it affords them.

Findings from adolescents who had taken drugs during psychoanalytic treatment revealed a wide range of psychopathology, none of which again could be called pathognomonic for drug users or drug addicts (Hartmann, D., 1969). However, Hartmann did note that among the young adolescents she saw there was a low tolerance for frustration and tension. Some of the adolescents who had a healthy earlier development had used drugs in defiance of their parents or out of "experimental curiosity." Others had allowed themselves to be seduced into the simple way of avoiding displeasure through the use of drugs: "They remain in a group of other drug users in a pseudoclose relationship, without much emotional commitment; their sexual gratifications are on the level of masturbation; therefore they are as often homosexual as they are heterosexual; the more passive they were to begin with, the greater is the danger of their being seduced by this kind of gratification."

Attempts have been made to relate the choice of drug to specific psychological needs, even to the extent of hypothesizing that "different drugs induce different regressive states that resemble specific phases of early childhood development." The user is said to harbor wishes or tendencies for a particular regressive conflict situation, which the pharmacology of a particular drug is thought to facilitate; the repeated experience of "satisfaction" is then said to establish preference for the specific drug (Wieder and Kaplan, 1969). For example, Wieder and Kaplan assert that L.S.D. states are comparable to the autistic phase, opiate effects have similarities with the narcissistic regressive phenomena of the symbiotic state, and amphetamines are reminiscent of the separation-individuation phase. Alcohol is said to be experienced by the younger adolescent as releasing too much drive, leading to fears of loss of control, and marijuana is preferred because it is shorter acting, less diffuse, and more controllable: the healthier adolescent will "use alcohol or marijuana only casually and intermittently, in the manner of the healthier adult." What can be said with a little more assurance is that the adolescent's personality determines in large measure how he experiences the pharmacological effects of the drug he uses. For example, adolescents with emotionally unstable personalities may experience profound depersonalisation, depression, and ideas of reference that may recur spontaneously for several weeks, all following a single marijuana cigarette (Klein and Davis, 1969).

In many instances drugs are taken to ward off depression or feelings of inadequacy. For some it is a form of rebellion. For example, the Hippie group of adolescents in part express their anti-establishment feelings through drug taking. Other adolescents will say they take drugs because they like them and because they reject what they feel to be the hypocrisies of society, such as keeping marijuana illegal but allowing the production of tobacco and alcohol. Others are convinced that the drugs they take are helpful to them. Blum and his associates are careful to point out that there is no simple, universal motivation behind the use of drugs in the young (Blum, 1969). Furthermore, they note that student drug use is frequent enough that it must be considered within the "normal range of behavior, at least on some campuses." Chein, et al. (1964) go further and note that etiological factors change over a period of time, so that analyses of causes reported at one time may become "hardly more than an historical curiosity rather than germane to pressing contemporary problems" at another time.

Since most of the drugs taken are illegally obtained, the meaning of breaking the law for some adolescents is often an intrinsic part of the motivation. For some, the act is performed as part of the wish to be caught and punished. For others, it is a relatively safe and private means of defiance and ridicule.

In a general way, over a period of time, sedative drugs appear to be preferred to stimulants. Class factors in the choice of certain drugs are also present, but are less clearly defined. Until recently, for example, heroin was rarely taken among the middle class, but this no longer holds true. It is rare for an adolescent to believe that he takes drugs because of an emotional disorder, and he rarely comes for treatment with the purpose of being weaned off a drug. Yet, it seems so often that the drug taking, pleasurable as it may be, is still part of the adolescent's attempts to deal with all the turmoil he feels at this stage in his development.

normality

In summary, adolescence is a time of physical and emotional turmoil. Many of the phenomena just described are seen to some degree in the normal adolescent. Abnormality is a question of degree, or rate, or persistence of any of these phenomena. At the same time, there are adolescents who appear to have little trouble coming to a satisfactory resolution of the problems. For them, reality and good judgment rule the day. Yet, even here, a word of caution should be said about the adolescent who appears to have no trouble, but who at the same time is not actually resolving any of his developmental tasks. The clinical picture may sometimes deceive the clinician who may be lulled into a false sense of security. Such adolescents may be too perfect.

Nevertheless, it must be said that most adolescents are also a source of great pleasure. A good example was described by Calandra (see Guttman, 1965):

" . . . . a physics student who was fed up with college instructors trying to teach him how to think instead of 'showing him the structure of the subject matter.'

. . . . the student had been given a zero for his answer to a question on a physics examination. The question was: 'Show how it is possible to determine the height of a tall building with the aid of a barometer?' The student's answer: 'Take the barometer to the top of the building, attach a long rope to it, lower the barometer to the street, and then bring it up, measuring the length of the rope. The length of the rope is the height of the building.' Dissatisfied with this solution but conceding that it was not strictly incorrect the physics teacher gave the student another chance to answer, this time in a way that would show some knowledge of physics. Having selected what he said was the best of many answers he had in his head, the student dashed off the following: 'Take the barometer to the top of the building and lean over the edge of the roof. Drop the barometer, timing its fall with a stop-watch. Then, using the formula $S = 1/2gt^2$, calculate the height of the building.' (S = distance fallen, g = gravitational acceleration of the barometer, and t = time). This apparently satisfied the letter, if not the spirit, of the examination question, and the student received almost full credit for the answer. He was then asked what other answers he had had in mind and responded, in part, with the following: 'You could take the barometer out on a sunny day and measure the height of the barometer, the length of its shadow, and the length of the shadow of the building, and by the use of a simple proportion, determine the height of the building.' Or, if not limited to physics, you could 'take the barometer to the basement and knock on the superintendent's door. When he answers you say: "Here I have a very fine barometer. If you will tell me the height of this building, I will give you this barometer." ' . . . . ''

NOTE 15

Piaget, J., 1969. The intellectual development of the adolescent. In: *Adolescence: Psychosocial Perspectives*, G. Caplan and S. Lebovici (eds.). New York: Basic Books, Inc., pp. 22–26.

Now, the great novelty that characterises adolescent thought and that starts around the age of 11 to 12, but does not reach its point of equilibrium until the age of 14 or 15—this novelty consists in detaching the concrete logic from the objects themselves, so that it can function on verbal or symbolic statements without other support. Above all the novelty consists in generalising this logic and supplementing it with a set of combinations. . . .

The great novelty that results consists in the possibility of manipulating ideas in themselves and no longer in merely manipulating objects. In a word, the adolescent is an individual who is capable (and this is where he reaches the level of the adult) of building or understanding ideal or abstract theories and concepts. . . . the adolescent is capable of projects for the future. . . ., of nonpresent interests, and of a passion for ideas, ideals, or ideologies.

. . . . it is apparent how these intellectual transformations typical of the adolescent's thinking enable him not only to achieve his integration into the social relationships of adults, which is, in fact, the most general characteristic of this period of development, but also to conquer a certain number of fundamental intellectual operations which constitute the basis for a scientific education at high school level. The problem that remains unresolved, however, is the generality of these intellectual transformations. . . . It is probable that in underdeveloped societies which still have a tribal organisation the individual remains throughout his entire life at the level of concrete operations, without ever reaching the level of formal or propositional operations that are characteristic of adolescents in our cultural environment. But in these societies the younger generations remain under the authority of the "elders" of the tribe, and the elders in turn remain subject to the conservative traditions of their ancestors. . . .

NOTE 16

Erikson, E. H., 1962. *Childhood and Society*. New York (second edition), W. W. Norton and Company, Inc., pp. 261–263.

. . . . 5. IDENTITY VS. ROLE CONFUSION. With the establishment of a good initial relationship to the world of skills and tools, and with the advent of puberty, childhood proper comes to an end. Youth begins. But in puberty and adolescence all samenesses and continuities relied on earlier are more or less questioned again, because of a rapidity of body growth which equals that of early childhood and because of the new addition of genital maturity. The growing and developing youths, faced with this physiological revolution within them, and with tangible adult tasks ahead of them are now primarily concerned with what they appear to be in the eyes of others as compared with what they feel they are, and with the question of how to connect the roles and skills cultivated earlier with the occupational prototypes of the day. In their search for a new sense of continuity and sameness, adolescents have to refight many of the battles of earlier years, even though to do so they must artifically appoint perfectly well-meaning people to play the roles of adversaries; and they are ever ready to install lasting idols and ideals as guardians of a final identity.

The integration now taking place in the form of ego identity is, as pointed out, more than the sum of the childhood identifications. It is the accrued experience of the ego's ability to integrate all identifications with the vicissitudes of the libido, with the aptitudes developed out of endowment, and with the opportunities offered in social roles. The sense of ego identity, then, is the accrued confidence that the inner sameness and continuity prepared in the past are matched by the sameness and continuity of one's meaning for others, as evidenced in the tangible promise of a "career."

The danger of this stage is role confusion.* Where this is based on a strong previous doubt as to one's sexual identity, delinquent and outright psychotic

---

* See "The Problem of Ego-Identity," *J. Amer. Psa. Assoc.,* 4:56–121.

episodes are not uncommon. If diagnosed and treated correctly, these incidents do not have the same fatal significance which they have at other ages. In most instances, however, it is the inability to settle on an occupational identity which disturbs individual young people. To keep themselves together they temporarily overidentify, to the point of apparent complete loss of identity, with the heroes of cliques and crowds. This initiates the stage of "falling in love," which is by no means entirely, or even primarily, a sexual matter—except where the mores demand it. To a considerable extent adolescent love is an attempt to arrive at a definition of one's identity by projecting one's diffused ego image on another and by seeing it thus reflected and gradually clarified. This is why so much of young love is conversation.

Young people can also be remarkably clannish, and cruel in their exclusion of all those who are "different," in skin color or cultural background in tastes and gifts, and often in such petty aspects of dress and gesture as have been temporarily selected as *the* signs of an in-grouper or out-grouper. It is important to understand (which does not mean condone or participate in) such intolerance as a defense against a sense of identity confusion. For adolescents not only help one another temporarily through much discomfort by forming cliques and by stereotyping themselves, their ideals, and their enemies; they also perversely test each others' capacity to pledge fidelity. The readiness for such testing also explains the appeal which simple and cruel totalitarian doctrines have on the minds of the youth of such countries and classes as have lost or are losing their group identities (feudal, agrarian, tribal, national) and face world-wide industrialization, emancipation, and wider communication.

The adolescent mind is essentially a mind of the *moratorium,* a psychosocial stage between childhood and adulthood, and between the morality learned by the child, and the ethics to be developed by the adult. It is an ideological mind—and, indeed, it is the ideological outlook of a society that speaks most clearly to the adolescent who is eager to be affirmed by his peers, and is ready to be confirmed by rituals, creeds, and programs which at the same time define what is evil, uncanny, and inimical. In searching for the social values which guide identity, one therefore confronts the problems of *ideology* and aristocracy, both in their widest possible sense which connotes that within a defined world image and a predestined course of history, the best people will come to rule and rule develops the best in people. In order not to become cynically or apathetically lost, young people must somehow be able to convince themselves that those who succeed in their anticipated adult world thereby shoulder the obligation of being the best. We will discuss later the dangers which emanate from human ideals harnessed to the management of super-machines, be they guided by nationalistic or international, communist or capitalist ideologies. In the last part of this book we shall discuss the way in which the revolutions of our day attempt to solve and also to exploit the deep need of youth to redefine its identity in an industrialized world.

NOTE 17

Settlage, Calvin F., 1970. An editorial postscript. *J. Amer. Acad. Child Psychiat.*, 9(2):278–281.

. . . . Freed from the dependency and conformity of childhood, and not yet tied or firmly committed to the existing culture by the necessity of having to earn a living and assume all of the other responsibilities of adulthood, the adolescent just may have a clearer view of the culture than anyone else. Although his critical comment may not always be elegant and may be expressed as much in behavior as in words, it ought to be heeded and given thoughtful consideration.

If we accept this view of adolescence, what might the behavior of at least the most noticeable, *i.e.*, expressive, of our adolescents be saying about the current state of our society, about the values of the culture which they are expected to join?

In a general way, their behavior bespeaks a conviction that existing values must be challenged in a culture and a world of cultures threatened by man-made problems and disasters of the proportions of those confronting us. Nothing, but nothing, is sacrosanct. They seem to have perceived that collective values too often are born out of individual man's most immediate needs, desires and fears, and, once born, are justified, rationalized, and perpetuated, sometimes to the detriment of mankind.

As exemplied by adolescents in the Hippie subculture, but by no means limited to them, the disavowal of materialism can be seen as the rejection of a societal attitude which values products, whose offal is destroying our Earth's natural resources. An emphasis on simplicity in living devalues an ever-burgeoning technology which moves in the same destructive direction. A turning to naturally-grown health foods is a criticism of a policy which allows the continuing use of pesticides which are known to kill, not only insects, but birds, fish, and eventually, man. A deemphasis by young men of the image of masculinity in their dress and hair is a protest both against a culture which expends men in debatable wars, and against war in general. In the era of the nuclear weapon, a turning to drugs which heighten self-awareness may represent not only an escape from a society seen as intolerable, but an attempt to come to terms with the inner self, particularly with one's dangerous and destructive urges. An emphasis on love, and on what appears to be affectionate as opposed to sexual love, can be seen as pitting this value against the value which extolls the virtue of aggression and war. Unisex in dress and appearance may be a protest against sex for procreation, against the population explosion. Drug cults and other manifestations of a turning to belief in magic and mysticism may voice a criticism both against the established religions and a society which has failed to live up to avowed ideals.

In sum, the described behavior, regardless of its pathogenicity for these adolescents as individuals and as a generation, expresses a refusal to go along with a self-contradictory, destructive, cultural value system, one which is outmoded, not only for our society but, basically, for all societies. The concept of a world of peoples living together in reasonable harmony is no longer only an ideal; it is a necessity pressing upon us with increasing urgency.

references

1. Bennet, I., 1960. *Delinquent and Neurotic Children: A Comparative Study.* London: Tavistock Publications.

2. Berger, B. M., 1969. The new stage of American man—almost endless adolescence. *The New York Times Magazine,* Nov. 2., 1969, p. 32.

3. Berman, S., 1970. Alienation: an essential process of the psychology of adolescence. *J. Amer. Acad. Child Psychiat.,* 9(2):233–250.

4. Blos, P., 1962. *On Adolescence. A Psychoanalytic Interpretation.* Chapter III, Phases of adolescence. New York: The Free Press of Glencoe, Inc., pp. 52–157.

5. ——, 1967. The second individuation process of adolescence. *The Psychoanalytic Study of the Child,* 22:162–187.

6. Blum, R. H., 1969. *Students and Drugs.* San Francisco: Jossey-Bass, Inc., p. 399.

7. Bonan, A. F., 1963. Psychoanalytic implications in treating unmarried mothers with narcissistic character structures. *Social Casework,* June, XLIV (6):323–339.

8. Bowman, L. A., 1958. The unmarried mother who is a minor. *Child Welfare* (October), 37(8):13–19.

9. Bruch, H., 1962. Perceptual and conceptual disturbances in anorexia nervosa. *Psychosomatic Medicine,* 24(2):187–194.

10. Chein, I., Gerard, D. I., Lee, R. S., and Rosenfeld, E., 1964. *The Road to H. Narcotics, Delinquency and Social Policy,* New York: Basic Books, Inc.

11. Cohen, A. K., 1955. *GANG.* New York: The Free Press of Glencoe, Inc., p. 129.

12. Cohen, S., 1969. Drug abuse. In: *Psychiatry Medical World News,* New York: McGraw-Hill, Inc.

13. Courts, R. M., 1967. Family crises and the impulsive adolescent. *Arch. Gen. Psychiat.,* 17(1):64–71.

14. Eissler, K. R., 1955. Some problems of delinquency. In: *Searchlights on Delinquency,* K. R. Eissler (ed.). New York: International Universities Press, Inc. (2nd edition).

15. Elkind, D., 1967. Egocentrism in adolescence. *Child Development,* 38(4):1025–1034.

16. Erikson, E. H., 1956. The problem of ego identity. *J. Amer. Psychoanalytic Assoc.,* 4:56.

17. ——, 1963. *Childhood and Society.* New York: W. W. Norton and Co., Inc. (second edition), pp. 261–263.

18. Fawcett, R. L. and Jensen, R. A., 1952. Addiction to the inhalation of gasoline fumes in a child. *J. Pediat.,* 41:364–368.

19. Fountain, G., 1961. Adolescent into adult: an inquiry. *J. Amer. Psychoanalytic Assoc.*, 9:417–433.

20. Fraiberg, S. H., 1961. Homosexual conflicts. In: *Adolescents*, S. Lorand and H. I. Schneer (eds.), New York: Paul B. Hoeber, Inc., 78–112.

21. Freud, A., 1946. *The Ego and the Mechanisms of Defense.* New York: International Universities Press, Inc., pp. 154, 160–165.

22. ——, 1958. Adolescence. *The Psychoanalytic Study of the Child*, International Universities Press, Inc., 13:255–278.

23. ——, 1969. Adolescence as a developmental disturbance. In: *Adolescence*, G. Caplan and S. Lebovici (eds.), New York: Basic Books, Inc., pp. 5–10.

24. Galdston, R., 1967. Adolescence and the function of self-consciousness. *Ment. Hygiene* (New York), 51(2):164–168.

25. G.A.P. Report, No. 68, 1968. Normal adolescence. *Group for the Advancement of Psychiatry*, Vol. VI, pp. 756–758, 841–846.

26. Glasser, F. B., 1966. Inhalation psychosis and related states. *Arch. Gen. Psychiat.*, 14(3):315–322.

27. Guttman, S. A., 1965. Some aspects of scientific theory construction and psycho-analysis. *The International Journal of Psycho-Analysis*, 46(1):129–137. Quoting Calandra, A. (1964) as reported by J. A. Osmundsen in the New York Times, 8 March.

28. Halleck, S., 1967. Psychomatic treatment of the alienated college student. *Amer. J. Psychiat.*, 124(5):642–650.

29. Hartmann, D., 1969. A study of drug-taking adolescents. *The Psychoanalytic Study of the Child*, 24:384–398, New York: International Universities Press, Inc.

30. Inhelder, B. and Piaget, J., 1958. *The Growth of Logical Thinking from Childhood to Adolescence.* New York: Basic Books, Inc.

31. Jones, M. C., 1957. The later careers of boys who were early- or late-maturing. *Child Development*, 28:113–128.

32a. Keniston, K., 1970a. Youth: a "new" stage of life. *The American Scholar*, 39 (4): 631–653.

32b. Keniston, K., 1970b. Student activism, moral development, and morality. *Amer. J. Orthopsychiat.*, 40(4):577–592.

33. ——, 1970c. We have much to learn from youth. *Amer. J. Psychiat.*, 126(12): 1767–1768.

34. Kestenberg, J. S., 1961. Menarche. In: *Adolescents*, S. Lorand and H. Schneer (eds.), New York: Paul B. Hoeber, Inc., pp. 19–50.

35. Khlentzos, M. T. and Pagliaro, M. A., 1965. Observations from psychotherapy with unwed mothers. *Amer. J. Orthopsychiat.*, 35:779.

36. Kinsey, A. C., 1953. *Sexual Behavior in the Human Female.* Institute for Sex Research, Indiana University. Philadelphia: W. B. Saunders Co. p. 842.

37. Kleber, H., 1970. Personal communication.

37a. Klein, D. F. and Davis, J. M., 1969. Diagnosis and Drug Treatment of Psychiatric Disorders. Baltimore, The Williams and Wilkins Co., p 417.

38. Lewis, M. and Solnit, A. J., 1963. The adolescent in a suicidal crisis. In: *Modern Perspectives in Child Development. In Honor of Milton J. E. Senn.* A. J. Solnit and S. A. Provence (eds.), New York: International Universities Press, Inc., pp. 229–245.

39. Malinowski, B., 1966. Parenthood—the basis of social structure. In: *The Unwed Mother.* R. W. Roberts (eds.), New York: Harper & Row, pp. 25–41.

40. Masterson, J. F., Jr., 1968. The psychiatric significance of adolescent turmoil. *Amer. J. Psychiat.,* 124(11):1549–1553.

41. Mizner, G. L., Barter, J. T., and Werme, P. H., 1970. Patterns of drug use among college students: a preliminary report. *Amer. J. Psychiat.,* 127(1):15–24.

42. Mussen, P. H. and Jones, M. C., 1957. Self-conceptions, motivations, and interpersonal attitudes of late- and early-maturing boys. *Child Development,* 28:243–256.

43. Noshpitz, J. D., 1970. Certain cultural and familial factors contributing to adolescent alienation. *J. Amer. Acad. Child Psychiat.,* 9(2):216–223.

44. Offer, D., Marcus, D., and Offer, J. L., 1970. A longitudinal study of normal adolescent boys. *Amer. J. Psychiat.,* 126(7):917–924.

45. Paulsen, J., 1969. Psychiatric problems. In: *Students and Drugs,* Richard H. Blum and Associates (eds.), San Francisco: Jossey-Bass, Inc., pp. 291–304.

46. Pearson, G. H. J., 1958. *Adolescence and the Conflict of Generations.* New York: W. W. Norton and Co., Inc., pp. 101–126.

47. Piaget, J., 1962. Comments on Vygotsky's critical remarks concerning "The language and thought of the child" and "Judgement and reasoning in the child." Cambridge, Mass., M.I.T., 71:473–490.

48. Piaget, J., 1969. The intellectual development of the adolescent. In: *Adolescence: Psychosocial Perspectives,* G. Caplan and S. Lebovici (eds.), New York: Basic Books, Inc., pp. 22–26.

49. Proctor, J. T., 1958. Hysteria in childhood. *Amer. J. Orthopsychiat.,* 28:394–407.

50. Schonfeld, W. A., 1969. The body and the body-image in adolescents. In: *Adolescence: Psychosocial Perspectives,* G. Caplan and S. Lebovici (eds.), New York: Basic Books, Inc., pp. 27–53.

51. Scott, P. D., 1965. Delinquency. In: *Modern Perspectives in Child Psychiatry*, J. G. Howells (ed.), Springfield, Ill.: Charles C Thomas, pp. 370–402.

52. Settlage, C. F., 1970a. Adolescence and social change. *J. Amer. Acad. Child Psychiat.*, 9(2):203–215.

53. ——, 1970b. An editorial postscript. *J. Amer. Acad. Child Psychiat.*, 9(2):278–281.

54. Sours, J. A., 1969. Anorexia nervosa: nosology, diagnosis, developmental patterns, and power control dynamics. In: *Adolescence*, G. Caplan and S. Lebovici (eds.). New York: Basic Books, Inc., pp. 185–212.

55. Stafford-Clark, D., 1969. Drug dependence. *Guy's Hospital Gazette.* 83(2110): 298–305.

56. Tanner, J. M., 1962. *Growth at Adolescence*. Springfield, Ill.: Charles C Thomas.

57. Toolan, J. M., 1962. Depression in children and adolescents. *Amer. J. Orthopsychiat.*, 32:404–415.

58. Ungerleider, J. T., Fisher, D. D., Fuller, M. and Caldwell, S., 1968. The "bad trip"—the etiology of the adverse L.S.D. reaction. *Amer. J. Psychiat.*, 124(11):1483–1490.

59. Wardrop, K. R. H., 1967. Delinquent teenage types. *Brit. J. Criminol.*, 7(4): 371–380.

60. Wieder, H. and Kaplan, E. H., 1969. Drug use in adolescents. *The Psychoanalytic Study of the Child.* New York: International Universities Press, Inc., 24:399–431.

61. Williams, F. S., 1970. Alienation of youth as reflected in the hippie movement. *J. Amer. Acad. Child Psychiat.*, 9(2):251–263.

62. Wise, L. J., 1970. Alienation of present-day adolescents. *J. Amer. Acad. Child Psychiat.*, 9(2):264–277.

Chapter 7

PSYCHOLOGICAL REACTIONS TO BODY STRESS

Illness is perhaps the most common and widespread stress that may befall the developing child. Every child who is ill has a psychological reaction to his illness. Some reactions are general; others are specific to the illness. General reactions depend upon several general factors, including the developmental stage of the child (emotional and cognitive levels of development and the child's previous adaptive capacity); the degree of pain or mutilation and the meaning of the illness to the child and parents; the parent-child relationship and the response to the reaction of the parents; the psychological reaction to medical and surgical procedures, separation, and hospitalization; and the resulting interference with physical, psychological and social functions. Specific reactions depend, in part, upon the specific nature and severity of the illness. Illustrative examples of certain birth defects, acute illnesses, chronic illnesses, and lethal illnesses will be considered in the light of the general and specific factors just mentioned.

birth defects : (a) reaction of parents

Antecedents for psychological reactions of parents to a birth defect in the child are found in the pregnant woman's concerns and fantasies about fetal abnormalities. The actual presence of the live baby with a congenital defect mobilizes these latent fears and stimulates further reactions. General reactions may include feelings of revulsion, anger, and anxiety, as well as a precipitous drop in the self-esteem and sense of integrity in the mother. Parents feel guilty and resentful. The more visible the defect, the greater the reaction. Equally significant is the sense of loss that both parents experience as they painfully and slowly relinquish their ideal fantasies during the process of adjusting to the sharply different realities and the need to establish new goals (Solnit and Stark, 1961). Because of the continuing presence of the defective child, the process of working through of loss is also a continuing, changing process in that at each stage in subsequent development other expectations may have to be modified or given up. At each new stage in the development of the child, new problems, often unanticipated problems, confront the parents. Some defects may not become known until a later stage of development. For example, certain congenital heart defects may be missed initially, but may subsequently be discovered either routinely or as a result of a study for the cause of certain symptoms. Other defects may only present at a later period of development. The process of giving up long held expectations in such cases is often more difficult because of the tenacity of such expectations.

Specific reactions depend, in part, upon the type of defect as well as the personality of the parents. Ambiguity of the external genitalia, for example, or hypospadias, may affect the parents' gender attitude toward their child, who in turn may have a heightened difficulty in accepting a clear sexual identification. In the specific instance of cryptorchism, the parental attitudes appear to induce in the child a preoccupation with his testes, with associated disorders of behavior including hyperactivity, accident proneness, lying, and learning difficulties (Blos, 1960). Mothers of children with cleft palate, on the other hand, appear to make especial use of the mechanism of denial and later will avoid talking with their child about the deformity, but may instead point out to others how "bright" the child is (Tisza, et al., 1968). At the same time, since cleft palate is a more or less correctable defect, the drive toward restitution is strongly reinforced in these parents.

birth defects : (b) reaction of child

The psychological reaction of the child is in large part related to the parental attitudes just mentioned. At the same time, the child also has his own characteristic reaction to his defect. Sometimes the physical defect is the starting point for a widespread interference with development to which the child then reacts. In children born with a cleft palate, for example, the interference with pleasurable sucking and feeding experiences, as well as the imbalance between gratifying and painful experiences, may lead later to speech difficulties and to a depressing view of life as being essentially painful. Further, the frequent separations and surgical procedures required for this defect, especially during the first few years, may interfere with the critical need for continuity of affection required for the development of the capacity for gratifying object relations. Even when surgical correction has been achieved, previously established self-concepts and self-esteem may persist and may make the child more vulnerable to each succeeding developmental task through to adolescence and beyond (Schwartz and Landwirth, 1968).

blind children

The complexity of the mutual impact of birth defect and parental reaction upon the development of the child is well illustrated in the case of children born totally blind. In a series of longitudinal studies of infants born totally blind, Fraiberg and her colleagues found that approximately one quarter showed motor stereotypes such as rocking, lateral rotation of the head and trunk, empty fingering; no definition of body boundaries; and delayed speech (Fraiberg and Freedman, 1964; Fraiberg, et al., 1966; Fraiberg, 1968). Adaptive hand behavior (ordinarily predicated upon the coordination of eye and hand schemas), gross motor achievements, and the constitution of a body and self image were all delayed in the absence of vision. Most significant was the absence or failure to achieve stable human object relations. For most of their 24-hour day, these babies had lived in a "sensory desert."

The parents were markedly upset, often revealing their unconscious revulsion by a form of avoidance consisting of not touching the baby except when it was necessary. Some fathers had developed potency problems soon after the birth of the baby. There was also a conspiracy of silence on the part of other family members who rarely said anything to indicate that the baby was at all attractive.

However, when the parent was able to perceive and interpret the non-visual signals of the baby and respond appropriately to the infant's needs, the disastrous development just described could be avoided. For example, blind babies do, in fact, show a smile response to the mother's or father's *voice* at around the same time that sighted babies smile at the sight of the human face. With the help of this piece of knowledge, and with the sensitive support and encouragement of a skilled person, the parents were able to avert the common reaction of feeling rebuffed at the blind child's failure to respond with a smile to the visual presentation of the parent's face. Indeed, the parents could feel elated at the smile response to the auditory presentation of the parent's voice, and would then relate in a more affectionate way with their now "responsive" baby. Both mother and infant could then be mutually responsive instead of mutually repelling.

One particular non-visual mode of communication in the infant that was especially informative was the expressive hand movements of the infant. Interventions designed to bring the hands together in the midline prevented the "empty fingering" and instead promoted useful hand movement. Later, introduction of objects that had a sound as well as a touch led to the infant being able, at 10 months of age, to conceptualize without the aid of vision an object with a sound, *e.g.* a bell. The infant could then search for a bell "out there" on hearing the sound alone. Once the infant was able to reach out on sound cue, he was also then motivated to propel himself forward. At that point, creeping, which had until then been delayed, could now proceed.

acute illness: (a) general reaction

General childhood reactions to acute illness again depend to a large extent on the developmental level of the child and the reaction of the parents, and may be adaptive or maladaptive.

Specific reactions depend in part, as before, upon the nature and extent of the specific illness. Under the general impact of acute illness most young children regress. They may return temporarily to bedwetting, thumb sucking, crying, and clinging behavior. Further, the young child particularly tends to interpret his illness as a punishment for something he has done wrong, and since he sometimes has difficulty in distinguishing between fantasy and reality, the wrongdoing could have been imaginary or actual. At hospitalization, the young child, especially the child under 4 years of age, feels abandoned, and fears what harm may come to him without the love and protection of his parents. He may also feel confused and anxious about the more or less sudden confrontation with people who are strange to him and about the strange routines (feeding, clothing, sleeping, toileting, etc.), and special procedures (immobilization, injections, etc.). These observations have been repeatedly documented. In a well-controlled study by Prugh and his colleagues, for example, children under the age of 4 years screamed, had outbursts of anger when the parents visited, withdrew, and had difficulty eating and sleeping (Prugh, *et al.*, 1953; see Note 18). ". . . . In general, children with previously limited capacities for adaptation showed the greatest difficulty in adjusting comfortably to the ward milieu and showed as well the most severe reactions to the total experience of hospitalization." Furthermore, problems of adaptation occurred often about 3 months after the hospitalization, with persistent signs of emotional disturbance again tending to occur in children under 4 years of age and children who had relatively unsatisfactory relationships with their parents, who had undergone very severe stress in the hospital, and who had shown the greatest difficulty in adapting to the ward milieu.

Anxiety is heightened when the special vulnerabilities of a particular developmental struggle are touched upon. For example, an infant who needs a sense of security and trust may express through fretting and fussing his state of tension and insecurity when held by a mother made anxious because of his illness. The fear of loss of love and loss of autonomy may be reinforced by separation and illness in the young infant. Castration anxiety may be heightened in the young child who is undergoing surgical procedures. Separation from peers may temporarily rob the school age child of the comfort and sublimation activities which he had previously enjoyed. And the adolescent may find increasing difficulty in dealing with the upset around such developmental tasks as body mastery, impulse control, and independence.

Children deal with this immediate anxiety in different ways, depending in part on their level of development. The most common reaction, regression, has already been mentioned. On the other hand, some children fight hard to retain their recently acquired skills. They may, for example, resist bed rest when they have only just learned to walk (Freud, 1952). Other children deny their illness and their anxiety. Some children identify with the doctor or nurse who seems to them so aggressive. Aggression is particularly mobilized in the face of motor restraint (Wolff, 1969). Still others may withdraw, or become astonishingly compliant. The particular pattern of response depends upon the many factors mentioned earlier, *e.g.* the state of the previous personality development; the degree of stress caused by the illness; and the reaction of the parents to the ill child.

Sometimes the anxiety becomes manifest after the acute episode has passed (Levy, 1945; Langford, 1948; Neill, 1967). Night terrors and dreams about being left alone in the dark, or fear of the dark, may occur with increasing frequency. Negativistic behavior toward the parents often occurs on return home.

acute illness: (b) specific reaction (1) *burns*

Specific illnesses with special features tend to produce characteristic reactions in the child. For example, children who suffer burns often experience severe emotional reactions. MacG. Jackson once said, "an extensive burn is an accident involving thirty seconds of terror, and it is often followed by years of suffering" (Jackson, 1968). Pain, fright, and body mutilation are, in fact, primary sources of psychological disturbance in the burned child, or the child traumatized in any other way. Further sources of disturbance in the burned child include the guilt over disobeying a parent's admonition, say, never to play with matches; the chaotic turmoil during the period of acute care; the hospitalization and separation from parents; the immobilization, exposure, and repeated immediate and long-term surgical procedures; metabolic changes induced by the burns; and the reactions of distressed and guilty parents and frustrated and angry hospital staff.

Pain in itself is a significant factor, and often gives rise to anger, hostility, and depression in the child (Long and Cope, 1961). In an unusual study of the psychological reactions to a leg burn in a 5-year-old boy with no pain sensation below the waist because of a myelomeningocele, Nover (1970) found that there was much less adverse reaction, and the child was more cooperative in the extensive surgical treatments than most burned children.

Pre-existing emotional difficulties often seem to predispose the child to the "accident" of a burn. In a study of 13 families of severely burned children, 10 were found to have major psychological and social problems which were present prior to the burn (Holter and Friedman, 1969).

Fluid loss, medication, anorexia, and sleep interruption are important aggravating factors during the acute period. It has also been suggested that magnesium deficiency may aggravate the psychological symptoms associated with burns (Broughton, et al., 1968).

Equally important are the long-term reactions. Grafting operations frequently extend over a period of 5 years, and in some cases as long as 15 years. Numerous concerns arise during this period. Jackson (1968) has observed such questions as: "Will my breasts develop normally?", "Will boys look at me with these scars?", and "Will I be able to have a baby?" The importance of these questions in the context of adolescent developmental concerns is obvious.

tonsillectomy

A further type of specific reaction occurs in response to tonsillectomy. Here, the operation is performed on a well child who usually does not have a clear understanding of why he needs the operation or what is the nature of the operation. Curiously, the indications for tonsillectomy actually are not well defined, and there are no adequate controlled studies (Horstman, 1969). Indeed, in one study of 681 children in whom tonsillectomy was postponed because of a poliomyelitis outbreak, more than one third were judged not to need the operation when re-examined 18 months later (Dey, 1952). Certainly scientific data do not support the extent of the operation, where approximately 2,000,000 tonsillectomies are done each year, at a cost of about $150,000,000, and incurring approximately 200 to 300 deaths annually. Interestingly, a study performed in 1938 revealed that the operation was twice as frequent when the family income then was above $5,000 a year (Collins, 1938).

In any event the operation is most often performed at an age when fantasies of injury to body parts and fears of punishment and retribution are prominent. Moreover, for a number of reasons, the child is often inadequately prepared for the operation. Sometimes the circumstances of availability of a bed in the hospital in many instances requires a somewhat precipitous admission to hospital at short notice following a telegram. Few explanations are given to the child as he is separated from his parents, turned over to strangers, and is submitted to routines which seem remote from the sore throat he once had and has now almost forgotten.

Lipton (1962) has further postulated that at least three powerful psychological forces in the adult help perpetuate this onslaught upon children. First is the dread of passivity and of doing nothing. Second, there appears to be a mobilization of aggression by both parents and doctors against the child as he exists, in an effort to convert him into some projected ideal. Third, the ready availability of the tonsils ideally serve as concrete representation of all the undesirable impulses or attributes projected onto the child, which can then be readily removed.

The impact of a tonsillectomy upon the child under these circumstances is enormous and the risks are great (Jessner, et al., 1952; Robertson, 1956). The child distorts the whole procedure and uses the distortion as an active, external representation of his current internal fears and fantasies. Anesthesia may be seen by the child as an oral attack. Separation anxiety and castration fears are heightened. The hospital staff are perceived unconsciously or consciously as attackers and punishers, and fears of death arise.

Demandingness, irritability, aggressive behavior, temper tantrums, fears, and nightmares often run rampant. Defenses mobilized to contain this anxiety may include the mechanism of denial and psychosomatic symptom formation. According to Lipton, during such psychic trauma lasting character traits may be formed (Lipton, 1962). Fortunately, much of this harm can be attentuated and even turned into a constructive experience when the child is adequately prepared for, supported through, and helped after the operation (Robertson, 1956).

chronic illness: (a) general reaction

Chronic, non-lethal illnesses also produce both general and specific reactions and, once again, the specificity of the reaction is in part associated with specific syndromes. In general, however, chronic illnesses impose psychological as well as physical strain upon the developing child. The strains arise from a number of sources. For example, a particular treatment regimen, *e.g.* motor restriction, diet, medication, surgical procedures, etc., may foster passivity and dependence against which the normal child struggles. The feeling of being different from other children arouses feelings of resentment and subsequently guilt. Young children in particular find the illness and the treatment virtually incomprehensible, and develop distorted ideas and frightening fantasies about the illness.

A 5-year-old boy with nephrosis was observed by the nurse to be unusually quiet and immobile. He would sit still in his wheel chair, and would contrive not even to turn his head. In the course of an interview, the boy revealed his ideas and fantasies about his illness. He knew that there was something wrong with his kidneys, and that this caused "blood pressure." He was aware of everyone's efforts to keep down his blood pressure. He felt sure that if his blood pressure went up, it would blow off the top of his head. Not surprisingly, he avoided any movement that might increase the blood pressure and lead to such a feared disaster.

Children with chronic illness also react to the parents' attitudes and concerns, or to their distorted perception of the parents' attitudes (Wolff, 1969). On the other hand, the actual attitudes of the parents are often a real source of anxiety for the child. In a study of family adaptation to cystic fibrosis in children, for example,

McCollum and Gibson (1970) found first of all that in the pre-diagnostic stage incorrect or incomplete diagnoses generated in parents a mounting mistrust of, and hostility toward, the medical profession. Further, since the infant patients were often unsatisfied by their feeds and had periods of fussiness, the mothers initially had feelings of self-doubt and self-reproach at their incapacity to nurture their infant. Subsequently, this led to feelings of despair and moments of frank hostility toward the infant, often accompanied by guilt. With the confirmation of the diagnosis, the threat of a fatal illness in the child stimulated an acute, anticipatory mourning reaction in the parents. Feelings of helplessness aroused anxiety in the parents and stimulated thoughts about their own death. In an effort to avoid these thoughts, parents invoked such defenses as an apparent absence of affect, denial, avoidance, and forgetting. Parents suffered sleep disturbances and disturbances of appetite. They often displaced anger toward the child onto others. Many other problems connected with the illness (the transmission to other members of the family; the impact upon other family members, especially siblings; the need for separate accommodations to house a mist tent; the odor produced by the stool; the major medical expenses; the parents' efforts to master postural drainage in the child, etc.) contributed to the parents' anxiety. Long-term adaptation by the parent invariably involved some denial of the prognosis, a denial that was constantly tested by certain intrusive characteristics of the disease, notably the odor and persistent cough of the child. The child, in turn, reacted to all these attitudes with anxiety.

Lastly, children may learn to use their chronic illness in the service of achieving other aims, as seen in the case of the boy Johnny, who used his diabetes to satisfy certain psychological needs. (See page 162.)

chronic illness : (b) specifc reactions

Specific chronic illnesses often invoke characteristic constellations of reactions in the child and his parents. The reactions of parents to the child with cystic fibrosis have already been mentioned. One further example of a chronic illness invoking specific reactions will be described, that of hemophilia in children. In a study of 28 hemophiliac children and their families, Browne and his colleagues (1960) observed that the children tended to feel isolated and different. They often tried to conceal their illness, and felt constantly watched. The enforced passivity prevented the discharge of tension through activity, and led to anxiety about movement and action. Sometimes the children were outwardly docile and passive, although there would often be evidence of subtle rebellion. For example, a child might revenge himself or his parents by deliberately bumping himself, by threatening to bleed, or by telling the doctor that his parents spanked him. Curiously, however, trauma was not the over-riding factor in bleeding. Bleeding was often spontaneous, and sometimes seemed to be related more to anxiety, especially anxiety about increased activity and independence. The bleeding would then serve to prevent the child from participating in these activities. Many of the children experienced anxiety around feelings of loss of masculinity. They felt unable to be active the way boys usually are, and experienced their father's withdrawal as a denial of masculinity for themselves. Further, the episodes of uncontrolled bleeding were sometimes linked in their fantasies with the bleeding that occurs in females. Most of the boys also knew that the disorder is handed down through the female.

These specific reactions to this particular illness often lead to psychiatric disorders, the most frequent being the development of passive-dependent characters, a tendency toward risk taking (accident prone) behavior, psychophysiological responses such as bleeding in relation to anxiety, and sexual identity problems (Agle, 1964).

Part of these reactions are related to the interaction with parents who themselves showed characteristic responses to the illness. For example, Browne, *et al.*, (1960) found that the mothers frequently felt guilt and anger at being the carrier. They tended to be ambivalent and over-protective toward their ill child. On the one hand they saw themselves as the only effective protector of the child. On the other hand, they also saw the child as a cross to bear. The child was restricted in his activities, since activity was equated with injury. The mother often selected the child's playmates and usually selected younger, smaller, passive children. Indeed, quiet little girls seemed the most desirable.

Many of the fathers seemed to lose interest in the child, and were relieved that they were not involved genetically as carriers. They were afraid to play with their sons, saw school as dangerous, and sought "desk jobs" for their hemophiliac sons. The child resented the father who denied him any physical activity. In another study, the son tended to regard his father as a traitor to his sex in that he denied the son the expression of masculinity (Goldy and Katz, 1963).

Many other illnesses produce characteristic behavior traits. Sometimes the behavior traits seem to be secondary to the complex relationships and reactions to illness just described; at other times the behavior traits appear to be a primary factor in the production of the illness. Usually there is an inextricable interaction between both primary and secondary factors. Nevertheless, some life processes do elicit certain highly characteristic behavioral reactions. And of these, the process of dying and the phenomenon of death are perhaps the most poignant.

the child's concept of death

Development, of course, continues beyond adolescence; and during the whole of development the inevitability of death is ever present. The child's reaction to his own dying or the death of others is related in part to his concept of death (Anthony, 1940; Gartley, W. and Bernasconi, M., 1967; Schilder, P. and Wechsler, D., 1934; Wolff, 1969), which in turn is related to his developmental stage. (See schematic diagram in Table 2) During the first few years, the child has virtually no concept of death other than a disappearance.

Children between 5 and 10 years of age (approximately) are beginning to clarify their concepts, but are still at times confused. For example, a child may say, "When I die, my heart stops, I can't see, and I can't hear. But if I'm buried, how will I breathe?" Some of the difficulty in thinking clearly is developmental, but some of the difficulty is emotional. If the child has a heightened castration anxiety at this time, he may tend to think of death in terms of the harm to the function of a particular organ, the more so because he also tends to think in concrete terms at this stage.

Somewhere between 10 and 15 years of age, the child acquires a grasp of the meaning of mortality (Kastenbaum, 1959). His reaction to death at this time is influenced more by his emotional struggles than his intellectual capacities. Thus, a young adolescent who is concerned, among other things, with sexual performance, control of his impulses, his physical intactness, and separating from his parents, may react with anxiety if any one of the sensitive conflict areas is aroused by the dying process.

child's response to parents' reaction to death

An important determinant of the child's reaction to death is the reaction of those around him. These others may be parents, siblings, or hospital staff. The reactions of parents have a chronological sequence, starting before and continuing during and after the moment of death. Specific types of reactions may vary according to whether the death to which the parents are responding is sudden, acute, or chronic (Friedman, *et al.*, 1963).

reaction of parents : (a) rapid death

When the death is relatively rapid (*e.g.* perhaps as a consequence of a brief, fatal illness), the period prior to death is filled with anxiety and concern. The parents may be desperately hopeful, but they may also experience feelings of guilt and have a need to deny the possibility of death as an eventual outcome. After such a death the parents may again feel some anger at the physician, more often because they felt abandoned by him (whether or not that was the case) than because of any alleged neglect. This is particularly prone to occur if the physician does not provide a follow-up interview. Over a period of time the parents will then undergo their own characteristic mourning process. This may include some identification with the lost person, and occasionally an over-idealization of the lost person (particularly in cases where the parent also experiences the loss of fantasied expectations they had for the lost child). Further possible reactions may include a displacement of attitudes toward the dead child onto one or more of the surviving

TABLE 2
DEATH AND CHILDHOOD

	BEFORE		BEFORE Sudden	BEFORE Acute	BEFORE Chronic	DURING Sudden	DURING Acute	DURING Chronic	AFTER Sudden	AFTER Acute	AFTER Chronic
	Ideas on Death	Death & Stage Anxieties									
Child											
0—5	abandonment punishment	fear of loss of love					avoidance of pain need for love	withdrawal separation anxiety			
5—10	concepts of inevitability confusion	castration anxiety					guilt (bad) regression denial	guilt (religious), regression, denial			
10—15	reality	control of body and other developmental tasks					depression despair for future	depression despair, anxiety, anger			
Parents				anxiety concern hopefulness	premature mourning, anticipatory grief, guilt, reaction formation and displacements, need for information	disbelief displaced rage accelerated grief numbness	desperate concern denial guilt	denial remorse resurgence of love	guilt mourning	anger at M.D., need for follow-up, over-idealizing, fantasy loss	remorse relief and guilt
Siblings											
0—5	reactions to changes in parents (sense of loss of love and withdrawal)									1. respond to reaction of parents	
5—10	concern re their implication fearful for themselves										
10—15	generally supportive									2. survivor guilt	
Staff	anxiety conspiracy of silence										

reaction: withdraw

tasks: 1. correct distortions, e.g., "am I safe?"; "will someone be with me?"; "will I be helped to feel better?"

2. comfort parents

3. allow hope and promote feeling of actively coping

4. protect dignity of patient

need for after care of survivors
autopsy request tact
accurate information regarding disposal of body
delay billing

children; attempts to fill the loss by another pregnancy; or a period of withdrawal. These and other normal reactions are usually respected by the sensitive physician and left alone.

reaction of parents : (b) prolonged dying

A different constellation of reactions may occur in parents when the period of dying is one of prolonged suffering, *e.g.* in leukemia (Richmond and Waisman, 1955). Sometimes unacceptable thoughts arise. For example, a parent may find himself wishing that the child would finally die and relieve everyone of the burden and suffering. Such a wish might horrify a parent, and lead to immediate defense reactions. Thus, one common defense reaction that occurs is a reaction formation, in which the parent is extra protective in caring for the dying child. Guilt may also be experienced. Such guilt (and anxiety) may be expressed in repetitive questions, which require tactful answers. Occasionally, a premature mourning may occur, with anticipatory grief and decathexis of the dying child, perhaps accompanied by a displacement of feelings onto an infant child in the family. As a chronically ill child nears death, the parents may be filled with remorse, and a resurgence of love occurs. Rarely, a denial of the imminence of death may remain in force. After the death of the chronically ill child, parents may feel a mixture of relief and guilt, with perhaps feelings of remorse uppermost in some instances.

sibling's reaction to death

The reactions of siblings prior to and during the death of a child is in large measure a function of the developmental level of the sibling, the sibling's reaction to the parents' response, and the sibling's relationship to the parent. For example, very young children, especially under the age of 5 years, sense the withdrawal of the parent and consequently themselves experience a sense of loss of love. Such young children view the death of significant other persons as an abandonment, or as a punishment, or both. This view occurs, in part, because the child at this time is almost entirely egocentric in his thinking, has very little capacity to distinguish between fantasy and reality, and is dominated by the fear of loss of love. Children between 5 and 10 years of age (approximately) are generally somewhat more concerned for the dying child and may also be fearful for themselves. Older children can usually muster a supportive attitude, and may temporarily assume parental roles for the younger siblings at home. Children as well as adults may experience survivor guilt after the death of a child. (Lifton, 1967.)

physician's reaction to death

Pediatric hospital staff naturally also experience anxiety when in the presence of a dying child or a grieving parent (Solnit and Green, 1959), and tend sometimes to deal with that anxiety by withdrawal and a conspiracy of silence. This reaction may hamper their optimal care of the dying child and his family and prevent them from carrying out certain essential psychological tasks. Besides comforting the parents, such tasks involve, for example, providing the child with an optimum feeling of being active in his attempts to cope with his anxiety as well as allowing some hope. Furthermore, the dignity of the child requires protection, and certain distortions require correction. A child, for example, may be quite concerned about such questions as "Am I safe?", "Will someone be with me when I need them?", "Will I be helped to feel better?" The continuing need for tact carries through into the period of after care for the survivors.

child's reaction to his own dying

The child who is himself dying experiences a variety of reactions. The very young child is mostly preoccupied with the discomfort of the illness, whether acute or chronic, and the separation and withdrawal that occurs with hospitalization. A somewhat older child interprets his illness according to his level of cognitive development and emotional conflicts. Thus he may interpret his illness as an act of "immanent justice" for the guilt he feels about some misdeed he may have done (or imagined). However, at the same time, there may be regressive behavior in the face of the illness, hospitalization, and treatment techniques. Occasionally, there is a denial of discomfort or dread (Solnit, 1965). An older child who is aware of the finality of death may deny his own anxiety, but will also exhibit a depression, occasionally mixed with outbursts of anger and anxiety. This is especially common in adolescents. On the other hand, some children are astoundingly courageous and steadfast in the face of death.

The range of reactions is great. Each child is an individual and a myriad of variables influence the ultimate behavior of the child, his family, and the helping persons around him. In a sense, all that has gone before contributes to the child's understanding of, and reaction to, death.

The physician who is aware of the many needs, fantasies, and thoughts of the developing child and his family is in a better position to offer sensitive care to the normal as well as the ill child. The care of the dying child and his family in particular is a special challenge to the physician. It is a challenge that makes most demands and is at times most poignant. The physician who learns to deal with his own reactions to death is that much better prepared to meet this challenge.

NOTE 18

Prugh, Dane G., Staub, E. M., Sands, H. H., Kurschbaum, R. M., and Lenihan, E. A., 1953. A study of the emotional reactions of children and families to hospitalization and illness. *Amer. J. Orthopsychiat.*, 23(1):70–106.

. . . . Two groups of 100 children each were selected for study, one designated as the *control* and the other, the *experimental* group.

. . . . A base-line study of the control group was carried out initially, covering a period of approximately four months. The circumstances under which hospitalization was encountered by children during this period were those involving traditional practices of ward management, existing prior to the experimental nursing program.

. . . . Following an interval sufficient to allow complete turnover of patients who had been in the control study, an experimental program of ward management was put into effect. This involved many of the practices employed in other hospitals and included daily visiting periods for parents, early ambulation of patients where medically feasible, a special play program employing a nursery-school teacher, psychological preparation for and support during potentially emotionally traumatic diagnostic or therapeutic procedures, an attempt at clearer definition and integration of the parent's role in the care of the child, and other techniques. Attention was paid to the handling of admission procedures, with parents accompanying the child to the ward to meet the staff and to assist in the child's initial adjustment. As a part of admission routine, parents were given a pamphlet prepared especially to enhance their understanding of their child's needs and their own role in his care.

In order to coordinate the activities of the professional staff in the management of patients, a weekly Ward Management Conference was held, directed by a pediatrician with psychiatric training. In attendance were the ward physician, head nurse, play supervisor, occupational therapist, dietitian, social worker, psychologist, and frequently a public health nurse. An attempt was made to discuss the adjustment of each child on the ward, although children presenting particular difficulties in adaptation received the most attention. Among other measures discussed and implemented in this interdisciplinary conference were: the assignment of one nurse to the principal care of a particularly anxious child; the scheduling of injections or other medical procedures at times other than feeding, nap, or play times; the use of appropriate psychological preparation for forthcoming procedures by physician, nurse, or play supervisor; the selection of particular play activities designed to meet the emotional needs of particular children; the special handling of feeding or other activities; the flexible arrangement of visiting periods or the encouragement of parental participation in ward care; and the provision of special psychological support for particular parents. Psychiatric consultation and psychological appraisal were provided where indicated, but the essential approach was in the direction of the coordination and potentiation of the efforts of all professional personnel involved in the care of the ill child. . . .

Results

Immediate reactions

. . . . 92 per cent of the children in the control or unsupported group exhibited reactions of a degree indicating significant difficulties in adaptation. . . . In the experimental group, this figure totaled 68 per cent. . . .

. . . . Immediate reactions to hospitalization were noted to be most marked in children from two through five years of age in both groups. . . .

. . . . In general, children with previously limited capacities for adaptation showed the greatest difficulty in adjusting comfortably to the ward milieu and showed as well the most severe reactions to the total experience of hospitalization. . . .

Long-range reactions

. . . . Children under four years of age and children who had relatively unsatisfying relationships with their parents, who had undergone very severe stress in the hospital, and who had shown the greatest difficulty in adapting to the ward milieu were those who tended to show persistent signs of emotional disturbance at three months following hospitalization. . . .

Types of individual reactions of children in the hospital

. . . . The most common manifestation of disturbance in adaptation at any age level or in either group was that of overt anxiety. . . .

. . . . (In) children from two to four years of age (in the) control group. . . . anxiety over separation from parents was the most common manifestation and the most intense of any age level, occurring equally in both sexes and to some degree in all children. Anxiety was often associated with fear or anger at the time of departure of the parents. Constant crying, apprehensive behavior, outbursts of screaming, and acute panic when approached by an adult were frequent, together with occasional somatic concomitants of anxiety such as urinary frequency, diarrhea, vomiting, etc. Depression, at times resembling the anaclitic type described by Spitz. . . . , homesickness and withdrawal were observed in this group more than in older children, particularly at the outset of hospitalization. The need for tangible evidence of home and family, such as dolls, items of clothing, etc., was particularly manifest in this group, as demonstrated by the anxiety of many children over giving them up. At times, shoes and socks, for example, seemed to be incorporated into the body image, with marked anxiety shown whenever they were removed.

Reactions to the experiencing of overwhelming fear or anxiety showed some specificity for the children in this age group, ... Disturbances in feeding behavior, including anorexia, overeating, and refusal to chew food, often combined with regressive smearing of food or the demand for a return to bottle feeding, were more frequent and severe than in any other group. Changes in toilet behavior were next in incidence, involving regressive loss of control of bladder or bowel functions, most marked in the early phases of hospitalization. Fears of the toilet or of the loss of the stool, fear of loss of control of bowel or bladder functions, as well as guilt and fear of punishment over wishes to soil or wet, were handled by mechanisms of denial, projection, and other modes of adaptation available to the child of this age. Fears of the dark or of physical attack were common and were associated with sleep disturbances—insomnia, nightmares and restlessness. Increase of bedtime rituals and other compulsive acts during hospitalization was often seen.

. . . . Open acting-out of infantile wishes and aggressive impulses appeared most frequently in this age group, with wild outbursts of frantic aggression and attendant guilt and anxiety. Marked inhibition of aggressive drives was observed in some children, together with turning inward of hostility. Restlessness, hyperactivity and irritability, with associated rocking, thumb-sucking or aggressive behavior, appeared in many children, particularly if they were confined to bed with the use of a "restrainer," as had been the practice for small or acute disoriented children in order to prevent their falling from bed. With ambulation, this behavior often disappeared or diminished markedly.

A variety of primitive gratifications of pregenital character. . . . were employed to greater degree than prior to hospitalization. Thumb-sucking and rocking were common, associated with withdrawal and with masturbation in one third of the children. Headbanging was relatively infrequent. In many instances, as children established parent-surrogate relationships, often with the play supervisor or one particular nurse, gratifications of this type diminished, no longer interfering with adjustment to the group.

Among the defense mechanisms available to this younger group, regression was the most widespread. Libidinal regression was often uneven, associated with feeding, bowel and bladder symptomatology. Oral components were manifest through enhanced sucking, overeating, and demanding behavior, with occasional biting and other manifestations. Cruelty, sadistic enjoyment of the pain of others, pleasure in handling or smearing feces, and other regressive anal components of behavior were transparently or openly evident, particularly in children isolated for medical reasons.

In some instances, a nearly total regression of the ego to a relatively narcissistic level of psychosexual development, associated with disturbances in reality testing, was manifest. . . .

Denial of illness or of the loss of the loved object, the mother, was observed in a number of children of this age. For example, one child, a boy of three and a half, insisted for three days that his mother was "downstairs" and that he was "all well now," in spite of the persistence of his dyspnea from a bronchopneumonia.

(In the) experimental group . . . . the same types of disturbances in adaptation were noted as among the control or unsupported group. In general, however, manifestations were less severe and lighter in incidence. . . .

Reactions to specific types of treatment or diagnostic procedures

. . . . The impression was gained that any or all . . . . procedures seemed to be interpreted by a child at a particular level of libidinal development in terms of the specific anxieties and fears characteristic of that level, and to be dealt with by means of his own previously developed defenses, rather than in terms of the exact nature of the procedure itself. . . .

In the main, the younger children tended to react to such threatening procedures as to hostile attacks, often interpreted as punishment. . . . The impression was gained, however, that a great deal of the small child's fear of unknown procedures, of separation from the parents, of punishment, and of overwhelming attack was displaced much of the time onto such objectively less threatening but directly visible things as needles, tourniquets, etc. In the experimental group, aggressive responses in particular to various procedures were only half as frequent and were less intense than those in the control group; . . . .

Post hospitalization reactions

. . . . Following discharge, most of the regressive manifestations in the younger age group appeared to subside rather promptly. Behavior of an infantile or demanding nature, together with greater dependence on parents, persisted for several months in a number of children under five years of age. Wetting, soiling, and intensified pregenital gratifications, however, were ordinarily given up within three months' time.

The most common manifestations among children showing continuing disturbances were related to anxiety over separation from parents, appearing most intensely in younger children but arising also in latency children. . . . All of these manifestations appeared to be milder in children in the experimental group (e.g., sleep disturbances were five times as common in the control as the experimental group) . . . .

In general, symptoms which persisted were fewer in number and milder for each child at home than in the hospital. Such symptoms appeared to be related more directly to the personality structure and characteristic patterns of adaptation of the child prior to hospitalization. . . .

Reactions of parents and families

. . . . Realistic fear in proportion to the severity of the child's illness, overt anxiety, guilt over possible involvement in the causation of illness or over previously hostile feelings toward the child, and other feelings were handled in various ways, dependent upon the character structure of the parent, the nature of the relationship with the child, experiences immediately preceding hospitalization, and other factors. . . .

. . . . Marked ambivalence, even on the part of well-adjusted parents, was frequent in the face of behavioral regression on the part of the child, either during or following hospitalization.

. . . . In general, the well adjusted parents whose children were hospitalized under the experimental program seemed more satisfied with visiting regulations than those in the control group, where visiting was strongly curtailed. . . .

Problems in ward management

. . . . The common conception that crying occurs more frequently among children whose parents visit frequently was found to be erroneous in the experimental phase of the study. . . .

. . . . (Moreover) the hazard of cross-infection is not appreciably increased under circumstances involving more frequent contact with parents.

references

1. Agle, D. P., 1964. Psychiatric studies of patients with hemophilia and related states. *Arch. Int. Med.,* 114(1):76–82.

2. Anthony, S., 1940. *The Child's Discovery of Death.* New York: Harcourt, Brace & World Inc.

3. Blos, P., 1960. Comments on the psychological consequences of cryptorchism: a clinical study. *The Psychoanalytic Study the Child,* 15:395–429.

4. Broughton, A., Anderson, M. B., and Bowden, C. H., 1968. Magnesium-deficiency in burns. *Lancet,* 2:1156–1158.

5. Browne, W. J., Mally, M. A., and Kane, R. P., 1960. Psychosocial aspects of hemophilia. *Amer .J. Orthopsychiat.,* 30:730–740.

6. Collins, S. D., 1938. Frequency of surgical procedures among 9,000 families, based on nation-wide periodic canvasses 1928–31. *Public Health Reports,* 53(16):587–628.

7. Dey, D. L., 1952. A survey of 681 children awaiting tonsillectomy and the indications for operation in childhood. *Med. J. Australia*, 1:510–514.

8. Fraiberg, S., 1968. Parallel and divergent patterns in blind and sighted infants. *The Psychoanalytic Study of the Child*, 23:264–300.

9. Fraiberg, S. and Freedman, D. A., 1964. Studies in the ego development of the congenitally blind child. *The Psychoanalytic Study of the Child*, 19:113–169.

10. Fraiberg, S., Siegel, B. L., and Gibson, R., 1966. The role of sound in the search behavior of a blind infant. *The Psychoanalytic Study of the Child*, 21:327–357.

11. Freud, A., 1952. The role of bodily illness in the mental life of children. *The Psychoanalytic Study of the Child*, 8:69.

12. Friedman, S. B., Chodoff, P., Mason, J. W. and Hamburg, D. A., 1963. Parental behavior before death of child. *Pediatrics*, 32:610–625.

13. Gartley, W. and Bernasconi, M., 1967. The concept of death in children. *J. Genetic Psychol.*, 110:71–85.

14. Goldy, F. B. and Katz, A. H., 1963. Social adaptation in hemophilia. *Children*. 10(5):189–193.

15. Holter, J. C. and Friedman, S. B., 1969. Etiology and management of severely burned children. *Amer. J. Dis. Child.*, 118:680–686.

16. Horstman, D., 1969. Personal communication.

17. Jackson, D. MacG., 1968. What the burnt child goes through. *Proc. Royal Soc. Med.*, 61:1085–1087.

18. Jessner, L., Blom, G. E., and Waldfogel, S., 1952. Emotional implications of tonsillectomy and adenoidectomy on children. *The Psychoanalytic Study of the Child*, 7:126–169.

19. Kastenbaum, R., 1959. Time and death in adolescence. In: *The Meaning of Death*, H. Feifel (ed.). New York: McGraw-Hill Book Co.

20. Langford, W. S., 1948. Physical illness and convalescence: their meaning to the child. *J. Pediat.*, 33:242.

21. Levy, D. M., 1945. Psychic trauma of operations in children and a note on combat neurosis. *Amer. J. Dis. Child.*, 69:7.

22. Lifton, R. J., 1967. *Death in Life*. New York: Random House, Inc., p. 594.

23. Lipton, S. D., 1962. On the psychology of childhood tonsillectomy. *The Psychoanalytic Study of the Child*, 17:363–417.

24. Long, R. and Cope, 1961. Emotional problems of burned children. *New England J. Med.*, 264:1121.

25. McCollum, A. T. and Gibson, L. E., 1970. Family adaptation to the child with cystic fibrosis. *J. Pediat.*, 77(4):571–578

26. Neill, C. A., 1967. The child and his family at home after hospitalization. In: *The Hospitalized Child and His Family*, J. A. Haller, Jr. (ed). Baltimore: The Johns Hopkins Press, pp. 67–77.

27. Nover, R., 1970. Personal communication.

28. Prugh, D. G., 1963. Toward an understanding of psychosomatic concepts in relation to illness in children. In: *Modern Perspectives in Child Development, in Honor of Milton J. E. Senn.* A. J. Solnit and S. A. Provence (eds.), New York: International Universities Press, Inc., pp. 246–370.

29. Prugh, D. G., Staub, E. M., Sands, H. H., Kirschbaum, R. M. and Lenihan, E. A., 1953. A study of the emotional reactions of children and families to hospitalization and illness. *Amer. J. Orthopsychiat.*, 23:70.

30. Richmond, J. B. and Waisman, H. A., 1955. Psychological aspects of management of children with malignant disease. *Amer. J. Dis. Child.*, 89:42.

31. Robertson, J., 1956. A mother's observation on the tonsillectomy of her four-year-old daughter, with comments by Anna Freud. *The Psychoanalytic Study of the Child*, 11:410–436.

32. Schilder, P. and Wechsler, D., 1934. The attitudes of children toward death. *J. Genet. Psychol.*, 45:405–451.

33. Schwartz, A. H. and Landwirth, J., 1968. Birth defects and the psychological development of the child: some implications for management. *Connecticut Medicine*, 32(6):457–464.

34. Solnit, A. J., 1965. The dying child. *Develop. Med. Child Neurol.*, 7:693–704.

35. Solnit, A. J. and Green, M., 1959. Psychologic considerations in the management of deaths on pediatric hospital services. 1. The doctor and the child's family. *Pediatrics*, 24(1):106–112.

36. Solnit, A. J. and Stark, M., 1961. Mourning and the birth of a defective child. *The Psychoanalytic Study of the Child*, 16:523–537.

37. Tisza, V., Selverstone, B., Rosenblum, G. and Hanlon, N., 1968. Psychiatric observations of children with cleft palate. *Amer. J. Orthopsychiat.*, 28(2):416–423.

38. Wolff, S., 1969. *Children Under Stress*. London: Allen Lane, The Penguin Press, pp. 53, 66, 75–93.

Index

Abstract operations, 148
Accidental poisoning, 33, 68–70
Accommodation, 26
Acculturation, 122–23
Acute phobic reaction, 86
Activity types, 16–17
Adaptation, 6–7, 20, 71, 123–24, 189
Adaptive sequence, 40, 51
Adoption, 89–91, 165
Aggression, 58–60, 132–33
Alienation, 123, 151–53
Amatruda, C. S., 15, 35–42
Anaclitic depression, 21, 33
Anencephalitic infant, 6
Animism, 57, 94
Anorexia nervosa, 167–68
Anticipatory guidance, 6, 7–8
Anxiety, 28–30, 95, 132–35, 189–90
Assimilation, 25–26, 94
Attempted suicide, 151, 155, 163–64
Autism, infantile, 30–33
Autistic state, normal, 22, 32, 55
Autonomy, sense of, 56

Bed wetting. *See* Enuresis
Birth defects, 185–88
Blindness, 19, 128, 187–88
Body image, 21–22, 29, 54
Bornstein, B., 85, 111–15, 121
Bowlby, J., 19, 21, 44–45, 63
Brain damage. *See* Minimal cerebral
 dysfunction
Breast feeding, 7–8
Burlingham, D., 63, 78–79

Burns, 190–91

Case illustrations: accidental poisoning, 69; acute phobic reaction, 86;
 adolescent turmoil, 157–58; at-
 tempted suicide, 151; diabetes,
 162–63; encopresis, 70; incest and
 repetition, 138, 155; maternal
 fantasies, 160; nephrosis, 193;
 oedipal conflict, 85
Castration anxiety, 64, 107, 108, 189,
 196–97
Cathy, age 7 and 15 (incest and re-
 petition), 138, 155
Child abuse, 33
Circular reactions, 25, 27, 45–47
Cleft palate, 186, 187
Cognitive development, 25, 56–57,
 93–95, 107, 124–25, 148–50
Complemental series, 31–32
Compulsive tendencies, 126
Congenital activity types, 16–17
Conservation, 125
Conversion reaction, 168
Critical period, 12, 13, 14
Cryptorchism, 186
Cystic fibrosis, 193–94

Daniel, age 15 (attempted suicide),
 151
Death, 196–201
Defense: hierarchy, 107–08, 109;
 mechanisms, 24, 30, 59–60, 88, 126, 157
Delinquency, 169–70

Depression 33, 66, 133, 154
Depressive position, 28
Deprivation, 13, 14, 33–34
Development: concept of, 11–12; stages of, 35–42
Developmental Quotient, 13
Developmental tasks, 58, 66–67, 71, 106
Diabetes, 162–63
Displacement, 59
Dreams, 20, 95–96, 190
Drive regression, 156–57
Drugs, 2,5; abuse of, 170–75, 179
Dyslexia, 128

Eating disturbances, 84, 167
Ego, 24, 29, 120, 126, 127, 135–38, 143, 150
Egocentrism, 57, 94, 148–49
Encopresis, 61, 70–71, 95, 127
Enuresis, 95, 104–06, 127, 189
Environment, prenatal, 1–2
Epigenetic principle, 11
Erikson, E. H., 11, 20, 43–44, 56, 93, 122, 150, 177–78
Evelyn, age 15 (adolescent turmoil), 157–58

Failure to thrive, 13, 21, 33, 54
Familial retardation, 72
Family romance, 94, 121
Fantasy, 27–28, 30, 40, 52, 85–90, 91, 101–02, 106, 121–22
Fifteen-year-old boy (maternal fantasies), 160
Firesetting, 126
Five-year-old boy (nephrosis), 193
Food attitudes, 84, 167
Forty-three-month-old girl (accidental poisoning), 69
Four-year-old boy (acute phobic reaction), 86
Freud, A., 2, 34, 56, 63, 66, 78–79, 122, 136, 150, 157, 190
Freud, S., 22, 24, 31, 62, 83, 84, 88, 96, 100, 102, 108–11, 126, 135, 143

Gender identification, 14, 54–55, 91, 148, 187

Gesell, A., 14, 15, 35–42
Grief, 63, 65, 78–79
Guilt, 59, 97–100

Hartmann, H., 2, 6–7, 20, 56, 60, 120, 157
Harvey, age 5 (encopresis), 70
Hemophilia, 195–96
Hippie subculture, 152, 174, 179
Homosexuality, 91–92, 135–38, 166–67, 173
Hospitalization, 64–65, 189–205
Hypospadias, 187

Idealization, 91
Identity, 150–51, 177–79
Illegitimacy, 90, 92, 165
Illness: acute, 188–91; and adolescence, 162–63; chronic, 193–96
Imaginary: audience, 149; companion, 121–22
Immanent justice, 94–95, 200
Incest, 138, 155
Infant needs, 19–21
Infantile autism, 30–33
Inhelder, B., 124, 148
Innate releasers, 19
Intellectualization, 157
Intelligence, and learning, 130–31
Intelligence Quotient, 72
Introjection, 24
Intuitive stage, 94
Irreversibility, 12, 13, 14
Institutionalization, 13, 17–18, 72, 100–01

Johnny, age 13 (diabetes), 162–63

Klein, M., 28
Kurschbaum, R. M., 201–05

Language, 15–16, 17–18, 41, 51–52, 58, 107, 131. *See also* Speech
Latency, 120–21
Laterality, 51, 127–28
Learning, 12, 125–32
Lenihan, E. A., 201–05
Love relationships in adolescence, 154–55

Lying, 140

Mahler, M. S., 22, 32, 55, 67, 68
Malnutrition, 2, 5, 34–35
Masturbation, 95, 100–04, 126, 166,
173
Maternal: attitudes, 2–4, 7; be-
havior, 18–19; depression, 65–66;
fantasies, 160; insufficiency, 33–35;
unwillingness, 34
Maturation, 14–15, 83, 119, 127–28,
147–48
Menstruation, 148
Mental retardation, 71–73
Minimal cerebral dysfunction, 128–30
Motor sequence, 39, 51

Negativism, 68–69
Nephrosis, 193
Neutralization, 60
Nightmares, 95–96
Night terrors, 95, 190
Nursery school, 125, 131

Object: constancy, 23–24, 29, 55–
56; permanence, 56; relations, 22,
23, 24, 29, 53, 68
Obsessional tendencies, 126
Oedipal fantasies and conflicts, 84–89,
124, 126
Omnipotence, 28, 55, 56–57
One-parent child, 91–92

Paranoid-schizoid position, 28
Passive position, 58
Paternal role, 4, 8, 33, 137, 195–96
Pearson, G. H. J., 140–41, 143
Pediatrician and "anticipatory gui-
dance," 6, 7–8
Peer relationships, 53, 121, 140–43
Peller, L. E., 142
Persecutory anxiety, 28
Personal: fable, 149; -social sequence,
42, 52
Phobic: organization, 107; reaction, 86
Piaget, J., 25, 26, 45–46, 56, 57,
93–94, 97, 124, 125, 148, 176–77
Play, 16, 52, 53, 54, 92–93, 107, 124,
142

Pleasure principle, 56, 62–63
Postpartum depression, 3
Pregnancy, 2–3; illegitimate, 164–66
Prematurity, 5
Pre-operational stage, 94
Primary: circular reaction, 25, 27;
identification, 22; process, 25–26,
58
Projection, 24, 59
Prugh, D. G., 64, 201–05

Reaction formation, 59–60, 126
"Realism," 97
Reality: principle, 56, 63; testing,
22–23, 30
Regression, 64, 156–57, 173–74, 189
Regressive pull, 122, 166
R.E.M. sleep, 19–20, 96, 100, 105
Repression, 59, 126
Role confusion, 177–79

Sands, H. H., 201–05
Schema, 25–26, 45
Schizophrenia, 157–58, 164
School phobia, 127, 134–35
Secondary: circular reaction, 26–27,
45–46; process, 24, 58, 120
Self, 21–22, 29, 54
Senn, M. J. E., 6, 7–8
Sensory-motor stage, 57
Separation, 29, 30, 44–45, 63–66,
78–79, 134, 153; -individuation
phase, 55, 68, 174
Settlage, C. F., 179
Sexual: deviancy, 55, 127, 135–39;
drive, 60, 100, 156–57; promiscuity,
138; theories, 83–84, 108–11
Sibling: reaction to death, 199–200;
rivalry, 88–89
Sleep, 19, 20, 95–96. *See also* Dreams,
Nightmares, Night terrors, R.E.M.
sleep
Social deprivation, 34–35
Society and adolescence, 161–62
Soiling. *See* Encopresis
Spanking, 103–04
Speech, in infantile autism, 31, 32.
See also Language

Spitz, R. A., 13, 14, 21, 23, 45, 103
Stealing, 45, 138–40
Stimulation, 17–18, 29
Stranger anxiety, 23, 34, 64
Student, age 19 (passive oedipal conflict), 85
Stupidity, apparent, 133
Sublimation, 60, 88, 126
Superego, 98, 121, 126, 138–40, 143; consolidation of, 88
Symbiotic: phase, normal, 55; psychosis, 67–68, 132
Symbolic: association, 133; pre-conceptual stage, 57, 174

Tertiary circular reaction, 27, 45–47
Thumb sucking, 22, 25–26, 189

Tics, 127
Toilet training, 61–62
Tonsillectomy, 107, 108, 191–93
Transitional: object: 52, 74–78; phenomena, 74–78
Transvestite behavior, 55, 136–38
Truancy, 133–34
Trust vs. mistrust, 43–44
Turmoil in adolescence, 157–61

Unusual sensitivity, 32

Visual attention, 18

Winnicott, D., 6, 20, 52, 74–78
Wolff, S., 5, 35, 190, 193, 196